Astrol.

8680

The
PRACTICE of
PREDICTION

The **PRACTICE** *of* **PREDICTION**

the astrologer's handbook of techniques used to accurately forecast the future

Nancy Anne Hastings

SAMUEL WEISER, INC.
York Beach, Maine

First published in 1989 by
Samuel Weiser, Inc.
Box 612
York Beach, Maine 03910

Library of Congress Cataloging-in-Publication Data
Hastings, Nancy Anne.
    The practice of prediction.

    Bibliography: p.
    1. Astrology. 2. Forecasting. I. Title.
BF1711.H275 1989 133.5 89-33879
ISBN 0-87728-684-1

Cover art ©1989 Michael Martin

Printed in the United States of America by
Capital City Press

CONTENTS

PREFACE

In the mid 1970s, I was asked to fill in for someone on a panel of astrologers at a conference in New York City. The discussion dealt with the function of astrology in current society. I don't think the people who asked me to substitute realized what kind of astrology I did, and I certainly did not know what kind of astrology the rest of the panel practiced, for I had not even read the list of panelists. One was a psychiatrist, another was completing a master's degree in psychology, and a third called herself a therapist. When the microphone came to me, I announced that I was a predictive astrologer. Immediately, the rest of the panel moved physically and psychologically away from me. The only people who seemed to understand what I meant, and what I did, were the members of the audience, God bless them. The panel members did their best to make it seem as if I worked from a tent, using a crystal ball, incense and amulets. Several of them looked uncomfortable when I said that if transits and progressions indicated that a client was due for a difficult time, I would tell the client to call me as the situation unfolded, if he or she needed to talk to someone. But I apparently made another, more fundamental error. Someone in the audience asked what I would do if the client didn't call. I answered that if I knew the client well, I would call to make sure that everything was alright. Two of the panel members reprimanded me, in front of the audience, for unprofessional over-involvement. Basically, their attitude was that predicting difficulty was unthinkable (perhaps impossible) and offering moral support during rough periods unprofessional.

I have thought about that panel for the last twelve years. With Saturn conjunct my Midheaven, it has taken me this long to say publicly that they were and are wrong. Astrology is not merely a useful adjunct to the fields of psychology and psychiatry. Although your natal chart certainly can help you understand yourself and your response nature quite well, you don't have to stop at natal analysis. "Great learning experiences" need not catch you by surprise. I feel a sense of achievement when my clients make it through incredibly difficult transits and progressions with a hangnail or two instead of a stay in the hospital. You see, you have to have the background symbolism filled in before an event happens, regardless of the aspects. No matter what kind of aspects you have in your natal chart, you are not likely to be mugged or raped while at a church social or a PTA meeting. You may drop your tuna hot dish or you may get into a heated argument with the president of the PTA, but those events leave your physical self intact.

Some people call this kind of predictive work negative astrology. What is so negative about being able to avoid getting hurt? It's pretty arrogant to assume clients are so dumb that they can't duck when the you-know-what is about to hit the fan. This arrogance ranks on a par with the physician who does not tell the patient the possible side effects of medications because the patient might then imitate or feign the side effects.

We can't control everything that is coming up in life, but I wouldn't drive a car I knew had bad brakes the day that transiting Mars squares my natal Sun. If transiting Uranus was within a degree of opposition to my natal Sun, and progressed Saturn within a few minutes of square my progressed Sun on the same day, I might decide to stay home and chance stubbing my toe in the backyard because I was in a hurry.

Astrology is a wonderful tool which gives you insight not only into your basic personality traits, but also about how to maximize your internal energy for positive gain while minimizing the negative possibilities in your life. There is not a lot you can do about a flood or hurricane, but you can do quite a bit about your reactions to the people or events in your life.[1] Our charts aren't excuses for failure any more than they are guarantees of success. Each of us chooses how to use the energy symbolized in our own charts. Each of was dealt a specific hand at the start of this life. Some of us didn't begin with a terrific set of cards. Theologians and philosophers can debate whether we chose our own hands or someone else gave them to us, but the real issue is what we decide to do with them. For example, hard aspects that indicate problems with interpersonal relationships often can be transferred into the business world, where they can provide the impetus to success. Deflecting that energy doesn't necessarily equate with avoiding the issue, for when we direct the squares and oppositions, we relieve the stress. Then we are more likely to use the easier symbolism in our charts in our personal lives.

---

[1] If you spend hours every day combing over the transits and progressions in your chart, and you have studied astrology for more than a year, you are probably avoiding something. You may be avoiding the process of living.

This book tells you how I do predictive work. If you combine it with my first book, *Secondary Progressions: Time to Remember,* you can find the troublesome times, and decide what to do about them. No book can do what a practicing astrologer does, for there are simply too many variables to cover. The more advanced techniques which I use are only to amplify the groundwork covered here. You *can* determine the approximate date of events without dials and midpoints, asteroids, heliocentric positions, harmonic sorts, or trans-Neptunian points, although these methods may help you to add details. It is more likely, however, that you will get confused if you turn to the additional techniques before you have a clear idea of probability from some pretty basic combinations. The basic combinations I use with every client are the natal chart, the progressed chart, and the transits.[2]

I didn't invent the techniques I've put in this book. They are a result of the experience I've had working as an astrologer since 1968. My teachers may recognize some ideas of theirs, and people who have lectured at conferences or written books themselves may see similarities to their views. Students and clients have provided the bedrock of experience which allowed me to evaluate information I learned from other astrologers. Finally, special thanks go to those who have let me use their charts in this book. These are special people, indeed.

---

[2]You could use the natal and solar arc and transits, or use the natal and a 90 degree dial and transits, but if you get beyond about three major techniques, you'll wind up with a headache and confusion.

INTRODUCTION

It is important to keep in mind that making a prediction is not the same as causing something to happen. When we make a prediction based on a set of astrological indicators, we are really describing a number of possible outcomes. These probabilities depend on the actions taken by the person involved. Once you know the potential of the symbolism occurring at a specific time, you can create an environment around yourself which eliminates the most negative possibilities. Thus, you have taken control of your own life. When you direct the energy, you can influence the outcome. However, if you do not know the negative possibilities, you may inadvertently place yourself in a position where the most difficult symbolism can manifest. The point of predictive astrology is to know yourself, know the possibilities, and master the possibilities.

Whenever the topic of prediction comes up, someone asks about predictions concerning death. It is very difficult (not to mention unethical) to make predictions concerning death. All of us will have hundreds of combinations during our lives which could be interpreted as death aspects—after the fact. We'll probably check out on one of those combinations. Our charts will continue to be aspected, and will continue to have terrible and terrific combinations long after we've shed our bodies and current ego structures.

There are three major predictive techniques defined in this book. These are secondary progressions, solar arc directions, and transits.

Secondary progression is an ancient technique in which the symbolism of each day after birth is equated to each year of life. Thus, the events occurring when you are ten years old are symbolized by the aspects which occurred when you were ten days old. Secondary progressions imply a strictly symbolic rather than causal connection between astrological events and life events. Appendix I on page 291 describes methods of erecting a secondary progressed chart for any year in your life.

Solar arc directions derive from the motion of the secondary progressed Sun. Since the Sun is the symbol of the basic life force, moving all the planets and angles at the same rate as the Sun moves provides a symbolism for events which connects to your fundamental life principle.

The techniques of secondary progression of all of the planets and solar arc direction of the planets do not conflict, nor do they provide conflicting information. However, most of us choose one of the techniques for daily work, and use the other as a type of back-up, primarily to avoid confusion.

Transits are simply the record of the daily motion of the planets. Transits alone were not widely used for precise predictive work until the late 1500s, when reasonably accurate and inexpensive ephemerides became available, giving the daily positions of the planets. Now that we can look up positions for the next ten years simply by flipping pages in a book, transits have become one of the most used techniques in astrology.

Transits are an extremely powerful predictive tool. Yet without the addition of one of the other techniques, it is often difficult to differentiate between major and minor events in life.

This book concentrates on aspects between planets. Whether the connection is from a secondary progression, a solar arc position, or a transit, the symbolic meaning is similar. The differences come from the duration of the connection. For instance, transiting Pluto can combine retrograde periods and make a zero-orb aspect to a natal planetary position for as long as two years. If you have a secondary progressed planet station with a zero-orb aspect to a natal position, you can have an exact aspect for several years. There is one more way that an aspect can stay in effect for a year or more. If your progressed Sun, Mercury, Venus, Mars or Midheaven aspect each other, the planets or positions involved may be progressing at nearly the same rate of speed, and the aspect can stay within fifteen minutes of arc for a few years. Aspects which last a year or more are background aspects. They color all the faster connections.

Calculating aspects within a secondary progression or between a secondary chart and the natal chart[3] isn't quite like calculating transit aspects to the natal chart. The major difference between the transiting aspects and the progressed aspects is time. The fastest moving secondary planet is the Moon, which travels at an average rate twelve times faster than the next fastest planet, or a degree a month. The Sun has a progressed monthly motion of about five minutes, while the fastest Mercury

---

[3]See Nancy Anne Hastings, *Secondary Progressions: Time to Remember* (York Beach, Maine: Samuel Weiser, Inc., 1984).

can move is about seven minutes. The outer planet transits seem positively speedy by contrast; for transiting Pluto and Neptune often move as fast as the progressed Moon (1° per month—although the progressed Moon has never gone retrograde, so far as I know!).

This means that if you're going to be able to time anything with the secondary planets, you must use orbs measured in minutes rather than degrees. A fifteen minute orb for the progressed Sun gives a three month lead time on an aspect. This is reasonable, for the aspect is strongest in the middle of the six month period (three months coming, three months going). Then, during the six months when the aspect from the progressed Sun is in orb, check the transits to see if anything can trigger this aspect.

The word "trigger" means that last little aspect which gets the larger configuration moving. Except for the Moon, the secondary planets don't usually symbolize events directly. The positions and aspects of the secondary planets really symbolize the *potential* for activity. This situation is like a pile of rocks on the side of a mountain cliff, which could sit there forever if nothing changed. However, if it rains heavily and dirt begins to pile up behind the pile of rocks, there is an increasing potential for a rockslide. If the rain continues, that could start the rockslide. If the rain stops just before the pressure is great enough for the rocks to start to move, something minor, such as an antelope jumping on one of the rocks, or a sonic boom from an airplane could start the slide.

Now, to translate this metaphor into astrological terms, continuing rain is like pressure from progressions or outer planet transits finally creating the environment for change in your personality to start. Although the progressed Moon or the three outer planets (Uranus, Neptune, and Pluto) can act like triggers in this kind of scenario, they usually don't. Most of us just don't have the kind of continuous rain (in the form of unremitting pressure) to force inner change in the absence of a specific event that starts the change process. Generally you feel the pressure building, but manage to hang on to your habits until some antelope or airplane (or some darn fool with a few blasting caps) starts stirring things up. Transiting Mars, Jupiter and Saturn are the usual triggers. But if you are perfectly primed for an internal rockslide, then the inner planets (transiting Sun, Venus or Mercury) can get it moving.

Sometimes the positions of the progressed planets don't indicate a rockslide, but show that the transits won't be as clear as expected. This is the case when a progressed planet aspects its own natal position. This aspect between the progressed and natal chart is quite unique, for as long as there are no transiting aspects to the progressed and natal positions, nothing much happens. As soon as a transit occurs, you feel the effect of the aspect between the progressed and natal positions of the planet.

Jupiter, Saturn, Uranus, Neptune and Pluto don't make new aspects to their natal positions by secondary progression except the conjunction, and then only if the planet was about to make a station and turn direct or retrograde just after your birth. These five move so slowly when making a station that the conjunction is likely to last several years. During the years of the conjunction, transits will simultaneously aspect natal and progressed positions. Thus, the effect of each transit is increased.

Part One

Predicting with Astrology

CHAPTER 1

Checking Out the Options:
ASPECTS

Most of life's memorable events correspond to several major indicators in the chart. Which is the most important aspect is not necessarily relevant, for the combinations will be different for each of us. What is significant, as the examples given in this chapter show, is a piling up of indicators. When this occurs you know that something is about to happen.

When I use solar arc directions, I track the following aspects: semi-octile (22-1/2°), semisextile (30°), semi-quintile (36°), semisquare (45°), septile (51.428°), sextile (60°), quintile (72°), and square (90°). By the time you are ninety years old, you will have had each one of these aspects from your solar arc Sun to your natal Sun. Instead of trying to memorize the names of these aspects, jot down the degrees. The aspect will occur during the year equal to the number of degrees in the aspect.

Minor aspects involving progressed positions other than the solar arc may influence events, but most major events will be characterized by major aspect patterns. You won't miss many major events if you use the major aspects for progressions and transits. If you want to analyze minor aspects between progressions and transits, you can associate them to the following major patterns. The semi-octile (22-1/2°) is a doubly hidden square, thus the stress/action analysis applies. The septile (51.428°), biseptile (102.856°) and triseptile (154.384°) fit between the tension and the ease aspects. Read both definitions and combine them. The semi-quintile or decile (36°), quintile (72°)

and biquintile (144°) are ease aspects with a bit of creativity, stubbornness, and insight thrown in.

Lots of us don't use these little aspects mainly because we can't just look at the chart and see them the way we can see any of the 30 degree aspects. The only minor aspects which I've found consistently acting like major aspects are the semisextile, semisquare, sesquiquadrate (135°) and inconjunct.[4] Instead of calculating the other minor aspects, I simply remember the degree of separation and think of that as years: one degree equals one year. When a client is the appropriate age I calculate the date when the solar arc will be exact for the minor aspect.

THE SEMI-OCTILE (22-1/2°)

This is half of a semisquare. Any of you who have worked with harmonics or 90 degree dials are familiar with this. Often this is simply called "22-1/2°." It's part of the series of stress/action aspects. I treat it like a doubly hidden square. Unless I'm working with a dial, I don't use it except with the progressed/solar arc Sun.

THE SEMISEXTILE (30°)

My teachers taught me that a semisextile was a slightly favorable aspect. For almost ten years I tried to force the semisextile into slightly favorable

---

[4]If you follow the rule of ten, a rule that I think I made up, you know that accuracy in mental mathematics depends on using numbers whose sum or difference does not exceed the number of fingers on both hands. In a pinch you can add one foot, but whenever you have gone beyond fifteen as a total number, you need a pencil. This rule of ten explains why most of us simply don't use the semisquare or sesquiquadrate aspect. The usual directions for finding it are to go to the next sign and add fifteen. Now this is inevitably going to get you to try to carry numbers (as well as signs) in your head, thereby creating confusion. I have made many errors by trying to do this in front of an audience or class. Under those circumstances it is impossible for me to add numbers over ten in my head.

There is a way to figure out these aspects using only the fingers of two hands (the original abacus) below the table or podium. 0 degrees cardinal equals 15 degrees fixed. 0 degrees fixed equals 15 degrees mutable. 0 degrees mutable equals 15 degrees cardinal.

status, but it just would not fit. My experience with clients has caused me to put this aspect in the slightly difficult file, regardless of what I had been taught.

SEMI-QUINTILE (36°), QUINTILE (72°) AND BIQUINTILE (144°)

The semi-quintile (36°) is one-tenth of 360 degrees.[5] The quintile and biquintile come from dividing 360 degrees by five. These three aspects are related by harmonic, and in fact, mean about the same thing. In the secondary chart, and in particular, when one of these aspects occurs between the progressed and natal position of the same planet, it seems to offer a creative or new means to resolve a problem. Unlike the septile, the solution doesn't seem to come from left field. Both the quintile and the semi-quintile provide the means for an "aha!" that not only resolves the problem, but holds up under later scrutiny as a logical way to have gotten out of a fix. In contrast, the septile seems to set the stage for an "aha!" for which you later can't find any logical connection, but which works fine. Using these aspects is most valuable when a difficult aspect (other than conjunction) is made with one of the planets connected by the quintile series. The transit or progression won't aspect both planets in the connection, so you can use one end of the aspect easily. The presence of one of the quintile series of aspects gives you the ability to create a new way out of the problem.

SEMISQUARE (45°) AND SESQUIQUADRATE (135°)

I've put these two aspects together because I have not been able to find any difference between their effects. These aspects act like hidden

Mumble to yourself "cardinal, fixed, mutable" a few times to get the order straight in your mind. Then go backwards or forwards from fifteen or zero.

[5]Some people call this a decile.

squares. They stir up as much action as a square, but they are not as obvious before the fact. You get a surprise when they are activated. This connection between two planets is a bit like a connection with a person who is nice to your face, but will stab you the moment you turn your back. You are never at ease with this person, because you don't know what will happen next. The two planets in these aspects are "on edge." It doesn't take much to get an event out of this combination.

SEPTILE (51.428°), BISEPTILE (102.856°) AND TRISEPTILE (154.384°)

The septile (51.428°) results from dividing 360 degrees by seven. It's a sextile minus 8–1/2 degrees. The biseptile is two times the septile, the triseptile three times the septile. These aspects form the seventh harmonic, since they derive from the division of 360 degrees by seven. These aspects are often described as "karmic." Regardless of how you define karma, the septile series seems to mean that you dredge up a wonderful solution to a problem without knowing how you arrived at the solution. It's almost a "deus ex machina" aspect, working on some inner instinctive level. If you'll let go and let your inner instinct take over, you'll resolve whatever conflict is at hand when you have this aspect exact from a progressed to natal position. The tension of the septile series arises from an adult disinclination to trust the universe. Little kids don't have too much trouble accepting wonderful solutions, but most of us get trained into distrusting solutions which don't have any logic attached.

SEXTILE (60°)

The sextile is a working aspect. This means that although it is an ease aspect, it packs more bounce than a trine does. Sextiles form a line along which the two energies can combine harmoniously. This creates a stable base from which action can arise. Progressed sextiles soften any difficult aspects from other progressions or outer planet transits.

SQUARE (90°)

Squares indicate stress that is out in the open. You need to do something to readjust the energies involved. Natal squares push you to act, to grow, to compromise between the two symbolisms. When a square is exact by progression, whether between two progressed planets or a progressed and a natal position, it usually signals an event. A square between an outer planet transit and a progressed position signals an uneasy time during which you know you should act, but outside events may not force the action upon you. During squares between two progressed positions or a progressed position and a natal position, the inner planet transits can be used to time the event(s). The transit to the natal position of either of the planets involved seems much stronger as a trigger than the transit to the progressed position itself. If you take a known event (such as an accident) and look at the natal chart, progressed chart and transits, you'll often find that the strongest trigger is the point *between* the natal and progressed position of one of the two planets involved in the square.

TRINE (120°)

Trines are a little like flowers: they don't feed you or pay the rent, but they are satisfying to the soul. Trines set up ease lines wherein you can relax. The combination of the two planets' energies brings an almost lethargic flow of simplicity. Progressed trines give you a period of quiet meditation when you can recover from stress aspects. If you've got a progressed trine going on while you are in the midst of a transiting mess, you may become pretty complacent about your wonderful ability to transcend the lower meanings of the difficult symbolisms of the transiting planets. This is fine, for as long as the trine holds out you will be able to get by even nasty Pluto. I usually advise clients who are starting a difficult outer transit pattern with a progressed trine protecting them that they still need to work on some of the issues involved with the difficult symbolism, for if the trine separates while the transiting planet (Pluto, for instance) is turning around to make another pass across their natal T-squares, they will have a tough time adjusting to the changed circumstances. It's very hard to actually dig in and make changes under a trine.

After all, your kids are gathering up all kinds of awards, getting into super colleges, your spouse is being promoted to big cheese, you are the golden-haired marvel at work, your car is running fine and your parents are supporting every decision you make. Well, maybe some of the above. Relax. Even type A personalities get progressed trines now and then. Let yourself smell the flowers.

INCONJUNCT (QUINCUNX) (150°)

Trying to define the inconjunct aspect reminds me of a story about a minister who was asked to give a eulogy for a thoroughly despicable character. The dead man had cheated, lied, stolen, pillaged, raped and killed, and otherwise spent his life attempting to break at least one commandment a day. The minister thought and thought and finally said, "His brother was worse."

Though some astrologers may differ with me, I can't think of any brother aspect to call "worse." The tension ranges from having the local bully call you names to getting raped. The results range from mild irritation to a stroke. Health issues often come up when an inconjunct is present by progression. It is a good idea to have a physical exam before the inconjunct aspect moves into position. Then DO whatever the doctor tells you to do. Be nicer to yourself. If you learn how to reduce stress before a progressed inconjunct, at least your body won't bear the brunt of the aspect.

Inconjuncts bring up issues of mortality. We Americans don't like to think about (much less talk about) death and dying. But pets and people do die, and you're likely to be thinking about this when an inconjunct is exact in your chart by progression. It's not always someone or something directly connected to you. For example, on November 22, 1963, President Kennedy was assassinated. I was eighteen years old. This death affected me very deeply, although I had no real connection to politics or the Kennedy family. Suddenly I realized that death didn't just happen to old people (like my grandparents) who had been ill for a long time. My progressed Sun was at 17° Aquarius 50', inconjunct my natal North Node (average node) at 17° Cancer 51', and my progressed Moon was at 5° Sagittarius 30', inconjunct my natal Saturn at 5° Cancer

39'. The only thing a counseling astrologer seeing these aspects approaching could have said would have involved an emotional connection to loss of a father figure, to thoughts of mortality, to a possible realignment of North Node career direction (which did not happen at that time). The two inconjuncts measured my reaction to the event.

OPPOSITION (180°)

Like the square, the opposition demands some sort of action by setting up a stress line between the two planets involved. The opposition is usually a little easier to resolve than the square, perhaps because it joins planets in the same yin or yang polarity. Oppositions usually indicate an event, an event timed by transit triggers to the natal position of one of the planets involved in the progressed opposition. Occasionally, the transit will be to the progressed position or to the position between the progressed and natal position of one of the planets involved in the opposition itself. Oppositions are out in the open. Folk wisdom has a thousand clichés describing the opposition by progression. The cleanest one is that it's time to fish or cut bait. You'll have to make a decision, and then you'll have to act on that decision. Oppositions are clearly not the end of the world, but they do mark out the times in your life when you have to pick which road you'll pursue. Oppositions from progressed planets (other than the Moon) involve fairly permanent choices.

CHAPTER 2

Combining the Possibilities:
ASPECT INTERACTION

To do predictive work, you have to combine aspect patterns. As you will see when you go through the example charts, single aspects rarely indicate events all by themselves. Instead, transits, progressions and natal positions interweave in almost endless patterns. In the following discussion, the background aspect could be a natal aspect, although I'm focusing the discussion on a background aspect consisting of a very slow progression. You can use the information here to interpret a transit to a natal combination. The strongest point in that aspect is *not* when the transit (or progression) is exact to either of the natal planets, but when the transit is precisely *between* each aspect.

This is not quite the same as looking at a midpoint. A midpoint is the degree and minute halfway between any two planets.[6] A transit or progression is between two aspects when it is approaching one aspect and separating from another. There is a "hot spot" in any pattern of two or more

---

[6]To calculate a midpoint, change the degree and minute to 360 notation, and subtract the smaller number from the larger. Divide your answer by two, and add this to the smaller original number. For example, to find the midpoint between a natal Sun at 25 Taurus and a progressed Sun at 15 Cancer, change to 360 notation, and 25 Taurus becomes 25 plus 30 (for Taurus) or 55, while 15 Cancer becomes 15 plus 90 (for Cancer) or 105. Then 105 − 55 = 50. 50/2 = 25. The last step is to add 25 to the smaller original number, or 55. 25 + 55 = 80. Now this has to be changed back to zodiacal notation. Gemini = 60, so 80 − 60 = 20 Gemini, which is the midpoint.

natal positions. This "hot spot is really the *average* of all the positions. Don't get into math anxiety over this; it is simply an easy way to find out when the influence of a transit or progression to a natal pattern is strongest.

I find that if a method takes too long or prints out too many pages from the computer, I never use it. This is my Libra rising (read lazy) way to get the important information. Simply write down the degree and minute of each of the planets in a configuration. Forget the signs. If you have Mars at 2° Taurus 47′, and Saturn at 4° Leo 23′, and the Moon at 5° Scorpio 32′, you have a T-square. To find the hot spot, add up the degrees and minutes and divide by the number of planets.

2	47
4	23
5	32
11	102

11/3 = 3-2/3 which is 3° 40′ and 102/3 = 34′. 40′ + 34′ = 74′, or 1° 14′, which you add to 3° to get 4° 14′. The hot spot for this T-square is 4° 14′ of any sign. Whenever a transit or progression is at that degree and minute it is equally distant from an aspect to each of the three planets in the configuration. Thus, the effect on the pattern is strongest at this degree and minute.

While calculating the hot spots for three or more planets in a natal configuration can pinpoint times of events, the progression of the chart creates another pattern situation which is unique. Whenever a progressed planet is exactly at its natal position (no orb), all of the major aspects and several of the minor aspects create situations in which transits can make simultaneous aspects to both natal and progressed positions. Each of these combinations has its own set of symbolism. In the following discussion, I'll look at the kinds of combinations possible, and their meanings.

SEMISEXTILE COMBINATIONS

When you are about thirty years old, your progressed Sun will semisextile your natal Sun. All your solar arc progressed positions will be 30

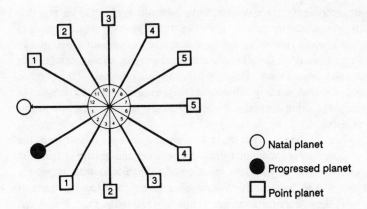

Figure 1. Combination aspects. Any planet in position ⬜1 forms a sextile and a semisextile simultaneously to either a natal planet or a progressed planet. In a similar manner, a planet located at positions ⬜2 , ⬜3 , ⬜4 or ⬜5 would also make combination aspects to a natal or progressed planet.

degrees from their own natal positions simultaneously with the Sun. When this occurs, any transit will aspect both natal and solar arc positions at the same time, but the aspects may be of quite different tone. If your natal Sun is 17° Taurus and your progressed Sun is 17° Gemini, transiting Saturn at 17° Virgo trines your natal Sun and squares your progressed Sun. (See figure 1.) You may decide that all of the aspects from Saturn stink, because the square to your progressed Sun indicates you won't see any benefits from the trine at this time. If you can resolve the complications arising from your current self-image (the progressed Sun) you can eventually reap the rewards of the trine to your natal Sun.

The Midheaven, Venus and Mars all can move about a degree a year by secondary progression, or at about the same rate as the Sun. Thus, you can have semisextiles between the natal and secondary progressed positions of any or all of these five positions within a year or two of each other. Add to that the cycles of the progressed Moon and transiting Saturn (both about twenty-eight years to conjunct the natal position) and you've got the potential for all sorts of things happening between ages twenty-six and thirty-two.

When the aspect from a transiting planet is easy to the natal position (trine or sextile) and difficult to the progressed position (square, opposition or inconjunct) you may have some difficulty arriving at the positive results symbolized by the transit. When this happens, you are getting in your own way. However, the square to the progressed position can simply give you that little kick in the pants most of us so often need to make a soft aspect work. Easy transits can lull you into such a state of somnolence that nothing whatsoever happens, but that square to the progressed position can wake you up and prod you to grasp the opportunities at hand.

When the set-up is the other way around, and the aspect from the transit is square or inconjunct the natal position and sextile or trine the progressed position, you have to let go of old habits in order to get the best out of the transit. Every time you revert to a natal pattern of response, the square (or inconjunct) hits you full in the face. If you can adapt and use your progressed symbolism (the new you) to full effect, you can pull your chestnuts out of the fire before they burn.

There are two more ways you can have transiting planets aspect both natal and progressed positions while the semisextile is present. You can have an opposition/inconjunct combination or a conjunction/ semisextile combination. Both of these combinations are difficult.

Opposition/Inconjunct

The opposition suggests action, while the inconjunct suggests tension. If the opposition is to the natal position, the action is a little clearer, and the tension involves whether or not you like your new projection of whichever planet is involved.

Let's suppose you have natal Mercury at 12° Capricorn and progressed Mercury at 12° Aquarius. Jupiter comes along to 12° Cancer, opposing your natal Mercury and inconjuncting your progressed Mercury. Jupiter oppositions are usually positive, but they can symbolize expansion of the current situation. If the current situation is difficult, Jupiter can make it worse than you ever thought possible. This particular transit has added tension from the inconjunct to progressed Mercury. If you give in to the hyperbole often associated with Jupiter opposed natal Mercury, you will be tense or upset with your own bragging. Or, you may offer to do everything for someone else (putting yourself in service to that other person) as the opposition prompts you to think that you can take on all of the world's problems, while the inconjunct sets you up to work for that promise. You may worry that someone is going to demand that you put your money where your mouth is, a thought quite different from the opposition alone.

What if transiting Jupiter were at 12° Virgo, opposing the progressed position and inconjunct the natal position? Now the action is going on through the progressed position while the tension is going on through the natal position. It's like your basic inside way of thinking and talking (your natal Mercury) doesn't approve of your current way of expressing yourself (or your current way of thinking). So that little voice inside nags and picks on you every time you open your mouth. "Are you sure you can do it?" "That wasn't quite the truth." "You know better than that." And so on and so on until you're ready to draw and quarter the owner of that little voice inside. This aspect combination will force you to clarify your progressed position, for you won't be able to act on that opposition unless you smooth out the tension with your natal pattern of thought.

Conjunction/Semisextile

In many ways, the conjunction/semisextile combination of transit to natal and progressed positions is similar to the opposition/inconjunct pattern described above. The tension implied in the semisextile is quite a bit like the tension of the inconjunct. The difference is that the inconjunct involves either a sexual tension or a tension revolving around service to others, while the semisextile involves either an unconscious dislike for the manifestation of energy present or a tension around the materialistic components of what's going on.

When the transit is conjunct the natal position and semisextile the progressed position, you are busy worrying about whether you're acting on the conjunction purely from a materialistic point of view. Alternately, you may find that action along the conjunction involves changing your value system. When the transit is semisextile the natal position and conjunct the progressed position, you may discover new things about yourself to dislike. This combination is rarely strong enough to make you want to do anything about these new things you dislike, but it does point out to you a few more imperfections in your natal position or response nature. After the aspect goes away you can decide whether to live with this newly discovered wart or go through the aggravation of getting rid of it.

Semisquare/Sesquiquadrate

The semisquare and sesquiquadrate only combine with conjunctions, oppositions and squares. If your progressed Sun is semisquare your natal Sun, any transit which conjuncts, squares or opposes your natal Sun will either semisquare or sesquiquadrate your progressed Sun. Thus, any stress/action aspects will involve both the symbol of your inner (natal) self and your current projection of your self. Whenever you have a semisquare or sesquiquadrate exact by progression, direction or outer planet transit, the effect of any square, opposition or conjunction to either end of the semisquare or sesquiquadrate will double.

SEXTILE COMBINATIONS

When you have a sextile exact by progression, direction or outer planet transit, the two planets will combine with any other transit or progression at the same degree and minute of any sign. The combinations possible (see figure 2 on page 18) range from very easy (sextile and trine) to extremely tense (semisextile each or inconjunct each). We'll start with the bad news and move on to the difficult, then to the fun combinations.

Semisextile Midpoint/Yod

Figure 2a is without a doubt the most difficult pattern possible with a sextile. The semisextile position between each end of the sextile sets up a powerful direct midpoint. The action of each of the planets in the sextile focuses through the planet in the middle. This is an uncomfortable action, for you must compromise the ease of the sextile to use the force of the center planet. When the third planet moves into the position opposite the center of the sextile, you have a figure commonly known as a yod. The word *yod* means "finger of God." This is the same finger God showed Job in the Old Testament. Events which occur with a yod pattern almost always bring up sacrifice, letting go, change. It seems that you can't have the ease of the sextile unless you abandon the symbol of the point planet. If you keep the symbol of the point planet, you must give up the sextile. The great lesson of the yod is to somehow compromise enough to function with all three symbolisms.

Yods bring pressure as inevitably as a hurricane brings wind. The longer the yod is present, the more pressure is possible. When you have close natal yods, you learn over and over again how to balance the discordant combination of symbolism. But when the yod is exact only by progression, direction or outer planet transit, you have a period of several months within which you must make compromises and adjustments between the energies indicated. If you have no natal inconjuncts, you are not well prepared for the resistance you will encounter.

Not all of the resistance is internal. This is probably the hardest feature of a yod. You may be as flexible as possible, as reasonable as any human could be, and either the situation or the people involved won't budge. Fairness, truth, responsible behavior may not make any difference when the pattern involved is a yod. Before you blame yourself for everything occurring, however, talk the situation over with friends or a counselor. While you may have some input or causal connection, at least half of the situations symbolized by yod patterns are not connected to anything the person with the yod did, thought, felt or subconsciously wished to have happen.

Square/Inconjuct or Semisextile/Square

The next combination is the square/inconjunct or semisextile/square (figure 2b). Action is possible along the line of the square. If you don't notice the semisextile or the inconjunct, you won't be ready for the tension involved in what otherwise might seem a straightforward choice situation. Guilt is attached to any decision when a tension aspect is involved. This pattern typifies any situation in which you can't please everyone. If the semisextile or inconjunct is the aspect which will last longer, there will be after-effects from any decision you make—even a decision to postpone making a decision. If the square is the longer-lasting aspect, the decisions and action needed will take more effort than you expected, but you will be able to overcome criticism of your choices.

Opposition/Trine

The opposition/trine combination (figure 2c) usually provides exactly the kind of punch a trine or sextile needs to get moving. This pattern doesn't let you vegetate through the sextile, but at the same time offers

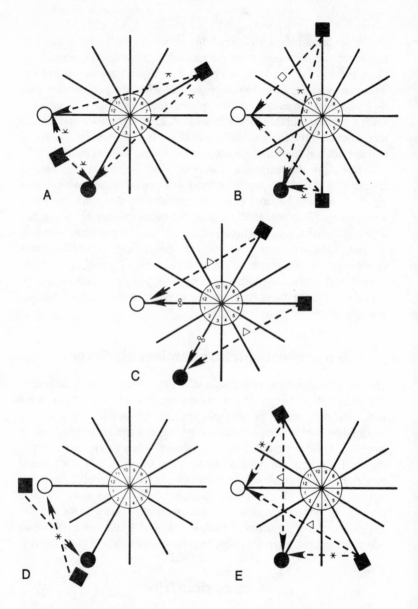

Figure 2. Sextile combinations. A) shows semisextile midpoint/yod; B) shows square/inconjunct or semisextile/square; C) shows opposition/trine; D) shows conjunction/sextile; and E) shows trine/sextile.

excellent rewards for effort expended. The explosive power of an opposition from transiting Pluto or transiting Uranus, for instance, removes obstructions in your path, allowing you to move along the path of either the trine or the sextile. Whenever you have this combination by progression, direction or outer planet transit, pay attention to the aftermath of the opposition. Often the opposition itself works like a cosmic chiropractor. You hear an alarming popping and snapping, after which you can walk again without stiffness.

Conjunction/Sextile

The conjunction/sextile (figure 2d) isn't as dramatic as the opposition/trine. It's more like a massage therapist than a chiropractor. Most of us don't get the alarming popping and snapping with a conjunction. But the action implied by the conjunction can start that sextile moving in some fashion. The presence of the sextile pushes the conjunction towards the more favorable possibilities inherent in the symbolism of the conjunction.

Trine/Sextile

The final possible combination, trine/sextile, emphasizes easy flow all around (see figure 2e). You get a double dip of ice cream in a sugar cone with chocolate sprinkles. Don't put a work trip on this one; it won't take it. Enjoy the time to relax. Let life flow around you. Plan a vacation. When does the next one come up?

SQUARE COMBINATIONS

When we think about combinations with a progressed square, we tend to focus on something conjunct or opposed one of the ends of the square, doubling the square or forming a T-square. It isn't hard to analyze these combinations, for they emphasize the need for action already indicated (see figure 3). If you have not decided to jump in and do something about whatever is happening in your life, the universe will shove you into the middle of it. If your life is going along quite nicely, don't over-schedule during this combination. Then you can take advantage of whatever shows up, rather than have to decline the gift.

Semisextile or Inconjunct/Sextile or Trine

There is another way the square can be triggered, which involves either a semisextile or inconjunct with either a sextile or trine. Action is more likely when the faster aspect is one of the ends of the square rather than the sextile, trine, semisextile or inconjunct. (See the previous section on sextile combinations.) When the slowest aspect is the square, the addition of the ease and tension combination tends to muddy the waters.

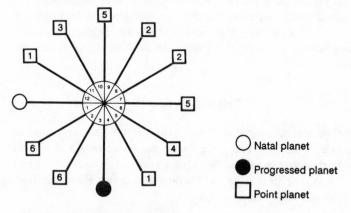

Figure 3. Square combinations.

[1] Any planet in this position forms a semisextile and trine to the natal and progressed planet.

[2] Any planet in this position forms an inconjunct and trine to the natal and progressed planet.

[3] Any planet in this position forms a sextile and inconjunct to the natal and progressed planet.

[4] Any planet in this position forms an inconjunct and sextile to the natal and progressed planet.

[5] Any planet in this position forms a square and an opposition to the natal and progressed planet.

[6] Any planet in this position forms a semisextile and sextile to the natal and progressed planet.

You can evaluate your choices or decisions much more easily before or after the ease/tension combination occurs.

Suppose transiting Jupiter sextiles natal Mercury while inconjuncting progressed Mercury. If you ignore the aspect to progressed Mercury, you may wax eloquent about relationships, material goods, fun and games. Your client may become very confused when he or she suffers a major bout of foot in mouth disease in the presence of an ideal other person.

TRINE COMBINATIONS

A background trine aspect from a slow progression to a natal position is often either ignored or over-emphasized in an analysis. (See figure 4.) Trines don't indicate events. Trines symbolize the easiest way over, around or through other difficulties. Sometimes people won't use their trines because they don't like to do things the easy way. If, for instance, you have a natal Venus-Pluto square, and your progressed Venus trines natal and progressed Pluto, you may be so used to having love relationships involve power and pressure that you simply can't relax and let yourself get the goodies the easy way. When another planet comes along to excite the background trine, you have an easy way to deal with the situation. It *is* up to you to decide to let it flow. Background trines can function to soften any other aspects coming through at the same time. If you are quite determined to do things in the hardest way possible, background trines may let you ignore a nasty situation until the trine separates and absolutely nothing can be done to correct the mess.

When the slowest combination is a trine aspect, the faster transit or progression can trigger the trine in some surprising ways. All through this book, the references to sextiles and trines indicate that they don't symbolize action, but rather ease the action of other aspects. The major exception to this general rule occurs when the slowest combination is a trine, and the faster aspect makes two sextiles (is in between the two ends of the trine) or makes two trines (opposite the point exactly between the two planets trining each other). Because these two positions are also midpoints, they mean action. The grand trine or double-sextile/trine starts life moving quickly. If the slowest combination isn't the trine (see section on sextiles) you won't have as much push towards action as you will when the trine itself is the background aspect.

The second surprise in this combination comes if you expect the usual trine/sextile goodies. Yes, there are usually more nice than nasty things associated with this combination, but it won't work as easily as a sextile/opposition. The problem arises because you usually try to do everything at once when the trigger planet hits the midpoint. You may not have a focus for activity. You're bursting with energy, like an eager kid the coach sends into the soccer game, who then runs the ball the wrong way down the field. Before the trigger planet hits, find out which goal is yours.

Sextile/Opposition

The sextile/opposition works on a background trine exactly the way a trine/opposition works on a background sextile. This combination gets

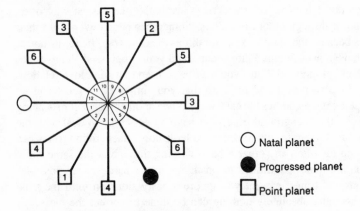

Figure 4. Trine combinations.
[1] Any planet in this position forms a sextile to both natal and progressed planets.
[2] Any planet in this position forms a trine to both natal and progressed planets.
[3] Any planet in this position forms a sextile and an opposition to the natal and progressed planet.
[4] Any planet in this position forms a semisextile and square to the natal and progressed positions.
[5] Any planet in this position forms a square and an inconjunct to the natal and progressed positions.
[6] Any planet in this position forms a semisextile and an inconjunct to the natal and progressed positions.

the lead out and moves that background trine into action. The background trine insures that you can turn the opposition into opportunity, regardless of the outer difficulty of the symbolism. Suppose you have transiting Uranus opposing your natal Sun, while progressed Saturn is exactly trine your natal Sun. That Saturn progression will be there at least as long as transiting Uranus. Uranus will loosen any over-control that progressed Saturn might indicate, while progressed Saturn will stabilize the sudden shifts that Uranus brings.

Semisextile/Square or Inconjunct/Square

The semisextile/square or inconjunct/square aspects tend to shake up the complacency of a background trine. The square urges you to take action, while the tension aspect nags at you with guilt or fear. If the trigger aspect is a fast one (like transiting Mars in fast, direct motion) most of us don't do anything but think about what we could have done. The longer the trigger aspect hangs around, the more likely you are to move that trine. Inner planets usually can't budge a background trine from the tension-action position.

Semisextile/Inconjunct

The semisextile and inconjunct combined with a background trine are unlikely to indicate action. When the trigger planet is one of the inner planets, the semisextile/inconjunct stirs up a little guilt and makes you think a bit about what you might do. That inner planet actually will trigger the trine when it gets to the conjunction/trine position. As it passes the semisextile/inconjunct you get a foretaste of what you'll need to do when the trigger planet comes to the conjunction. Sometimes, with a slower trigger, this combination symbolizes a distasteful set of circumstances which you handle quite well.

Conjunction/Trine

The last of the combinations with a background trine is the conjunction/ trine. The background trine provides a steady line of ease along which to take that conjunction to a positive result. A conjunction from an inner planet may not have enough energy to overcome the lethargy of a trine without some other action aspects in the chart. However, if combined with other stress/action aspects to anything else in the chart, this combination yields extremely positive results.

INCONJUNCT COMBINATIONS

As you can see from figure 5, there isn't any simple, easy combination possible to trigger a background inconjunct. Every trigger position involves a combination of ease and stress/action, or tension and stress/action, or ease and tension. No wonder the inconjunct aspect is so difficult.

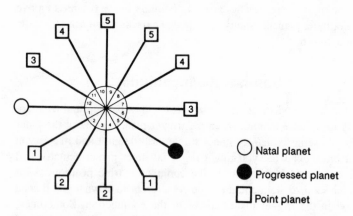

○ Natal planet

● Progressed planet

□ Point planet

Figure 5. Inconjunct combinations.
1 Any planet in this position forms a semisextile and trine to the natal and progressed positions.
2 Any planet in this position forms a sextile and square to the natal and progressed positions.
3 Any planet in this position forms an opposition and a semisextile to the natal and progressed positions.
4 Any planet in this position forms an inconjunct and a sextile to the natal and progressed positions.
5 Any planet in this position forms a square and a trine to the natal and progressed positions.

Semisextile/Trine or Inconjunct/Sextile

Of the possible combinations, the semisextile/trine or inconjunct/sextile is probably the least outwardly troubling. Most of us choose to stand pat during these patterns, and for good reason. You're up to your ears in alligators with the background inconjunct. You don't have time to fuss over whether or not there are mosquitoes in the swamp. Don't expect these positions to trigger much: at most they intensify the dilemma.

Sextile/Square or Square/Trine

In contrast, a trigger planet in either the sextile/square position or the square/trine position starts to break up the rigidity of the inconjunct. Maybe you grab hold of a big stick with which you can bash alligators. The square part of the pattern indicates the line along which you can take action. In order to get out of the inconjunct, you have to do something. The square gives you something to do, and the sextile or trine provides some basis for the action. Often the type of action which relieves the tension follows the symbolism of both the trigger planet and the natal house the trigger planet is transiting.

Conjunction/Inconjunct or Opposition/Semisextile

The conjunction/inconjunct or opposition/semisextile trigger positions work along similar lines. You have to take action along the line of the conjunction or opposition in order to relieve the tension of the background inconjunct. For most of us, it doesn't feel much like compromise. It seems more like you are abandoning the planet not involved in the conjunction or opposition. It would be lovely to assure you that you can have that other symbolism back if you only let go of it. Sometimes it works that way. Sometimes it takes a long, long time before you can use that other planet's symbolism with any kind of ease. Playing guilt games is what got you stuck in the inconjunct in the first place. Don't go back to sit in the trap by blaming yourself if you don't heal immediately.

OPPOSITION COMBINATIONS

A background opposition demands attention. It is very difficult to ignore or suppress the symbolism of the two planets involved. Opposition

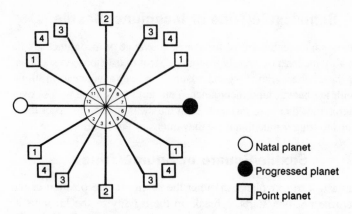

Figure 6. Opposition combinations.

1 Any planet in this position forms a semisextile and an inconjunct to the natal and progressed positions.

2 Any planet in this position forms a square to both natal and progressed positions.

3 Any planet in this position forms a sextile and a trine to the natal and progressed positions.

4 Any planet in this position forms a semisquare and a sesquiquadrate to the natal and progressed positions.

energy is so intense that even the trine/sextile will bring activity. Opposition energy often indicates a time during your life when you finally understand the areas of yourself that are symbolized by the two planets involved. You might not like yourself a whole lot during a progressed Mars opposition to your natal and progressed Pluto. But every time a transit kicks off that opposition, you'll learn more about how you deal with anger, how you respond to pressure, and most importantly, just what you've got inside for personal power. Most people find that during the slower progressed oppositions (progressed Jupiter oppositions take about a year, Saturn, Uranus, Neptune and Pluto take longer) events that all have a similar message occur. Eventually, if you are paying attention to what's going on in your life, you figure out how to put the two energies together, resolving the opposition (see figure 6).

Semisextile/Inconjunct

There are three combination patterns possible with a background opposition. The first of these, the semisextile/inconjunct position, inhibits the action orientation of the background opposition. While the semisextile/ inconjunct is present, you tend to worry about the outcome of any action you initiate. If you've been popping off all over the place with every other trigger to this background opposition, the semisextile/inconjunct may indicate a need to slow down and consider directing the energy of the opposition. If the trigger isn't an inner planet, but is transiting Jupiter or Saturn, you'll have more than a twinge of guilt over inappropriate uses of your background opposition. The progressed Moon can toss you into emotional turmoil about the use of the opposition. Before one of these closes in on an inconjunct/semisextile to that background opposition, clean up your act. The more clearly you understand the stress symbolism of the opposition, the less difficulty you'll have with the tension triggers.

Square/Square

This combination is the double-action combination, where a triggering planet squares both ends of the opposition, conjuncts one end, or semi-squares one end and sesquiquadrates the other end. Differentiating between these combinations is like talking about the difference between two tons, three tons or four tons of TNT. It only matters if you are not standing next to it when it goes off. For those of us on the observation deck, the square is the four-ton load, the semisquare the three-ton load and the conjunction the two-ton load of dynamite. The tighter the opposition is, the smaller the spark you need to set it off.

Dynamite is quite useful when you want to get rid of obstructions, build roads, or dig foundations for future construction. If you approach these aspects with some idea of what you want to use the energy to accomplish, you can establish a certain amount of control over the effect of these combinations. Engaging in sky-diving or motorcycle scrambles while you have one of these triggers hitting off a background opposition, however, is rather like tossing a cigarette butt into the pile of dynamite. It might not light one of the fuses. But then again . . .

Sextile/Trine

The third combination possible comes from the sextile/trine position. Now you have a way to move the opposition energy into positive focus. Grab this one and run with it. Watch for these times, because you can make the best use of that background symbolism every time something moves into one of the four sextile/trine positions. The inner planet transits provide quite a few opportunities to resolve the stress of the opposition. If transiting Jupiter or Saturn or the progressed Moon makes an ease pattern to both ends of a progressed opposition, use the time period to pull the two planets in the opposition into a positive connection. It is possible, under these circumstances, to have results which mimic a positive conjunction rather than an opposition.

CHAPTER 3

Let's See
How They Run:
EXAMPLE CHARTS

The following charts are examples of combinations of secondary progressions and transits which could be used to predict an event. All of the names have been changed to protect the privacy of the people involved. Sometimes events show up quite clearly with the transits alone, as the fourth example, Lucky Lucy, shows. The first two example charts belong to a friend who has an interest in astrology. Neither she nor her astrologer had worked with progressions, and Kay told me that neither of these events showed astrologically. As you will see from the charts, the progressions in each case outlined the possibility of an event. The first incident had a 0 degree orb conjunction between Mercury and Neptune by progression; the second incident had a combination of conjunction and semisextiles by progression.

The third example shows two things. First, the combination of progressed Saturn square natal Sun and progressed Sun inconjunct natal Saturn set off warning bells in my head. I had birth information for more than one person in the family, so instead of turning to more complex techniques to unearth the outcome of this combination of aspects, I looked at Seth's wife Stella's chart. By analyzing the progressions and transits to her chart during the days surrounding the most difficult aspects in Seth's chart, I was able to make an accurate prediction of the result of the event indicated by the planetary positions.

This third example may provide the most valuable information for you, the student of astrology, for it clearly shows two things. Not only must you treat the chart as a whole, avoiding making judgments based upon only one aspect; you also must gather information about the gestalt of the person involved. In this case, Stella and Seth are happily married and very much in love. Nothing which had a major effect on one of them could have no effect on the other. Even if Seth and Stella hated each other, there would have to be some change in each chart if a major accident occurred involving the family breadwinner. If you see something which looks awful coming up in the chart of someone you care a lot about, look at your own chart for the same date. Is there anything going on? If not, the event may be scary, but the person will pull through just fine.

When you are doing this kind of person-to-person analysis, you have to be totally honest. One of my clients had been caring for her mother, who was extremely ill for three years. My client loved her mother dearly, but moving her mother from the hospital, to the nursing home, to her own house time and again certainly was wearing. Her mother's chart showed some difficult aspects just when all the trouble in my client's chart separated. Her mother died. My client's mother was ninety-one years old. It was not a negative event. But my client had a hard time accepting the fact that the death of her mother was a blessing.

This case had to be analyzed quite differently from Seth and Stella's combination. Had I not asked all sorts of questions about the kind of relationship that this client had with her mother, I might have assumed that her mother would recover, in spite of the medical evidence to the contrary.

Events which affect children (no matter how old the "child" is) affect the charts of their parents, as long as the parent has contact with the child. If your thirty-year-old son, who doesn't live with you, breaks his leg, your chart will show some sort of sharp aspect. If the son then comes to convalesce with you, your chart will show more stress.

If you have not spoken to a brother for ten years, you won't find much in the way of hard aspects in your own chart when something happens to that sibling. If the event brings your parents into focus, the indicators may be difficult to decipher, for you may respond to your parents' stress more than to the event involving your sibling.

We are all connected, not only to the universe, but to other people who touch our lives. Use your knowledge of these connections to sharpen your skills in predictive astrology. It certainly isn't cheating to use every available source of information when you want to know what is going to happen!

KAY'S CONCUSSIONS:
A ONE-TWO PUNCH

Kay is extremely bright, has a Ph.D., and is involved in so many projects she makes us ordinary mortals tired just watching her. Her father is a professor at a university in the midwest, where Kay grew up. Kay's mother taught elementary school and did the traditional things that a faculty wife had to do during the fifties. Kay's brother also is bright and successful.

Kay had two concussions, ten years and three days apart. The events surrounding the two concussions were quite different; the aspects in her chart were also different. Yet there are certain similarities between the aspects, as we will see in the analysis.(See Chart 1 on page 32.)

Kay has not had any other concussions so far in her life. Her Sun-Mercury conjunction trines her natal MC, squares her natal Jupiter and sextiles her natal Uranus. The trine and sextile indicate that she can usually move fast enough (Uranus) to extricate herself from difficult situations. With her Sun square Jupiter, she may get into bigger predica-ments than many of us. This particular square doesn't suggest that she is accident prone so much as that she is likely to be opinionated and/or climb up on soapboxes to champion "good causes." Kay does just that. With the Pluto-Mars-Ascendant conjunction, Kay can be quite forceful when she believes in what she's doing. A certain sense of invincibility comes with this combination of Ascendant power and righteousness from Jupiter. She really believes Davy Crockett's dictum: When you know you are right, go ahead.

With all her planets on the east, Kay is a self-starter. It's hard for her to share power, so she works for herself. Her planets are all contained in the trine from Jupiter to the Saturn-Neptune conjunction. Here we have a concentration of energy. I don't think that Kay is fully aware of the enormous impact she has on the people around her. She isn't afraid to make waves, but knows the importance of doing her homework before

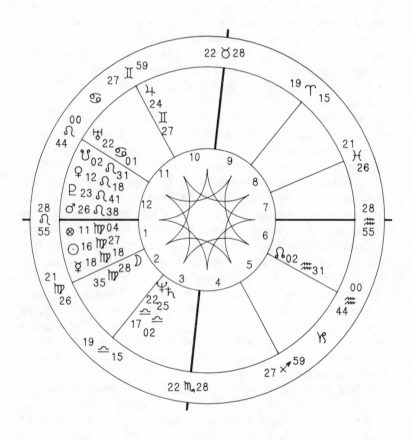

Chart 1. Kay's natal chart. September 9, 1953, at 4:35 AM CST, 42N16, 95W52. Data from birth certificate; Placidus Houses.

she stirs something up. That Saturn-Neptune conjunction helps her understand the needs of this particular reality plane, while the Jupiter trine to that conjunction provides the background to successfully defend even extremely unpopular positions.

The first event occurred in 1973. Kay had recently graduated from a midwestern college, and had been living in the "big city" for a little over nine months. She was collecting money at a college dance, when four young hoods snatched the cashbox. Not a seasoned city girl, fueled by the invincible Pluto-Mars-Ascendant conjunction and Sun-Jupiter square, Kay (who is about 5'3" tall) vaulted the table and chased the group. Two of the hoodlums jumped on a campus bus (the police later arrested them). The other two turned on Kay and punched her in the head. That was concussion #1.

The incident occurred on October 6, 1973, at about 10:00 P.M. EDT. Kay wasn't thinking too clearly—she had progressed Mercury conjunct her natal Neptune with 0 degree orb. (See Chart 2 and Chart 3 on pages 34–35.) Kay's progressed Jupiter was 35 minutes of arc from sextile her natal Mars while her progressed Saturn was 35 minutes of arc past the sextile to her natal Mars. The point exactly between Kay's progressed Jupiter and progressed Saturn was Kay's natal Mars. This kind of combination often indicates dealing with money.

The transiting positions give us information about the possibility of accident or violence, for transiting Uranus was 48 minutes of arc (separating) from square to her natal Uranus. If you add up the degrees and minutes (disregarding signs) of natal Uranus, progressed Uranus and transiting Uranus, then divide by three, you get what I call a "hot spot" or the middle of the influence of the three planets. The average is 22° 14′, 3 minutes of arc from that progressed Mercury–natal Neptune conjunction. Transiting Jupiter was 7 minutes of arc from conjunct Kay's natal Node, 57 minutes of arc (separating) from sesquiquadrate Kay's natal Sun, 55 minutes of arc (approaching) sesquiquadrate Kay's natal Mercury. Jupiter was only 1 minute of arc from sesquiquadrate the natal Sun/Mercury midpoint. Both the progressed midpoint and the transiting Jupiter hits to the Sun/Mercury midpoint are easy to see without using any dials or extra tools. If you want to analyze further with a 90 degree dial, you will see many more midpoints indicating challenge of control, running after the crooks, etc.

One of the aspects I would use to time this doesn't involve Kay's own chart directly. At the time of the robbery, transiting Saturn was

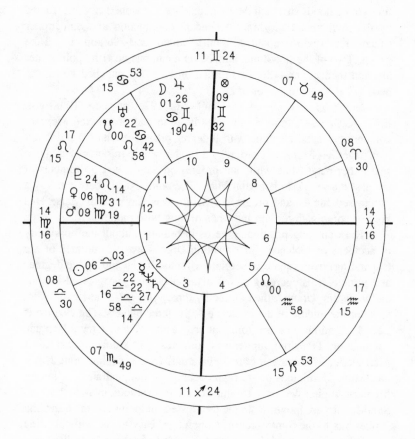

Chart 2. Kay's progressed chart for October 6, 1973, her first concussion. The Midheaven is progressed by the traditional (Naibod Arc) method.

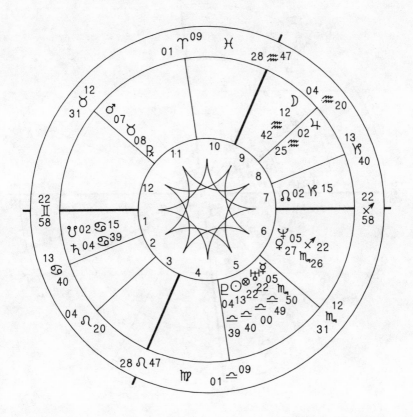

Chart 3. Kay's transit chart for the approximate time (10:00 PM EDT) of the incident on October 6, 1973, which occurred at 40N21, 74W39.

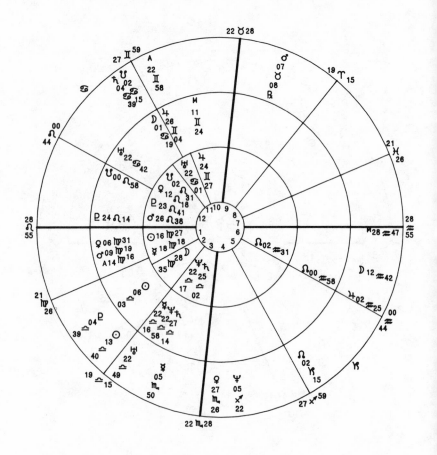

Chart 4. Kay's triple wheel. Kay's natal chart is on the inside, her progressed positions are in the middle, and the transits are on the outside for October 6, 1973, at 10:00 PM EDT.

exactly square transiting Pluto in the sky. The two planets are not precisely aspecting Kay's chart, although they're within 2 degrees of square her North Node. The key is that this aspect occurs on a day that Kay does have precise aspects to her chart by progression. Somewhere in this world existed someone else whose planets were aspected precisely by this square. Without branching into the more detailed dial analysis, I would have told Kay to be careful on that day because her head wasn't screwed on particularly tightly.

The next time Kay got banged on the head was October 9, 1983. It was Sunday and Kay had gone to her office to catch up on a few things before she left on Tuesday for a business trip. No one was in the office except Kay. At about 2:30 P.M., she climbed on a desk to adjust something, slipped and fell, hitting her head on the side of the desk. There was no one around to help out. Kay had to keep from passing out long enough to get some help for herself.

When we look at the progressed chart (see Chart 5 on page 38), we see progressed Mars 19 minutes of arc (separating) from semisextile progressed Sun. Mars was progressing slowly, only moving 38 minutes during the year. The Sun was progressing at a rate of 59 minutes per year. That semisextile had been exact on November 24, 1982. Mars wouldn't conjunct Kay's natal Sun by progression for over a year, even though the two are only 51 minutes apart. Kay's progressed Sun was 21 minutes of arc (approaching) semisextile her natal Sun. That semisextile would be exact on April 19, 1984. She was just about exactly between the two semisextiles. This means that the tension aspects were both in force, although neither was exact. There had to be some sort of trigger to pull that tension into the open. It didn't have to be a very big trigger, because she was so close to the time exactly between both aspects.

Kay's progressed Ascendant was 7 minutes of arc from exact semi-square to Kay's progressed Mercury. With the angles, a 7 minute arc is about as exact as you'll ever get, because we simply can't time the birth to the second. The Ascendant often symbolizes your physical surroundings. Here we have some sort of mental difficulty within or due to the immediate environment. Kay's progressed Moon was 52 minutes of arc (separating) from semisquare her natal Sun, while 1 degree (approaching) semisquare her natal Mercury. The progressed Moon was only 8 minutes of arc from exactly between the two aspects. Further, the progressed Moon was in a 12 minute applying square to Kay's natal

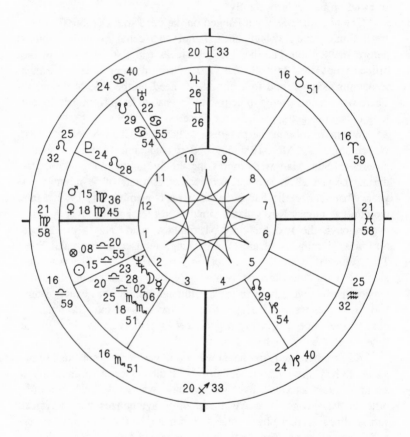

Chart 5. Kay's progressed chart for October 9, 1983, the second concussion. The Midheaven is progressed by the traditional (Naibod Arc) method.

Nodes. Stress/action aspects between the Sun and Moon involve conflict between the emotional and the physical self. Thus, they can indicate physical stress. Mercury is related to the brain or nervous system. Mars (the head) is already present symbolically. I often use the Nodes to indicate business connections. Kay was at work, in spite of the fact that it was Sunday.

There are two protective aspects from the progressed positions to the natal positions. Progressed Pluto is 1 minute of arc from sextile natal Jupiter, and the progressed Ascendant is 3 minutes of arc from sextile natal Uranus. Kay would be able to pull herself together and go get help.

On the triple wheel you can see the combinations of transiting positions and progressed positions. The transiting Sun at 15° Libra 52′ (2:00 P.M. position, could be a bit off) conjuncts Kay's progressed Sun, pulling together three positions: the progressed Mars conjunction to the natal Sun, the separating semisextile from the progressed Sun to Mars, and the approaching semisextile from the progressed Sun to the natal Sun. Besides the transiting Sun conjunction to the progressed Sun, transiting Neptune was 19 minutes of arc past the opposition to progressed Jupiter, transiting Pluto 30 minutes past the conjunction to progressed Saturn, transiting Jupiter 10 minutes past semisquare progressed Neptune, and the transiting Node 28 minutes from sesquiquadrate the progressed Moon. These are all stress/action combinations. The background is certainly set.

If the transiting Sun were the only trigger, my argument here would be pretty flimsy. The most powerful push to the combination in Kay's chart comes from the transiting Mars-Uranus square (exact later in the day) which is approaching semisquare/sesquiquadrate Kay's natal Uranus. Although transiting Uranus won't be exactly sesquiquadrate natal Uranus until October 22, transiting Mars will be exact two days later. (When I mentioned this to Kay she told me that on Tuesday, when she had to fly to the west coast on business, she had a monumental headache. All her business negotiations were more difficult because she was understandably irritable.)

If you noticed the transiting Mars square transiting Uranus on October 9 (see Chart 7 on page 41), you could have pinpointed that day as a target for activity in Kay's chart, primarily because the transiting Sun pulled in all the tension and action surrounding both Kay's natal and progressed Sun.

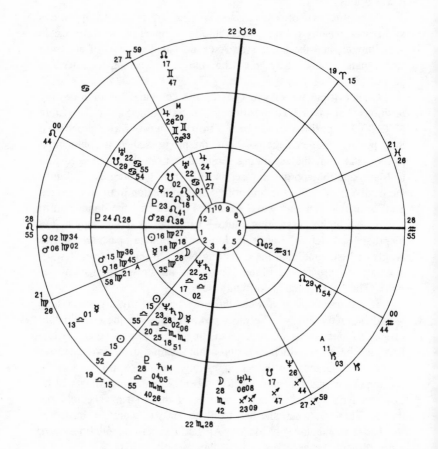

Chart 6. Kay's triple wheel for October 9, 1983. This wheel has Kay's natal chart on the inside, her progressed chart in the middle, and the transits on the outside for the second concussion, October 9, 1983, at about 2:00 PM EDT.

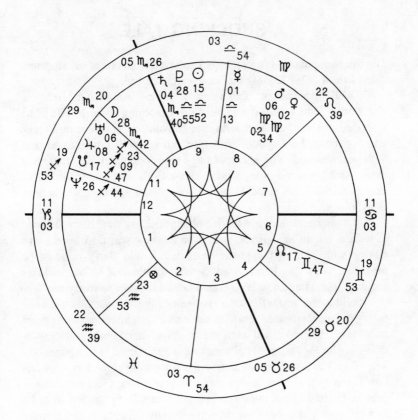

Chart 7. Kay's transits on October 9, 1983. This is a chart erected for the approximate time of the incident (2:00 PM EDT), which occurred at 40N21, 74W39.

Curiosity prompted me to see if there was anything going on around Kay's natal Neptune at the time of the second concussion, since Neptune had been involved (with progressed Mercury conjunct it) the day of the first concussion. The transiting Jupiter transiting Uranus midpoint was exactly (0 degree) semisquare Kay's natal Neptune at the time of the second concussion!

A SHOCKING TALE

The following quote is from a letter I received from one of my students, dated June 17, 1987. Only the names are changed.

"Well, it happened! Seth's narrow escape around June 10th! He was working in a confined area last Friday morning about 10:30 and he sustained an electrical shock with enough voltage that he couldn't break away or speak. Luckily Joe, his helper, ran and pulled the breaker, and Seth was released! You also told me—after looking at my progressed chart—that I was just going to say 'Thank God,' and I must admit I've said that a few times since! How is it possible for anyone not to believe in astrology!

"Of course Seth didn't tell me about this. My son, Barry, learned of it from one of his friends, and asked me how was Dad when I was talking with him on the phone yesterday. I told Barry he must be mistaken, but today I had to ask Seth point blank if he had had this accident. He admitted to it, and said he didn't want to worry me!"

Stella, who wrote the letter, is one of my students. She had been taking private lessons to learn to use secondary progressions during April and May, 1987. We had used the charts of her family members as examples for the lessons. (Follow along with Charts 8–11 on pages 43–47.) When I'm giving private instruction in astrology, I teach my students how to put up the charts, unless they own computers. I feel that students need to be able to ask questions and get charts fairly quickly in order to keep their enthusiasm for the answers alive. Furthermore, being a Capricorn, I don't want my students calling me at odd hours and asking me to calculate their charts on my computer. Hand calculations had brought us to a prediction concerning Seth for about June 10. The event actually occurred on June 12. The computer calculations place the prediction precisely on the twelfth.

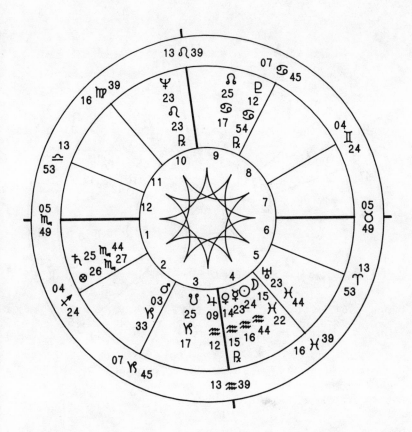

Chart 8. Seth's natal chart, February 13, 1926, 11:15 PM EST, 42N22, 71W04. Information from birth certificate; Placidus Houses.

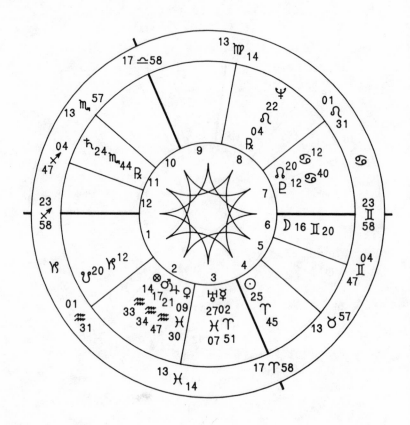

Chart 9. Seth's progressed chart for June 12, 1987, 10:30 AM EDT.
The Midheaven is progressed by the traditional (Naibod Arc) method.

Stella attended an intermediate class for several months. Seth drove her to class because Stella has poor night vision, and it is a forty-minute drive from their house. During our classes, Seth sat in the kitchen and worked on electrical design prints or listened to the radio. All the class members grew to love both Seth and Stella, who demonstrated a kind of loving which let the rest of us see that sometimes there is a "happily ever after." They are openly affectionate, although Stella is usually the initiator.

Seth has Sun, Mercury and Venus in Aquarius. He has the Moon in Pisces and Scorpio rising. With Saturn in Scorpio in his first house, square his Sun, Seth is somewhat shy. He really enjoys Stella's outgoing nature. Seth has a grand trine involving Saturn, Uranus and the North Node. He works as head engineer for a small town in New England, maintaining the town's electrical systems.

On June 12, Seth had his progressed Sun inconjunct natal Saturn with a 1 minute orb, while his progressed Saturn was exactly square his natal Sun. Saturn only moved 4 minutes in this progressed year, so that exact square was a background aspect, exact for three months. The other aspects between the progressed chart and the natal chart were progressed Sun 28 minutes past square natal Node, progressed Venus 18 minutes past inconjunct natal Jupiter, and progressed Moon 58 minutes past square natal Moon. Seth's progressed Ascendant was making four aspects. Since his birth time is from hospital records, it may be quite accurate. Nonetheless, before this event, I would have hesitated to use the progressed Ascendant to time anything. The progressed Ascendant was 13 minutes past square his natal Uranus, 35 minutes past trine his natal Neptune, 42 minutes approaching sextile his natal Sun, and 40 minutes past sextile his natal Mercury. This combination, after the fact, tells me that his birth time is about as precise as you can get. The fact that Seth survived his accident with no ill effects inclines me to believe that the 2 minutes arc separating orb sextile from the progressed Ascendant to the natal Sun-Mercury midpoint was more operative than the progressed Ascendant square to natal Uranus, just as the orbs indicate.

The triggers for the two Sun-Saturn aspects by progression were all transits. The transiting Mercury-Mars conjunction was inconjunct Seth's Venus, with transiting Mercury 11 minutes approaching and Mars 19 minutes separating at the time of the accident. The planet Uranus also is often involved in accidents. Transiting Uranus is only 9 minutes of arc from square Seth's natal Uranus and 9 minutes from sextile Seth's

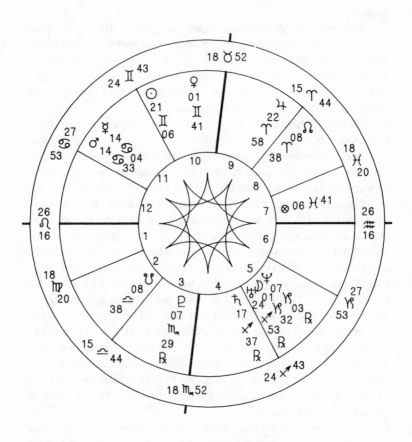

Chart 10. Seth's transits for June 12, 1987. This is a chart erected for the approximate time of the incident (10:30 AM EDT), which occurred at 42N45, 71W28.

Sun. Transiting Jupiter was making four aspects to Seth's ...
within 1 degree (approaching). It was 25 minutes from trin... hart
Neptune, 18 minutes from sextile Seth's Mercury, 45 minutes ...
sextile Seth's Sun, and 45 minutes from semisextile Seth's Uranus. W...
certainly have a pile-up of aspects on June 12!

The reason I didn't believe this event would put Seth in the hospital
didn't involve Seth's chart at all. When you examine charts of several
family members who live in the same house, you can see several different
perspectives on any event which involves the health or safety of one of
the people. Instead of confusing the issue with dials and midpoints and
asteroids and trans-Neptunian points, use the materials that will give
you the fastest answer.

In this case, that means use Stella's chart. If you inspect the aspects
on Stella's triple wheel for June 12 (see Chart 12 on page 49), you see
that Stella's closest progressed aspect was a 0 degree orb sextile from
progressed Saturn to natal Pluto. This aspect is a "protective" combina-
tion. Stella's progressed Sun is 4 minutes of arc from semisquare her
natal Mercury, and 19 minutes of arc past semisquare her natal Saturn.
The Sun won't hit the midpoint of those two natal positions for several
months. Stella's progressed Moon is 21 minutes from sesquiquadrate
her Ascendant (which is close enough, given the inevitable uncertainty
of a 5 A.M. birth time), and progressed Venus is 5 minutes past semisextile
Stella's natal Moon. These combinations of aspects just are not powerful
enough to cancel that progressed Saturn sextile to Pluto. Within the
progressed chart, progressed Mars is 3 minutes past semisquare Stella's
progressed Sun, and progressed Mercury is 2 minutes from semisquare
Stella's progressed Saturn. The only other exact aspect by progression
is a quintile from progressed Pluto to natal Venus.

The progression doesn't look too bad, for the two good aspects
both involve symbolism which could stand for Seth: Venus and Saturn.
The next step is to look at the transiting positions for this time frame.
Transiting Pluto is separating (37 minutes) from the square to Stella's
natal Sun, and approaching (32 minutes) a trine to Stella's natal Pluto.
These two should cancel each other. Transiting Neptune is only 6 minutes
of arc from opposing Stella's Pluto. This can be an exasperating aspect,
but it usually reflects some sort of unrecognized power struggle. Transit-
ing Uranus is 51 minutes from sesquiquadrate natal Neptune—another
exasperation aspect, because you don't know what is going on. The
most bothersome transit here is Mars. Mars is the most common trigger

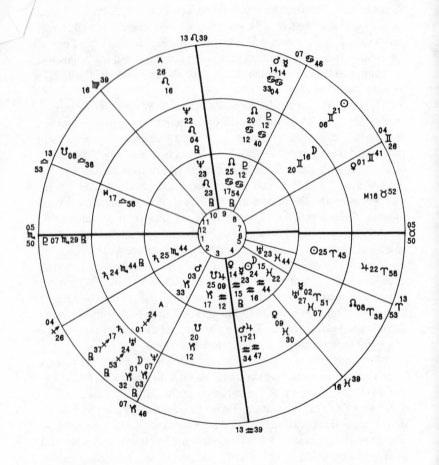

Chart 11. Seth's triple wheel. Seth's natal chart is on the inside, his progressed chart in the middle, and the transits for June 12, 1987, on the outside.

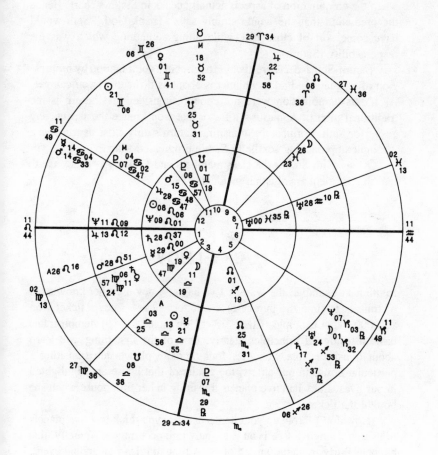

Chart 12. Stella's triple wheel. Birth date August 1, 1919, at 5:00 AM EST, 42N45, 71W28. Data from birth records; Placidus Houses. Her natal chart is on the inside, her progressed chart for June 12, 1987, in the middle, and the transits for June 12, 1987, at 10:30 AM EDT on the outside.

planet, and here it is semisquare both Mercury and Saturn, although separating from each. Mars is approaching a sesquiquadrate to Stella's natal Uranus. It is clear that something will happen. The problem with all of this is that it looks like Stella won't be affected until June 16, when the combination of aspects actually peaks in Stella's chart. Hence the prediction that she would simply say, "Thank God." Seth would have some sort of close call while doing something which was his responsibility (Saturn).

Saturn-Sun aspects are always tough, but a combination by progression of a square and an inconjunct is about as difficult as you can get. As if this combination were not enough, consider that Saturn is the traditional ruler of Aquarius—a factor that won't make the aspects any easier for Seth. Fortunately, transiting Saturn's only close aspect was a 2 minute approaching sextile to Seth's progressed Mars.

Along with Stella, the class members and I all say, "Thank God" that this incident was just an incident.

LUCKY LUCY

In the next example, the woman I've named Lucy used her knowledge of transits to time the purchase of a lottery ticket. Lucy's ticket won $50,000. This example (Charts 13–17 on pages 51–55) demonstrates basic astrological principles clearly. One of the first things we learn about transits is that whenever four or more planets are transiting a particular house in our charts, the affairs of that house are highlighted in our lives. Lucy had five planets transiting in her fifth house when she bought the ticket.

Now don't throw up your hands because you think that five planets transiting a single house is an extremely rare occurrence. Actually, this happens fairly frequently to all of us. Although it isn't an annual event, there will be times during your life when you have four or five planets transiting your fifth house. In general, you are luckier during the month each year that the Sun transits your fifth house. During that month, the Moon will join the Sun for a couple of days. And, since both Mercury and Venus stay fairly close to the Sun, every few years there is a time during which the Sun, Moon, Venus and Mercury are in your fifth house.

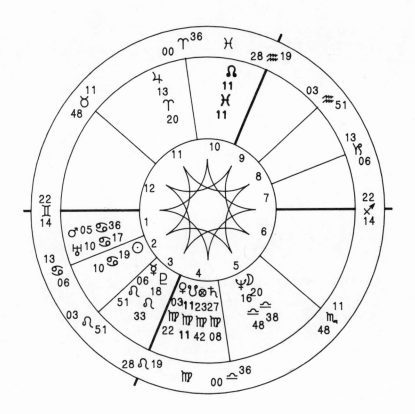

Chart 13. Lucky Lucy's natal chart. She was born July 12, 1951, at 2:45 AM EST, 39N57, 75W10. Data from her birth certificate; Placidus Houses.

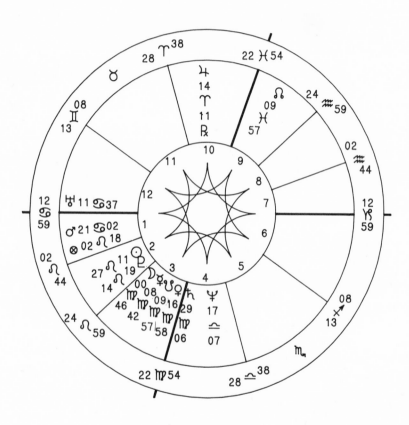

Chart 14. Lucy's chart progressed to November 11, 1974, at 7:00 PM when she bought the winning ticket. The Midheaven is progressed by the traditional (Naibod Arc) method.

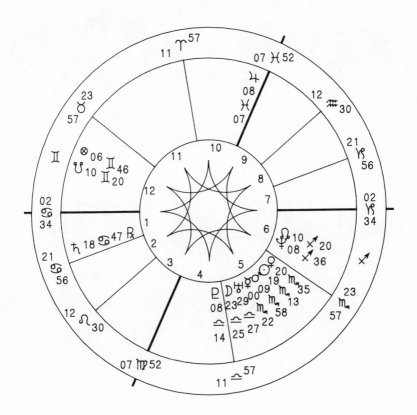

Chart 15. Lucy's transits. This is a chart erected for the approximate time that Lucy bought the ticket on November 11, 1974, 7:00 PM EST, 42N21, 71W12.

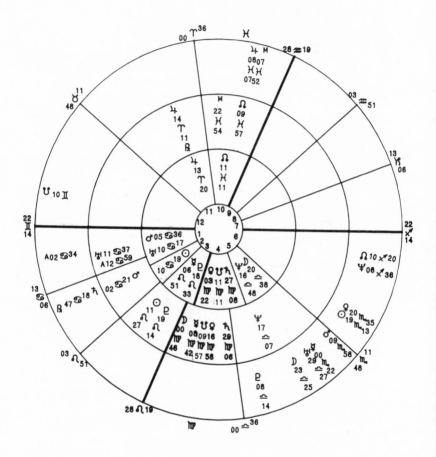

Chart 16. A triple wheel with Lucy's natal chart on the inside, her progressed chart in the middle, and the transits for November 11, 1974, 7:00 PM EST on the outside.

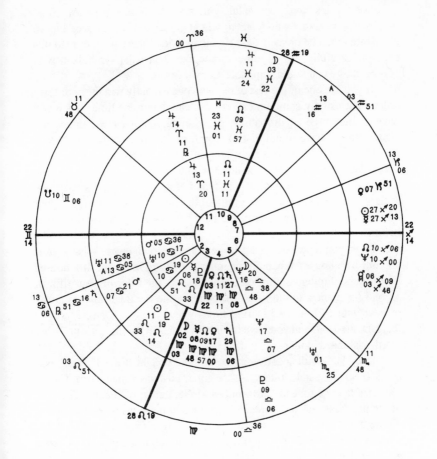

Chart 17. A triple wheel with Lucy's natal chart on the inside, her progressed chart in the middle, and the transits for December 19, 1974, 10:00 AM EST (when she was paid by the lottery commission) on the outside.

If this coincides with a Mars transit (which happens every two years), or a Jupiter transit (once every twelve years), you have the five planets in place. Of course, if you happen to have Scorpio, Sagittarius or Capricorn on the fifth house cusp natally, you have had one of the outer planets in residence there by transit for quite a while.

Some folks have good natal symbolism for winning money. Most of us know someone who tends to win at games of chance (even bingo) more often than he or she loses. If you are one of these people, read this example carefully, for if you combine excellent natal symbolism with good timing, you could duplicate Lucy's results.

If you are one of the rest of us, who occasionally win thirty or forty dollars but usually come up empty, you can determine times when you have a slightly better probability of winning. During these times, my students and I have found that we can turn up a five- or ten-dollar win ticket fairly easily. If you have laid out five hundred dollars for your ten-dollar win ticket, you'll be upset with this method of timing. On the other hand, if you've bought one ticket (for one dollar) and won ten dollars, you had some fun figuring out the times, you didn't loose your money, and you can wait until the next hit to see if you can do a little better.

After you read Lucy's story, get out your own chart. What sign is on your fifth house? When do the inner planets go into your fifth house? Does Mars, Jupiter, Saturn or Uranus aspect the ruler of your fifth or second (or planets in the fifth or second) while the inner planets are in or near your fifth house? During times when you can answer "yes" to that last question, and you have the inner planets in the fifth, it's probably worth risking a dollar.

Lucy had studied astrology before she bought the ticket that won her $50,000 in a state lottery. At the time, this was a major win, for the state had not yet gone to multi-million-dollar games of chance. The time of the purchase was no accident—just look at her transits. I've included all the data (time of purchase, time of drawing, time of pay-off) so that you, as students of astrology, may be able to duplicate this in your own chart or that of someone close to you.

Lucy has won money several other times, although this example is her largest win so far. Lucy's natal chart indicates the possibility of winning money. The ruler of the second house, the Moon, is in the fifth house, conjunct Neptune, trine both the Ascendant and the MC, forming a grand trine. Lucy's natal Sun is in the second house, square Jupiter in the eleventh, and square the Neptune-Moon conjunction in the fifth, creating a T-square. The Mars-Uranus conjunction in the first is on the cusp of the second and sextile Venus, which rules the fifth. Jupiter is only 17 minutes of arc from square the second-eighth axis, and it trines both Mercury and Pluto. The North Node, in the tenth, trines Mars, Uranus and the Sun. Saturn rules the eighth house (gambling winnings), and squares the Ascendant, grounding the trine from the Moon-Neptune conjunction. Saturn also is conjunct the fifth house cusp, pulling that symbolism into reality.

When Lucy bought the ticket, transiting Jupiter was conjunct the transiting MC. Jupiter wasn't exactly aspecting Lucy's natal planets, although it was approaching a conjunction to her natal and progressed Node, approaching an opposition to her progressed Mercury, approaching a trine to her natal Uranus, and in her tenth house. By making the purchase while the transiting MC conjuncted transiting Jupiter, the transiting MC pulled in all the approaching aspects from transiting Jupiter. The astute astrology student can use transiting angles to amplify approaching aspects in any chart.

Lucy's fifth house was packed with five transiting planets. She had transiting Pluto, Moon, Uranus, Mercury and Mars in the fifth while the transiting Sun and Venus were trine her natal Sun from the sixth house. The strongest transiting indicator was Saturn, 23 minutes past conjunct Lucy's Sun and 25 minutes from semisquare Lucy's Venus, ruler of the fifth. Lucy had checked the previous cycles of transiting Saturn while studying astrology, and had noted that Saturn usually indicated a positive time for her, so she wasn't at all discouraged by the conjunction. When Lucy bought the ticket, her progressed Pluto was 4 minutes of arc past semisextile her natal Sun; progressed Venus was 10 minutes past semisextile natal Neptune and 9 minutes from semisextile progressed Neptune (1 minutes of arc past semisextile the point precisely between natal and progressed Neptune). Her progressed Sun was 11 minutes from semisextile progressed Uranus. The tensions of these semisextiles all seem to center on the money or material goods side of the symbolism for a semisextile.

The transits tell the tale here, both to the natal and the progressed positions. When the ticket was drawn at 8 P.M. the next night, transiting Saturn was 24 minutes past conjunct Lucy's natal Sun and 24 minutes from semisquare Lucy's natal Venus—precisely between the two aspects, when the influence on each aspect peaks. I call the point exactly between two aspects a "power point." Transiting Mars was 24 minutes past trine natal Uranus and 30 minutes from trine her natal Node—only 4 minutes of arc from the power-point exactly between the two aspects form a grand trine in Lucy's chart. The transiting Node was exactly inconjunct Lucy's natal Uranus.

The moral of this story concerns Saturn. Saturn isn't always an awful Daddy—every so often he pays off. When the reality that Saturn brings is $50,000, he's a nice parent after all.

The aspects when Lucy received the check seem slightly anti-climactic. They certainly are not as dramatic as the aspects on either the day of the drawing or the day of the purchase. Lucy's progressed Ascendant was 15 minutes of arc from square her natal Jupiter and 14 minutes from sesquiquadrate her natal MC, activating a 1 minute orb natal Jupiter-MC semisquare. The midpoint structures were more active than the clear direct aspects at this time. However, if you want to win, it is more important to know the time when you should purchase the ticket than the time they will pay you!

Part Two

Aspects of Prediction

CHAPTER 4

Different Strokes for Different Folks:
Methods of Prediction

In the United States, the three methods of prediction we use most often are transits, secondary progressions and solar arc directions. The first method, transits, takes the current positions of the planets and compares these positions to the natal chart. Most of us learn this method shortly after we learn how to analyze a natal chart. The Sun, Moon, Mercury and Venus move quite quickly. The Moon averages about 12 degrees per day, traveling through a sign in about two and one-half days. Unless there is a new Moon or full Moon (conjunct or opposing the Sun) or an eclipse of the Sun or Moon, we don't usually experience more than a mild response to the daily position of the transiting Moon. The mild fluctuation in response can be a useful teaching tool. In order to test this, use the delineations in this book and in *Secondary Progressions: Time to Remember*,[7] for the progressed Moon. Most of us notice the transiting Moon's house position a little more than the aspects it makes. Most of us also notice that any other transit will obliterate most of the effects of the transiting Moon.

The Sun, Mercury and Venus also transit too fast to have a major impact on our lives. However, when either Mercury or Venus makes a station, it will stay a day or two at a particular degree. If it makes this

---

[7]Nancy Anne Hastings, *Secondary Progressions:Time to Remember* (York Beach, Maine: Samuel Weiser, Inc., 1984)

station within a degree of an aspect to something in your natal chart, you will probably notice this transit. In the sections on Mercury and Venus, the delineations include the effects of a transiting station.

The second method of prediction, secondary progressions, is a symbolic predictive method based upon a correlation between the diurnal, or daily cycle, and the annual cycle. When you use secondary progressions, the inner planets (Sun, Moon, Mercury, Venus and Mars) assume much more importance in the analysis. When a day equals a year, the Moon's motion averages a degree a month. Thus, any aspect from the progressed Moon will be within a degree of exact for a month. Thanks to the accuracy of the ephemerides currently available, it is quite simple to calculate the position of the Moon to within a few minutes of arc accuracy. This allows us to focus on a week during which the effect of the aspect is maximized.

In a similar manner, we can find a two- or three-week span within which the effects of an aspect from the progressed Sun, Mercury, Venus or Mars will peak. If you have a computer, or have written for a computer calculation of the dates of progressed aspects, you need to remember that these calculations will only be within a few days of the exact aspect. At the time of this writing (1988) it simply isn't possible to calculate aspects to the exact minute during the day when they occur. Nonetheless, if you can combine the progression with simultaneous transits, you have a valid predictive technique.

You really can't time events well from outer planet progressions, because the planets from Jupiter through Pluto usually move too slowly. When a planet is moving at a rate of 3 minutes per day, this translates to one minute every four months in secondary progressions. An aspect from progressed Uranus could have a zero orb for several months. For outer planets, I use either transits or the solar arc method to time events.

Solar arc, the third major method of prediction, is based upon the arc of the secondary progressed Sun. In this symbolism, the distance between the natal Sun and the progressed Sun is measured and added to each of the planets and the angles. Since the Sun is the fundamental symbol of life itself, this method simply extends that symbolism to every area of life. Solar arc directions equalize the symbolic strength of all the planets, as each moves approximately 5 minutes per month, depending on the speed of the natal Sun. Most people seem to feel a solar arc aspect for about three months, although any events tend to peak during the week surrounding the exact (0° 0′ orb) aspect. All of the delineations in this book will work with solar arc directions.

My students always want to know two things. First, which method works best, and second, what aspect is the strongest. All that any teacher can ever tell you is what works best for that teacher. Although I do use all three, I concentrate on transits and secondary progressions. I urge students to try everything with a critical eye, settling on the method which works best for them.

The second question is a bit more difficult to answer. Up to a point, duration of an aspect is the simplest gauge of strength. Anything which is within a degree of exact for a month is stronger than anything which is exact for a day or two, then separates. But this answer is simplistic and ignores several major factors. Transiting Mars usually moves through aspects fairly quickly, yet when Mars is stationing a few degrees past a major aspect to your natal chart, you won't think that transiting Mars is inconsequential. Triple hits (direct, retrograde, direct) from any transiting planet beyond Mars spread out the action, and aspects from Neptune or Pluto can hang around for up to two years. Yet there are clear periods of increased intensity with an outer planet transit. Whenever that transit gets really close to the exact aspect, things start to move in the direction indicated by the planets involved. In contrast, a slow progression, within four or five minutes of exact for several years, often acts like a natal aspect. No matter what the aspect is, if it's going to be there for several years, we adapt to it. We feel it when a transit or the progressed Moon triggers the aspect. The changes indicated by slow progressions usually involve a whole chain of events which have the underlying message of the symbolism connected to the slow aspect.

Whatever method you ultimately choose to use in your own practice, consider the duration of the aspect in your assessment of its strength. I would pay more attention to a transiting or solar arc Uranus aspect to a natal position than to a progressed Uranus aspect to the same position, because the transit is much more likely to indicate an unexpected event. By the time Uranus progressed to a zero-orb aspect, you've had all kinds of transits kick this aspect off. You probably know it's raining, because you've already been soaked to the skin.

In this part of the book, I've delineated aspects from each planet to its own natal position and to the rest of the planets. These delineations are useful for each of the three methods of prediction.

CHAPTER 5

My Ever-Changing
Self:
SUN ASPECTS

The Sun symbolizes life itself. We can imagine living without our planetary neighbors. We can think of living on a planet without a Moon. But we can't think of living on a planet with no Sun. Life as we know it depends on the warmth and light which the Sun provides.

As the Earth circles the Sun the Earth goes through its seasons. Near the equator, the seasonal changes are from wet to dry, while at the poles the changes are from darkness to light. This annual rhythm is so much a part of our lives that it forms a constant backdrop for our activities. Since we base our measurement of time upon the motion of the Earth on its axis and around the Sun, we are in nearly the same position on the same day each successive year. The transiting Sun will conjunct your natal Sun within a day of your birthday every year of your life. Most of us start new projects as the Sun moves through our first houses. We attend to the areas of life symbolized by the houses in our charts as the Sun moves through those houses. One of my dearest teachers, Dorothea Lynde, says that the Sun "lights up" the part of the chart it is transiting. Stop a moment and think about your own personal annual rhythm. If you attune yourself to this rhythm, you will find you feel more comfortable in your activities.

The transiting Sun will only trigger events when there are close, powerful patterns of slow transits or progressions. Otherwise, the Sun is back the same time every year. However, whenever the Sun transits stress patterns in your natal chart, it symbolizes light thrown on the problem. Some years you may keep your eyes shut, because you just don't want to look at that issue now. Other years you take advantage of the brief spotlight to learn a little more about the reality of underlying stress.

The progressed Sun traces out the solar arc and your growth in this great adventure called life. This solar position symbolizes who you are right now. Aspects to and from this position indicate current events which affect your perception of who you are. Sometimes you like who you are, and at other times you are not so comfortable with yourself. Self-image isn't static, but a slowly changing perception of worth and ability.

Your natal Sun tells you whether you are an apple tree, a pine or an oak. Your progressed Sun tells how you grow. It symbolizes a late frost one year that means fewer apples, or a dry winter that slows the pine's growth. But it also traces the abundant years, the healthy growth. The progression of the Sun won't change you from an apple tree to a pine or an oak, but as you grow, the progression allows you to see your own unique gifts and liabilities, your own worth.

SOLAR ARC DIRECTIONS

There is a whole method of directing a chart which depends entirely upon the *solar arc*, or the distance between the secondary progressed Sun and the natal Sun.[8] Even though it looks different when you read the directions for calculation of the solar arc Sun, it really is the same as the distance between the progressed and natal Sun. Every time the progressed Sun makes an aspect to its own natal position, *all of the other planets as well as the angles* make the same aspect to their own natal positions from their solar arc position. Thus, whenever you are analyzing an aspect between the progressed and natal Sun it involves ALL of your symbolism.

In this section I'm going to talk about all of the possible aspects from the progressed Sun to the natal Sun. Since all the solar arc planets are also involved, the discussion will include parts of yourself that you

---

[8]Directions for calculating solar arc are in the appendix.

don't ordinarily associate with the Sun. Further, I'm going to talk about minor aspects that you won't see anywhere else in this book except in some of the example charts. Don't be scared by these minor aspects. They aren't very hard to calculate, because the Sun progresses at a fairly regular rate averaging 60 minutes per year. It moves a little faster in the winter and a little slower in the summer. The aspects usually occur right around the age equal to the degrees of the aspect. In other words, the progressed Sun is 30 degrees from the natal Sun when you're about thirty years old, and it's forty-five degrees from its natal position when you're about forty-five years old. These aspects help define different stages of life for all of us. When you combine the background symbolism of the aspects between the secondary Sun and the natal Sun with the symbolism of the particular transits and/or progressions going on in your chart, the differences in the manifestation of these aspects aren't very hard to discern.

Semi-octile (22-1/2°)

The first aspect that occurs between the progressed Sun and the natal Sun is a particularly aggravating minor aspect. This aspect is often masked by the cycle of the progressed Moon, making its third square to its natal position when you're about twenty-one years old, or by the cycle of transiting Saturn, which makes its third square to its natal position at about the same time. If you really do have either the progressed Moon or transiting Saturn hitting at exactly the same time that your progressed Sun is 22-1/2 degrees from its natal position, the cycle of the Moon or Saturn will seem horrid. The 22-1/2 degree aspect is a "No I won't" aspect. You don't want to change anything about your natal expression, but at the same time, you don't really like your natal expression. You're an adult and want to express your unique difference from your parents, but then again, you're getting tired of pointless adolescent rebellion. Whether you've been on your own for a while, or you're just finishing college, this aspect indicates an inner conflict between doing things yourself and asking for advice. Like many of us, you may get around this vacillation by forming friendships with people who are in their late twenties or early thirties. Then you can ask these friends for their opinions without getting roped into an argument or power play with Mom or Dad, who may not have realized that you have grown up.

Semisextile (30°)

The semisextile is not a minor aspect. Every major transiting aspect carries a double meaning when your progressed Sun is semisextile your natal Sun and the solar arc positions of each of your planets and angles are semisextile their natal positions.

During the six months that your progressed Sun enters orb of the semisextile to itself, makes the aspect exactly, and leaves the 15 minute orb of the aspect, you'll feel every single transit to any planet in your natal chart as a double entendre. It's small wonder that in our society, we've fastened on age thirty as a transition year![9]

Semi-quintile (36°)

Here is another aspect that I never use except with the progressed Sun. This aspect can ease the tensions surrounding the second waxing square from your progressed Moon and/or transiting Saturn, both of which occur when you're about thirty-five years old. The semi-quintile isn't a reciprocating aspect—transits which aspect the natal position won't aspect the progressed position, and transits to the progressed position won't aspect the natal position. This means that either the natal symbolism or the progressed symbolism acts freely while still functioning within a harmonious connection to the other.

Since the progressed Moon and transiting Saturn cycles rarely occur precisely at age thirty-five, the semi-quintile can occur before, between or after these cycles. When the progressed Sun and thus all the solar arc positions are 36 degrees from the natal position during the other two cycles, you'll have an internal sense of optimism or buoyancy in spite of the tensions around you. Often this perceived ease comes from an unrealistic appraisal of the situation(s) at hand. When the semi-quintile results in the "rose-colored glasses" syndrome, life can become totally bizarre before you notice that anything out of the ordinary is going on.

This unconscious mode of functioning lets you believe your spouse when he (or she) tells you about working late at the office or visiting a friend regardless of the obvious flaws in the excuse. On the other hand,

---

[9]See figure 1 on page 13 for combinations possible with the semisextile.

the semi-quintile may prompt you to believe that the little affair that you're considering won't affect your own marriage or career.

Thus, if you've got that little minor aspect from your natal Sun to your progressed Sun, even though the positions of both transits and progressed Moon indicate that you should be in the middle of a storm, you may insist that things aren't really all that bad.

Semisquare (45°)

This is the most important aspect between the progressed Sun and the natal Sun. The underlying tension that this aspect symbolizes activates every difficult aspect in your natal chart. You take apart all of the responses that have never worked very well for you and try to make sense out of them. Self-acceptance is rare during this aspect, for you usually amplify your negative side and ignore your positive behavior patterns.

It's as if you have an insistent, discordant background rhythm vibrating all of your natal squares, oppositions, semisquares and sesquiquadrates. The closer in degrees the natal aspect is to exact, the louder the noise gets. More than any other cycle, this semisquare defines the time of mid-life crisis.

If you have taken a good look at your own problem areas before you get to the semisquare, you can ride this aspect through with some minor adjustments, although most of us encounter some difficulties during this time.

If there are no major outer planet transits or other progressions occurring at the time of this semisquare, you will find yourself doing some internal housecleaning. You feel that it's time to get rid of many of the things that have been bothering you. All too often this includes current relationships, as it is frequently easy to blame someone else for your own inside hurts. However, some relationships actually serve the purpose of enabling you to confront the difficult sides of your own projection. Through these relationships, you learn who you are, and at that point may discover that the only reason for continuing the relationship involves self-punishment. If this is the case, the semisquare can give that last push that releases you from destructive relationship patterns.

The relationship you release may be a marriage. It is equally likely that a child may leave home, or you may let go of a parent. This is not an aspect that's directly connected to the death of a parent. It involves scrapping the tapes from your internal, critical Mommy or Daddy.

If you don't experience the semisquare through a relationship, you most likely will undergo a career change. Some of you do both at once, maximizing chaos. By age forty-five, you've probably been working more than twenty years. If you've spent all of that time developing a single career track, you should have achieved some kind of recognition for the experience you've accumulated. When you feel that this experience is discounted or ignored, depression sets in. All of us want to be able to tell those twenty-year-old kids how to do the job. Furthermore, we want them to listen to us. You don't need some kid fresh out of school to walk in and teach you how to run a word processing machine or use a spread sheet. If this kid is earning more than us, we don't want to know it. You've got to brush up on what's going on, no matter what career you've chosen. The painful part of this involves the difficult action symbolized by the 45 degree aspect. The changes are scary. Even though the shift doesn't have to mean starting over, it often feels that way.

The person who has "succeeded" or has come close to reaching his or her goals now needs to set some other goals for the rest of life. Even the self-made millionaire hits a snag here. What comes next?

This is the key to the semisquare. You're halfway home, not young or old. How will you choose to use the second half of your life?

Septile (51.428°)

The septile is one-seventh of a circle. This aspect is often referred to as "karmic" or fated, particularly in Hindu astrology. The experience of my clients has varied widely, depending on the choices they've made in their lives up to this point.

One group of clients seemed to have a sense of helplessness when they hit this aspect, compounded by depression about what they considered the inevitability of old age. These folks suddenly realized their own mortality. For some, this involved a desire to produce some sort of legacy so that they would not be forgotten.

Another set of clients gained a sense of priority. They trusted their inner instincts enough to accept the solutions to problems which seemed to pop up out of nowhere. By releasing their inner fears, this group of people gained a sense of peace, rather than a sense of hopelessness.

As you have probably gathered, there is still quite a bit of work needed in the analysis of this aspect. I have a sense that something is left out here, and that something may be Chiron, that new little planet which has a cycle of about fifty-two years.[10]

Sextile (60°)

The sextile between the progressed Sun and the natal Sun, occurring when you're about sixty years old, provides an island of calm. You can look forward to about twenty more years, and in these twenty years you can put together your philosophy of life. The sextile is a working aspect, which means that you can't find the good in it without a bit of effort. It will ease any difficult transits, for it seems to give a larger perspective to the whole thing.

If you've backed off enough from the petty annoyances of daily life, you can really develop the ability to sort out how important (or trivial) your daily grind has to be.

Some of my clients seem to get a second wind during the time of the sextile. They may start a new pursuit, or renew their interest in the things they've always done. Whenever you choose to work with the energy of the sextile, you can come up with a delightful new approach, or some insight into areas of cooperation and communication.

ASPECTS OTHER THAN SOLAR ARC

I've divided the aspects into four groups for the rest of the planetary combinations. The conjunction, a variable aspect, depends on house and sign for part of the delineation. In *Secondary Progressions: Time to Remember,*[11] I described the meaning of the sign positions of planets. Briefly, a planet gains strength if it is in its sign of rulership or exaltation, or if it is in a house of natural rulership or exaltation. (See Table 1.)

---

[10]Erminie Lantero, *The Continuing Discovery of Chiron* (York Beach, Maine: Samuel Weiser, Inc., 1984).

[11]Nancy Anne Hastings, *Secondary Progressions: Time to Remember* (York Beach, Maine: Samuel Weiser, Inc., 1984), p. 99.

Table 1. Planetary Expressions

Planet	Exaltation	Fall	Rulership	Detriment
Sun	Aries	Libra	Leo	Aquarius
Moon	Taurus	Scorpio	Cancer	Capricorn
Mercury	Aquarius	Leo	Virgo or Gemini	Pisces or Sagittarius
Venus	Pisces	Virgo	Taurus or Libra	Scorpio or Aries
Mars	Capricorn	Cancer	Aries or Scorpio	Libra or Taurus
Jupiter	Cancer	Capricorn	Sagittarius or Pisces	Gemini or Virgo
Saturn	Libra	Aries	Capricorn or Aquarius	Cancer or Leo
Uranus	Scorpio	Taurus	Aquarius	Leo
Neptune	Cancer	Capricorn	Pisces	Virgo
Pluto	Leo	Aquarius	Scorpio	Taurus

The tension aspects are the semisextile and the inconjunct. These aspects imply underlying discontent with the present state of affairs, but an unwillingness to change the situation. You have to make some compromises in order to use the energy of either planet connected by a semisextile or inconjunct. Although the inconjunct seems more powerful than the semisextile, both bring up inner fears. Unless or until a stress/action aspect occurs, most of you simply feel uncomfortable during tension aspects. Once triggered, these aspects characteristically map the most important events in your life.

The stress/action aspects (semisquare, square, sesquiquadrate and opposition) provide a push to do something about a situation. Inertia gets to all of us, so without the stress/action aspects, we might vegetate through our lives, unable or unwilling to get out of our own way. Stress/action aspects are often easy to shift from stress to action. If you see them coming, simplify your life. This means don't over-schedule yourself while they are present. One of my clients did this and had someone offer him a four-day, all expenses paid trip to the Bahamas. If he hadn't done all his work ahead and left those days unscheduled, he would have had to refuse the trip! Be aware that difficult aspects may indicate difficult things, but keep in mind that they also may indicate an adventure.

The ease aspects (sextile, trine) provide a time of R&R, a time when you can decide to sit around and enjoy yourself, or put some of the changes of the stress/action aspects to good use. It isn't always necessary to DO THINGS with each and every aspect in your chart. Those of us who are inclined towards workaholic behavior patterns frequently can't stand doing nothing, because we don't know how to do nothing. I've included things to do during ease aspects for the folks like me who can't imagine sitting around enjoying what life offers. Perhaps we can learn to do less, and eventually learn to relax.

When the progressed Sun aspects natal planets and angles, the aspect lasts for about six months, giving a 15 minute approaching and separating orb.

SUN–MOON ASPECTS

The progressed Sun symbolizes your present manifestation of your life energy. It is your own yang symbol, the symbol of action, life, and your physical body. Your natal Moon symbolizes your inherent yin nature. The Moon indicates how you respond to the inevitable ups and downs of life. It is your internal balance beam, absorbing the events around you and providing a means to cope with these events. When the progressed Sun aspects the natal Moon, you experience a six-month period of some type of connection between your present self-expression and your habitual response nature. The aspects between the progressed Moon and your natal Sun, on the other hand, indicate a current state of emotional response which either reinforces or challenges your perception of your internal life energy. Aspects between the progressed Moon and the progressed Sun almost always signify events or attitudes which relate to the here and now. These events or attitudes don't involve past perceptions or childhood experiences.

Aspects from the progressed Moon last about six months (3 degrees approaching, 3 degrees separating) but tend to peak rapidly just as they become exact. These aspects are excellent for prediction or for rectification because the events indicated usually occur during the two-week period when the aspect is within 15 minutes of exact. By looking at the transits for this two-week period, you can frequently pinpoint the time of an event.

Sun-Moon aspects by progression symbolize intensely emotional events, particularly any event involving relating to another person. Hence, they are extremely common at times of marriage, engagement to be married, or childbirth.

Variable: Conjunction (0°)

This combination of the symbols of "who I am" and "how I feel" brings an intense desire to combine the two sides of yourself in all of your interactions. By the end of this six-month period, you will know yourself and your response nature better. The conjunction alone doesn't tell anything about whether you'll like yourself any better, it simply indicates you'll know more about this person. If the conjunction is in a fire or air sign, the Sun will dominate. This means that you will explore the reasons why you respond the way you do. You'll be inclined to analyze your feelings, although when the two are in a fire sign, you may not do the analyzing until after you've taken some kind of action in response to the event. If the conjunction is in water or earth, the yin, or lunar, symbolism is stronger. In this case, you will be more likely to experience your responses completely as "who I am" gives in to "how I feel."

Tension: Semisextile (30°) and Inconjunct (150°)

These aspects indicate an underlying dissatisfaction with either the way you express who you are (the Sun) or the way you express how you feel (the Moon). Whatever appeals to the Sun (who you are) conflicts with the Moon (how you feel) and vice versa. The major difficulty with the semisextile or inconjunct involves your unwillingness to alter either of these expressions. Sometimes it's easier to get sick than to change the way you express who you are or how you feel. If you get sick, you can be uncomfortable without having to change too much. Sometimes you just get sick of your relationships, for then you can project the tension onto other people.

Many of us dredge up problems with or between our parents during this time. You may catch yourself doing or saying things that are exactly what your parents did or said while you were growing up. Even if you had a good relationship with your parents, you don't want to repeat their lives. It's important to remember that you are not your mother or father, and you don't have to repeat the relationship that either parent had with you or with each other if you don't want to.

As the aspect passes, you can begin to release the tensions involved. Other aspects (natal, progressed and transit) to the natal planet in this combination show the ways to get out of the stuck position of the semisextile or the inconjunct.

Stress/Action: Semisquare (45°), Square (90°), Sesquiquadrate (135°) and Opposition (180°)

Although the square and opposition are more likely to indicate an event that everyone can see (such as a marriage or separation), the semisquare and sesquiquadrate show up as major, albeit often more private occurrences. Any of the Sun-Moon aspects can affect health because they involve the response nature and the physical body or relationships— because they involve the strongest yin and yang symbols of the charts.

The stress part of these aspects leads directly to action: you have to do something before the aspect is done. With the square or opposition, you'll have a pretty clear idea of what is involved, for these aspects emphasize one of the quadruplicities in your life. If both planets are in cardinal signs, you may jump into the change a bit precipitately. The initiating impulse of cardinality may prompt you to implement a change before you consider the alternate possibilities. If the two planets are in fixed signs, you'll delay any change as long as possible. When you're finally backed up against the wall, you'll give in and make the change that's needed. When the two are in mutable signs, the events occurring may demand more than one shift before you're finally done with the matter. Some of you who have these aspects occurring in mutable signs try to keep all bridges intact, in case you decide to change your minds later. This attempt can backfire, because the hard aspects between the Sun and Moon usually indicate a complete change of attitude.

Regardless of the signs involved, you're going to make some choices during the square or opposition between the Sun and the Moon. You can help the process along by thinking about what's involved. Most of you are not resistant to change when the change is your own decision.

The semisquare and sesquiquadrate are often more difficult to deal with because they don't involve a clear choice or change. You may find yourself inexplicably irrational or upset during the aspect, without any obvious trigger. If your emotional discomfort appears when dealing with a spouse or partner, you may not be able to decide whether you need to change or your partner needs to change. Since it's your aspect, in your chart, the one most likely to change is you, regardless of who should have changed.

If you have any tight squares, oppositions, semisquares or sesqui-quadrates in your natal chart (even if they don't involve the Sun and Moon) you are likely to find them activated during the time that you have an exact hard aspect between your Sun and Moon by progression. The progressed aspect sets up a kind of vibrational background, pushing your natal hard aspects into activity. Transiting aspects then take on a greater intensity, an intensity involving the Sun-Moon symbolism. You'll tend to personalize all of the events going on when your Sun and Moon are in one of the stress/action aspects to each other.

Ease: Sextile (60°) and Trine (120°)

With these aspects, your physical health is usually excellent. The easy combination of how you express who you are and how you feel tends to smooth out any events occurring during the aspect. You can move mountains if you have enough difficult aspects going on at the same time. If all you've got going on in your chart is this trine or sextile, however, you're not likely to do anything at all. This aspect does not show up often in events unless there are a number of hard aspects occurring simultaneously. Thus, although the symbolism could suggest that these aspects would be fantastic for marriage, engagement or any other pleasant life event, the sextile and trine just don't provide enough push to motivate action.

However, if there are difficult aspects anywhere in the chart during the time of the sextile or trine, the easing of energies between the Sun and the Moon becomes both obvious and extremely helpful. You'll have the ability to swing through events with an emotional stability that is just about unshakeable. If you're dealing with a difficult Saturn aspect at the same time, then the trine or sextile between the Sun and Moon by progression often indicates marriage; the next most popular event is a career change (positive). The presence of the trine or sextile between the lights changes difficult transits or progressions to super opportunities for change and growth.

SUN-MERCURY ASPECTS

The Sun represents your basic internal self, while Mercury symbolizes how you think and act. When these two are aspected to each other, there is a strong link between your conscious thought patterns and your self-expression. You'll be much more aware of how your communication presents you to others in the world. If your natal Mercury-Sun combination indicates that you don't let others know you very easily (Mercury isn't in the same sign as the Sun, or is more than 15 degrees from the Sun, or you have planets between Mercury and the Sun), you'll become much more aware of how you hide from others while your progressed Sun or your progressed Mercury aspects your natal Sun or Mercury. You may find your barriers crumbling, or you may find yourself reinforcing those walls. If your natal Sun and Mercury are in the same sign, within 15 degrees of each other, and have no planet between them, you'll find yourself reevaluating the way you communicate during the aspect.

Variable: Conjunction (0°)

In older texts, anything within 5 degrees of the Sun is called combust. One of the ancient definitions of this concept involves being "swallowed up by the Sun" or lost in the power of the Sun. While I don't think that Mercury's influence totally disappears when Mercury is conjunct the Sun, its influence is muted. When your thought process is exactly the same as your inner self, you are expressing or communicating yourself exactly the way you see yourself. It's often hard for you to pull back and see how others are responding to you. Many folks with this conjunction in their natal chart cannot understand how some people can mentally step aside and look at themselves interacting with others. During the progressed conjunction, this same intensity and difficulty with objectifying occurs. Unless there are other aspects which pull the conjunction into interaction with other planets, symbolically pulling the person into interaction with other people, this conjunction can be quite solitary. While you gain insight into your own thought process or your own inner self, you lose objectivity. Watch out for mental ruts, for you'll dig them with amazing speed during this conjunction. After the aspect has separated, you may have quite a bit of difficulty dislodging the habits you formed.

Tension: Semisextile (30°) and Inconjunct (150°)

The inconjunct aspect between progressed and natal positions of Mercury and the Sun is rare, but can occur. The semisextile, on the other hand, happens to everyone. During these aspects, you experience a sense of dissatisfaction with the way you express yourself. You're aware of shortcomings in both the way you express yourself and the way you are inside. At the same time, you'll have a lot of fear about changing in either area, because you're just not sure what you'd like to change into. Before you can adopt a better way to do something, you have to find a way to do it that you like better. So most of you have a six-month period of inner irritation. Usually the outcome is quite positive, for it paves the way for you to accept that you've changed from the old self into a slightly newer version. As the aspect separates, you become more comfortable with the idea that consistency isn't always a virtue. Then you can use both natal and progressed symbolism, choosing whichever is more appropriate in any given situation.

Stress/Action: Semisquare (45°), Square (90°), Sesquiquadrate (135°) and Opposition (180°)

Although hardly anyone gets the sesquiquadrate or opposition between Mercury and the Sun by progression, most of you experience the semisquare and square during your lives. These aspects set the stage for change in your ability or means of communication, and more importantly, change in your way of thinking about yourself.

The change these aspects indicate usually involves some kind of study or mental activity which leads to an increased use of mental abilities in the working world. It's the decision the factory worker makes to learn something about electronics; it's the librarian's leap into social work; it's the technical editor's romance novel. The common thread in all these individuals' changes is the change in their mental images of themselves. The stress which prompts the change may be economic (the factory worker fears loss of job security), but often has little to do with money. The technical editor certainly has more job security and benefits in her position at a major computer company than through the possible career of romance novelist, and the librarian turned social worker doesn't earn any more counselling troubled teens than she did checking out books for them. All three of these clients were much happier with their new choices, because for each the *image* of the new choice is more prestigious. All three worried about whether or not they could achieve the new status. So far, although the technical editor hasn't sold anything yet and still works nine-to-five for the computer company, she and the other two are pleased with their decisions.

Ease: Sextile (60°) and Trine (120°)

Not too many of you will have the trine aspect between Mercury and the Sun by progression, but quite a few of you will experience the sextile. These aspects work nicely as background, for they tend to ease difficult transits. I can't tell you a single thing about using these aspects in predicting events, because neither the trine nor the sextile is an action aspect. However, you'll be able to think clearly and logically, and more importantly, be able to communicate effectively during the six-month period that these are exact. You won't waste time with useless worry about things you can't change. This is the single largest benefit of this aspect, but unfortunately, you usually don't notice the absence of worry—you only notice its presence!

SUN/VENUS ASPECTS

Sun-Venus aspects can be a bit tricky, for the obvious meaning of the combination (that you will fall in love and live happily ever after) is not the only interpretation. The Sun symbolizes your internal self, your physical body, the manifestation of your life on Earth. Venus symbolizes your way of giving and receiving love, but also represents your self-indulgence, your lazy side, your manipulative side. The problem in interpreting the aspects between the Sun and Venus by progression is determining which of the sides of Venus will show. The nice side (the loving part) won't necessarily manifest in the easy aspects and the difficult side (the spoiled child) doesn't always show up during stressful aspects. If you've never considered the darker side of Venus, you may find the following interpretations quite negative. So do I. Unfortunately, these problems all have manifested in real-life people: my clients. I made several mistakes in interpretation by assuming that the energy of Venus was usually positive. Perhaps I could have helped some of my clients more if I had devoted more time to delineating the potential abuses of the combination of Sun and Venus rather than dwelling on the rosy future indicated.

The most positive (and my favorite) event indicated by any Sun-Venus aspect is true love. And that does happen with this combination. Marriage, engagement, moving in with a wonderful person—all of these things can and sometimes do happen with Sun-Venus combinations. You have to do some digging into the other aspects to both your natal and progressed Sun to find out if this is what will happen to you when the Sun is connected to Venus by progression.

While most of us want a happily-ever-after loving relationship, many of us are terrified of that kind of relationship. This fear can come from a negative self-image, a self-image that says you are not worthy of being loved. If you know that you are not loveable, anyone who loves you anyway must be incredibly stupid. Then you may use the combination of Sun and Venus to manipulate your loved ones until they get sick and tired of being yanked around. At this point, your loved ones start to leave, proving your underlying premise—that you are not loveable.

Sometimes this fear of intimacy stems from a fear of being swallowed whole by a lover. If you can't imagine any type of love other than complete obsession in which you obliterate your own individuality, you develop an avoidance response. After all, who needs or wants to be a non-person? In this case, you may manifest the Sun-Venus connection by eating yourself into an unattractive mountain. This usually provides a pretty effective barrier to intimacy.

I have two cases in my files of Sun-Venus connections by progression which marked a year of self-indulgence through drugs, in both cases cocaine. Two examples don't even set up a theory, but they certainly made me re-think my automatic assumption that Neptune is always involved in cases of drug abuse.

In summary, be careful with your predictions based on Sun-Venus connections in the secondary chart, or between secondary and natal positions. Find out as much as you can about your underlying attitudes towards your body, your ability to love or be loved, your needs and fears in a love situation. Then be aware that you can do lots of things to sabotage an aspect which is usually interpreted as wonderful.

Variable: Conjunction (0°)

The easiest way to manifest the conjunction is to fall in love and get married. Your tendency will be to identify yourself with loved ones, which can be either very positive or positively horrible. If you are displaying love readily and are open to receiving love in return, you probably will reap the rewards of a strong and affectionate alliance. If you are submerging your wants and needs under those of a loved one, the self-sacrifice involved will become a burden as the conjunction passes. If you expect the final outcome of love to be a disaster (à la Greek tragedy), you may set yourself up for this during the conjunction.

Tension: Semisextile (30°) and Inconjunct (150°)

These are about the most troublesome connections possible between Venus and the Sun, because they do not indicate a conflict that is out in the conscious mind. The nagging worry and fear often surface as jealousy, whether or not your loved one has given you cause to be jealous. If you are not in a relationship, you can either be jealous of the gal or guy down the hall who seems to be doing pretty well, or you can get quite morose about real or imagined flaws in either your physical body or your ability to relate to other people. If you can latch onto a nice big Saturn aspect at about this time, you can use this energy to revamp your whole body, building up what needs building and slimming down what needs slimming. The point here is to avoid the frustrating rigidity of these aspects by preparing for a new outlook, even if you are not quite ready to fully accept a new you.

Stress/Action: Semisquare (45°), Square (90°), Sesquiquadrate (135°) and Opposition (180°)

These aspects point out the problem of interpretation of Sun-Venus connections, for the stress/action aspects are the ones most likely to result in positive motion. Far from being negative, these combinations usually do indicate love and relationships. You have a tendency to see the flaws as well as benefits in your relationships. Even though the stress/ action aspects rarely go along with the kind of relationships described in gothic romances, they seem to accompany the relationships real people set up in the real world. So along with starry eyes, you have jealousy. Then you have to figure out why you are jealous, and confront your lover or yourself with the causes of this insecurity. Along with visions of happily-ever-after, you have annoying habits. You have to decide whether you can live with bad table manners or camping trips. You have to decide what your comfort priorities really are. The stress/action aspects put you on the line. You can't procrastinate during these aspects; you have to decide.

When you have one of these aspects between the Sun and Venus, indecision usually results in getting fat or neglecting your body in some other self-indulgent way. The effect is so immediate that you have to be absolutely unwilling to deal with your own internal reality to ignore what you are doing to yourself. Even if you do try to ignore it, your friends will tell you about it.

Although you may experience a separation from a loved one during this kind of aspect, the separation is often connected to a positive desire to sort out your internal love responses, not due to strife per se within the relationship.

Ease: Sextile (60°) and Trine (120°)

Your desire for and determination to get comfort and pleasure increase. If this is a reciprocal agreement (and you are willing to give as well as get), this connection can be marvelous. Unfortunately, the person with this kind of aspect often does either all the giving or none of the giving. Both of these extremes work against long-term satisfaction. If you are busy being indispensable, caring and totally giving in all of your relationships, you may wind up exhausted and drained at the end of the aspect. If you aren't involved with that manifestation, but are busy manipulating the folks around you into catering to your every whim, you may wind up quite disappointed as these folks jump ship when your sextile or trine separates. The "charming child" of this aspect tends to resemble Cinderella's coach, disappearing when the aspect separates. If your internal script has you playing the part of one of the sister uglies, you won't get your foot into the glass slipper no matter how hard you try.

When Venus and the Sun are involved, the ease aspects often mean too much of a good thing. It may be possible to transcend the materialistic, selfish, self-indulgent sides of these aspects, but it isn't easy to do so unless you have some pretty strong natal aspects, or difficult aspects from other progressed planets or outer planet transits. If you have quite a few difficult aspects, this sextile or trine will symbolize balance by providing you with an underlying positive self-image.

SUN-MARS ASPECTS

Our society doesn't like to deal with Mars except indirectly or through euphemism. We have an inconsistent attitude towards energy, drive and competition—the positive attributes of Mars—and a tendency to deny or repress anger, aggression and temper—the negative attributes of Mars. Since the Sun represents both the physical body and the manifestation of your life energy, the combination of Mars and the Sun is one of the most powerful connections possible by progression. Almost all of the events indicated by aspects between Mars and the Sun are real-life events which manifest on the physical plane. After the aspect passes, you rarely wonder what happened, although you may spend some time unraveling *why* it happened.

Athletes provide excellent examples of Sun-Mars energy. The Sun-Mars aspect isn't the recognition of effort put out; it *is* the effort. In other words, if you're looking for an aspect to time winning an award or title for sports or any other physical activity, look for the time *after* the aspect between Mars and the Sun has separated. During the aspect, the person will be busy training, preparing, developing his or her body to peak performance. Mars gets the athlete moving, but some other combination of aspects usually indicates the outcome of this training.

What about the majority of you, who are not athletes? You have Mars-Sun connections, too. Sometimes you take up physical body-building or training while Mars and the Sun are aspecting each other by progression, but often you don't. If you go through the ephemeris, however, and pick out the years when your progressed Sun aspected natal or progressed Mars, and the years when your progressed Mars aspected natal or progressed Sun, you will discover that during those times you were incredibly busy. While living through that year, you may not have noticed your increased energy, but from the vantage point of a few years later, you will wonder how on Earth you managed to do all the things you did during those years.

If you aren't an athlete and are about to have a Sun-Mars aspect by progression, look for intense activity relating to the house positions and sign positions of the two planets. Connections between these two require some caution—you could be careless of your own safety or of your physical body, and thus be more accident prone at this time.

Variable: Conjunction (0°)

Many astrologers, in spite of what they say out loud, have a negative view of the action of Mars, the lesser malefic. An analysis of the effects of the conjunction based on the lives of real people rather than theory comes as a surprise to these astrologers. While you certainly will notice the conjunction, its influence is usually positive. Unlike the natal conjunction, which can indicate a rather abrasive manner, the conjunction by progression won't lead to temper tantrums or other kinds of obnoxious behavior unless there are a multitude of other aspects contributing to the negative expression of the energy.

The effect of the Mars-Sun conjunction depends largely on three variable factors. First and most critical in the analysis: what are the other aspects to the configuration? If the conjunction is between the progressed position of the Sun and the natal position of Mars, what are the natal aspects to Mars? If the conjunction is between the progressed position of Mars and the natal Sun, what are the aspects to the natal Sun? Whenever the closest aspects to the natal planet are positive, the conjunction increases physical vitality. You'll wake up any trines to your natal planet, making them lines of activity rather than comfy old shoes that you hardly notice. Sextiles to the natal planet start hopping as you use this working aspect to its fullest capacity. If the aspects to the natal planet are difficult, you'll either start working on these areas of stress or you'll find yourself coping with events which manifest the symbolism of the aspects involved. The Mars-Sun conjunction will magnify the energies involved until you just can't avoid doing something about your natal stress lines.

The second factor you should consider when analyzing the Sun-Mars conjunction by progression is the sign position. This tells you which energy dominates. If the conjunction is in Aries, where the Sun is exalted and Mars is ruler, you have an incredibly active combination, which probably will set off sparks no matter what the other aspects are. If the conjunction is in Leo, which the Sun rules, or in Cancer, Virgo or Taurus where Mars is weaker due to debility or fall, the Sun dominates the conjunction. When the Sun dominates, the physical effect of increased energy is more pronounced. Mars is stronger when the conjunction occurs in Aries or Scorpio, which it rules, or Capricorn, where it is exalted, and in Aquarius, where the Sun is weaker. When Mars is the stronger planet, you get into more activities. You may involve yourself in so many different things that you don't feel the extra energy you are expending.

The third factor contributing to the analysis of this combination is the natal house position of the conjunction. This provides the clue to the area of life or kind of event that's likely to occur. The second house concerns money, fourth house home, sixth house daily work, etc.[12]

Tension: Semisextile (30°) and Inconjunct (150°)

These aspects intensify any guilt you may harbor about the way you use your aggression, your competitive nature, and/or how you express (or repress) anger. Since all human beings have to express Mars one way or another, all of us have a large capacity for irritation with the way we

---

[12]Hastings, *Secondary Progressions: Time to Remember*, pp. 260–264.

handle these social outcast feelings. These aspects are not action ori-
ented, but are "mumble-grumble" aspects. Very often you find yourself
in daily contact with someone who drives you nuts while the semisextile
or inconjunct aspect is exact. If you examine *why* that other person
makes you feel slightly murderous, you'll probably discover that he or
she expresses Mars in a manner which mirrors all of the parts of your
own angry insides that you don't like. This is particularly true if you are
normally even-tempered and don't have huge reserves of anger. The
better you've integrated your natal Mars expression, the more the other
person's behavior can irritate you. Unless you married the aggravation,
which usually indicates that you've projected your angry insides instead
of integrating them, these aspects ease off quickly as they separate.

Stress/Action: Semisquare (45°), Square (90°), Sesquiquadrate (135°) and Opposition (180°)

These aspects really get you moving. You need to be careful, though,
for haste can lead to accidents while these aspects are exact. Being
careful is difficult during the stress/action aspects, because you're look-
ing for action. Your reflexes will be enhanced, which can give you a
sense of invincible strength.

If you don't or won't accept your own Mars and your own aggres-
sive needs, you may have to find someone else to act out this progressed
aspect for you. In this case, you may be the victim of some sort of Mars
activity. Someone else might batter you mentally, verbally or (worst
case) physically. If this happens, it doesn't make sense to run around
afterwards feeling guilty about being the victim. This only increases the
tendency to deny the anger, which was what got you into the mess in
the first place. It's much healthier to use this event as a pivot point,
expressing your rage and letting that fury out of the closet. Since the
universe didn't collapse when the rotten event happened, it probably
won't even shudder if you hop up and down and curse a lot. Once you
discover your ability to be angry without blowing up the world, you'll be
a lot more comfortable in all of your interchanges with life's irritations.

Ease: Sextile (60°) and Trine (120°)

These aspects bring out the best of your Sun and Mars. You can act
quickly and decisively in most situations. Although neither of these is

event-oriented, if there are other aspects from transits or progressions during the time that Mars and the Sun are trine or sextile by progression, you will find the most positive means to use the energies involved. Don't assume that the trine or sextile cancels any aggressive or angry responses, for they most emphatically do not. These aspects indicate that you will direct your energy towards a resolution of difficulties. You're not likely to waste energy on a useless display of temper, but you will be able to display that temper when it will bring about a positive result.

SUN-JUPITER ASPECTS

Since Jupiter is the greater benefic[13] most of us think of Jupiter aspects in positive terms. Jupiter energy is often easy to integrate, because it usually feels good. Jupiter represents expansion on all levels—physical, mental and spiritual. The darker side of this planet involves over-doing on any or all of these levels. When you combine the symbol of almost unlimited growth with the symbol of the self (the Sun), the result is an enlarging of everything connected to your manifestation of life energy.

You can become very lazy with the nicer Jupiter connections, because things just seem to come easily. When you don't pay any attention to the needs or rights of others, you can expand into arrogance and self-righteousness. If you're determined to ignore the spiritual or religious side of Jupiter, you can expand into sloth, indifference and wasteful indolence. If your whole world revolves around yourself, you can expand into the circus sideshow as the fat man or woman. Jupiter can enlarge a drinking or drug problem to outright addiction by encouraging excessive consumption.

Jupiter-Sun connections tend to make you popular, because others see the buoyant, optimistic and just plain fun side of Jupiter. At the same time, Jupiter sometimes can interfere with your ability to form deep relationships, because all of your relationships are so easy.

Variable: Conjunction (0°)

This conjunction sometimes resembles the wild optimism often present at Democratic national conventions. (For some reason, Republicans are

---

[13]Venus is the lesser benefic.

much too sedate for Jupiter.) You are singing "Happy Days Are Here Again" and waving your flags all over the place. Nothing keeps you down for long during the conjunction, because you're sure that good times are right around the corner. If you are financing your expansion with plastic, you may be near bankruptcy by the time the conjunction separates. While you could be more lucky during this time, you can also lose in a spectacular fashion, so caution is advised with gambling. Jupiter is the great-grandaddy of gambling, so it can be very difficult to quit while you are ahead. The best way to handle this urge is to look around for a Saturn aspect (the harder the better) and confine your gambling to the periods when you have both Jupiter conjunct your Sun and Saturn lurking around to keep you from blowing everything on a single throw of the die. Saturn is about the only planet that can scare some sense into the Jupiter-Sun conjunction, particularly if you think you're on a roll during the conjunction.

Tension: Semisextile (30°) and Inconjunct (150°)

When the Sun and Jupiter are connected by either of these aspects, the thing you don't need hanging around in the background is Saturn. The tension aspects between Jupiter and the Sun often make you afraid to expand, or cause you to worry about the results of exploring new territory. You may retreat when you could be moving into bigger experiences. These aspects indicate a fear of losing what you already have by risking something new. Sometimes the frustration surfaces as bigotry or religious fervor. When you're doing this, you're refusing to look outside of the narrow confines of the "right" way you've selected, and you are in real danger of limiting your own growth due to the blinders you've placed over your eyes. Somewhere inside you know darn well you are preventing your own development. This internal knowledge intensifies the frustration symbolized by these two aspects. Every living thing needs to have the ability to grow. When you (through the Sun symbolism) are thwarting this basic need, you can become very uncomfortable with yourself. Then you might try to escape the dilemma by filling your face with food, alchohol or drugs. Neptune isn't the only planet involved with alchohol or drugs. In fact, in my files, either Jupiter or Venus is more often directly connected to periods of drug abuse than Neptune.

Sometimes you are not the one who restricts your growth during the tension aspects. Sometimes you are in a position of having to cope with a very restrictive set of circumstances (such as being the go-for in a new job) during these aspects. If you can get off the sorry-for-myself feeling, believing that all avenues are blocked, you'll find that mental or spiritual growth does not depend on a non-restrictive work environment.

Stress/Action: Semisquare (45°), Square (90°), Sesquiquadrate (135°) and Opposition (180°)

Things usually start to move under the stress/action aspects. This means the show goes on the road, whether or not you've gotten your act together. You had better gather yourself together as quickly as possible, for the stress/action aspects between Jupiter and the Sun by progression only happen once. The news is good as often as it is difficult with Sun-Jupiter.

If the last statement is true, how can you tell which side (nice or nasty) will show up with a Jupiter-Sun stress/action progression? This is a rather crucial question if you're trying to predict anything from a chart. The answer is tough only because you have to take into account the basic honesty of the person whose chart you are analyzing. People who are looking out for #1 seem to get rotten Jupiter. And the rest of you cheer until you find out that even rotten Jupiter can still turn out well, regardless of your personal attitude.

During this kind of rotten Jupiter you could have your business go bankrupt, whereupon you write a book about how to negotiate the bankruptcy laws which sells a billion copies and earns more than your original business ever did.

Of course, this result infuriates the righteous among us who didn't wreck a business so didn't write a book so didn't get royalties. (Righteousness as well as writing are ruled by Jupiter.)

Now, some people would not be able to snatch the opportunity at hand when faced with a huge Jupiter mess. Whenever Jupiter precipitates a disaster, there is a compensating bonus. Grabbing the gold ring involves leaning out pretty far. Some of us would rather not reach as high as the stress/action aspects from Jupiter demand. Every single one of us has at least one of these stress/action aspects from the progressed Sun to progressed and natal Jupiter during our lives. If we believe in ourselves enough to go for the gold ring, our lives will change dramatically.

Ease: Sextile (60°) and Trine (120°)

If you have nothing else going on to push these aspects into action, you may not even notice them. It's easy to get into debt, but that's about the worst manifestation of these aspects. (Getting into debt can happen with any of the Jupiter aspects; it just feels nicer with the easy aspects!) If you do have other aspects from progressed positions or outer planet transits, an ease aspect from Sun to Jupiter by progression seems to enlarge the other aspects. It doesn't really make them any better or worse; it just makes them bigger. If your internal script about yourself has winning or success in it, you will find a positive solution to the events going on around you. On the other hand, you may have a script which says that you are not really very good and can't possibly succeed in the long run. If this is your hidden agenda, the ease aspects from Jupiter will make sure your expectations are fulfilled. When you have an easy aspect between your Sun and Jupiter and cannot find any way through a major problem, run, don't walk to some kind of therapy. You are, in psychological jargon, "ripe." This means that your hidden agenda is so close to the surface that unless you get a truly useless counselor, you will find out why you are afraid to grab that gold ring. Sun-Jupiter by progression usually signals that you can get at the hidden failure script even with an incompetent therapist.

SUN-SATURN ASPECTS

Since Saturn is the "greater malefic,"[14] we often regard Saturn with the kind of love reserved for cod-liver oil. Nasty but good for you. Sometimes it feels like rancid cod-liver oil; nasty and bad for you.

Saturn, like your bones (which it rules), gives form and reality to the life you live. It would be about as hard to get around in life without Saturn as it would be to walk without any bones inside. Whenever I hear something like that, some little voice inside me says, "Yes, but that doesn't mean I'm going to like it." You can grow awfully tired of getting

---

[14]Mars is the lesser malefic.

exactly what you deserve. You also can get fed up with great learning experiences.

Does that mean that none of the Sun-Saturn connections is ever decent? None of them is exactly fun, but most of them are not totally disastrous. Saturn rarely brings surprises, because deep down, most of us not only expect Saturn; we rely on it to keep things sane.

Saturn's reality says that if you throw a rock at a plate glass window, the window will break. You expect that if the window didn't break, either the rock wasn't thrown with enough force or the window wasn't plate glass at all. You don't expect the window to throw the rock back at you. Someone inside might throw the rock back, but this particular Saturn reality on Earth does not allow the window itself to throw the rock back anymore than it allows the window to dissolve, let the rock through and reform after the rock passes.

When your Sun connects with Saturn by progression, or Saturn transits your Sun, your inner self connects with reality. This can be hard to cope with regardless of the eventual outcome of the events involved. Something in this combination is resistant to change, resistant to growth. All of us will have Sun-Saturn aspects by progression and transit during our lives. All of us will have to reassess our relationships with the real world, with the outcome of our behavior, with our inner priorities and ability to accept responsibility for ourselves.

Variable: Conjunction (0°)

Your internal "shoulds and oughts" all seem to come due during the conjunction. Watch out for accepting responsibilities for things (or people) which are not really necessary. Somehow, during the conjunction, if you've already done all your shoulds, you can get yourself into extras. The conjunction brings a time for you to sort out just where your own liability begins and ends. If you hate taking any kind of responsibility for your own life (and it's always bad luck or someone else's fault when things go wrong), the conjunction may be extremely difficult. This aspect brings you nose to nose with the results of your own actions.

If you have a negative self-image, the conjunction can magnify this to positively impossible proportions. While this may result in low physical energy and/or depression, most people eventually recognize their need to straighten out priorities and deal with their internal critical parent. That's what Sun-Saturn conjunctions are all about.

Tension: Semisextile (30°) and Inconjunct (150°)

When you are not doing all that you could do, this aspect comes to bother you at odd hours. Practically nobody ever does absolutely everything perfectly, so this aspect gets to all of us. When this aspect is within 15 minutes of arc (progressed Sun approaching), or about 3 degrees for transiting Saturn approaching, you find all your little ways of shirking supposed duties. The aspect does not mean that you suddenly start doing everything; it just means that you are suddenly aware of your shortcomings. If your natal Saturn is strong by position or aspect, this aspect can really get to you, because you already have a keen sense of duty and responsibility. It seems that the stronger your desire to be perfect and upright, the harder this tension hits. You'll have to decide whether you want to take on responsibility for every stray person who crosses your path or whether you can bear to be a human being who has somewhat limited responsibility. You are not too sure of your own self-control during this aspect, nor are you certain about the amount of control you can exert on others (or they can exert on you). You may choose to get out of worrying about this by taking on the problems of neighbors, co-workers, siblings, parents, the old lady down the street and anyone else you can find. This leads directly to Dudley Doright, but doesn't lead to personal peace or happiness. Once you stop feeling responsible for everyone else, you can accept responsibility for yourself.

Stress/Action: Semisquare (45°), Square (90°), Sesquiquadrate (135°) and Opposition (180°)

Everyone who is over forty-five has had one of these aspects between the progressed Sun and Saturn (natal and progressed). Everyone over five years old has had the transit. That can be cold comfort when it's you in the middle of the aspect. This may not be the most difficult aspect you'll deal with during your life, but it will probably rank in the top ten. Even people who profess to like Saturn change their minds a bit while in the midst of the hard aspects from their progressed Sun to Saturn. The transit is not usually quite so memorable, for we experience many more of the transits.

There is one major exception to the gloom above. These aspects can be very strong marriage indicators when combined with progressed aspects between the Moon, Venus or Jupiter. When that is the case, the marriage has a very good chance at making it until "death do you part," because the stress/action aspects between Sun and Saturn symbolize an awareness of commitment and an assumption of responsibility.

The central theme in Sun-Saturn stress/action aspects is self-control or self-discipline. While you may wallow around in self-pity for a while, you'll have to do something about what's going on around you as the aspect gets closer. Sometimes the discipline required is the courage to say "no" to the unreasonable demands of the people around you. If your natal Saturn is strong by aspect or sign, you are more likely to have to limit your tendency to try to do everything during this aspect. If you can't or won't refuse to accept responsibility which should not be yours, your body will pay. This kind of over-responsibility often results in stiffness, arthritis, bursitis, problems of rigidity. You've taken literally the old order to "stiffen your backbone" and have accepted the burdens of your immediate world. Who appointed you Atlas? During this aspect it may be time to make the rest of the people around you carry their fair share of the burdens. If you can let go of carrying everyone (and also controlling them through your assumption of their responsibilities), you can use these aspects to free both your Sun (your internal self) and your Saturn (your perception of reality) to function with much less guilt.

Ease: Sextile (60°) and Trine (120°)

These aspects usually indicate that you can work towards your goals without too much distraction. You can let go of any perfectionist problems which interfere with your ability to get on with the realities at hand. If you are in the midst of other difficult progressed or transit aspects, the presence of the ease aspect between your progressed Sun and natal and progressed Saturn, or from transiting Saturn to your Sun, actually gives you the endurance and strength you need to make the best choices in each situation. This combined symbolism encourages you to discriminate between the things you can and should control and the things you cannot or shouldn't control.

There is a problem with the ease aspects which does show up every so often. You can get into really strong control situations with all the people around you. Then you've got your thirty-year-old kid living at home and kowtowing every time you walk by, or you've got your spouse so tangled up in your web that he or she can't possibly take control of his or her own life again. When the progressed Sun or transiting Saturn moves out of orb of the trine or sextile, you'll grow tired of having to make all the decisions for the people you controlled so easily during the time of the ease aspects. That's going to be too bad, because you'll probably be stuck with the situation, Saturn being the way it is, and giving you what you deserve as the result of your own behavior.

ASPECTS BETWEEN THE SUN AND THE OUTER PLANETS

Uranus, Neptune and Pluto move so slowly by progression that the only new aspects between any of them and the Sun are made by the progressed Sun. Neptune and Pluto often stay within a degree of their natal position for your entire life. Thus, the progressed Sun will aspect both natal and progressed positions within the same year. Each of these three planets will aspect your natal Sun by transit during your life. Uranus moves about 4 degrees per year. Whenever Uranus is within 4 degrees of an aspect to your Sun, you will notice the itchy desire to change things. That desire won't become a drive until Uranus is actually within a few months of making the exact aspect. The speed of Neptune and Pluto depend on their position in their orbits. Right now Pluto is near perihelion, moving about as fast as it can go. Neptune is now the planet farthest from the Sun, and the slowest planet. Both of these can dwell at one degree for up to two years, going direct, retrograde, direct and retrograde again over the position. For most of you, the transits, because they last longer, will be more powerful than the progression.

The symbolism of the progressed Sun aspecting the natal and progressed positions of your outer planets always involves your current manifestation of life energy, or the here-and-now you. If your natal Sun aspects one of the outer planets (say you have natal Sun at 22° Taurus, square natal Pluto at 22° Leo), your Sun will progress to sextile your natal Pluto when you are about thirty years old. Then you experience a change in the way you use the natal combination. Your progressed sextile won't be quite the same as the sextile for someone who has natal Sun at 5° Taurus, with his or her natal Pluto at 22° Leo. The 5° Taurus Sun doesn't have the natal dynamic to change.

When your progressed Sun aspects an outer planet pattern which is not otherwise connected to any of your personal points (your natal Sun, Moon, Ascendant, Midheaven or Node), the generational effect of the aspect starts to function on a more personal level. For example, millions of you have Neptune sextile Pluto in your natal charts. If none of your personal points is making an aspect to Neptune or Pluto, you are not likely to notice the sextile other than being alive during a time when the world is becoming aware of a need to change some concepts about reality and power. However, during the years that your progressed Sun aspects either natal Neptune or Pluto, the sextile comes home to you, and you have to decide what you as an individual are going to do about your illusions concerning personal power. The closer the orb of the sextile in your natal chart, the more likely you are to experience it on a personal level at some time in your life.

Given the average life expectancy of a person in the United States, your progressed Sun will aspect each of your outer planets at least twice during your life. It's no use looking backwards in your life for causes of events that occurred during these aspects, for the symbolism shows that they don't have to do with your Daddy or Mommy; they have to do with you. You always have the choice of which side of the outer-planet symbolism you will incorporate into your life. All three planets have difficult symbolic expressions as well as the possibility of major spiritual transcendence of the ordinary.

The lower Uranus disrupts and changes, demands its own way, and is endlessly arrogant. The higher Uranus builds a new structure while dismantling the old.

The lower Neptune lies and cheats and cops out with drugs, alchohol or any means at hand. The higher Neptune lifts you to a new spiritual plane, introducing you to a vast, new awareness.

The lower Pluto destroys utterly, using whatever force is needed to cause the elimination of something. The higher Pluto transforms, bringing new life and vitality to all it touches.

When your progressed Sun approaches aspects to the three outer planets, you choose the level of response. Most of us go through at least a little of the negative side, for if we were so enlightened that we didn't experience any of the lower manifestations of the three outer planets, we would not need to be here at all.

The transits of the three outer planets to your natal or progressed Sun involve changes in your view of yourself. Of the two types of aspects, the transit to the natal position is stronger. We are always more flexible about our present views (progressed Sun) than about our internal self-symbols (natal Sun). Thus, most of us have more trouble with transiting aspects to the natal Sun.

SUN-URANUS ASPECTS

Uranus is the symbol of creative, inventive self-will, but it's also the two-year-old inside us who screams "I want to do it MYSELF!" Uranus symbolism isn't overflowing with cooperation. On the other hand, Uranus represents the flashes of insight that allow you to break old habits or create a new reality for yourself. When you combine the symbolism of the Sun (your inner self) with Uranus, you get creative change of self-image. Some of us accomplish this change in great exciting leaps; the rest of us are dragged into it kicking and screaming. The process of change is most difficult when you resist it. If you can flow with the tide of change, the power of these connections can bring you further along towards self-awareness than any other planetary combination.

I think of Uranus as a kind of cosmic joker who keeps you both flexible and alive. If you thought you had everything in your life under control and had become very satisfied with your own neat reality before you had a Sun-Uranus connection by transit or progression, you won't think so afterwards. Uranus wipes out apathy. Uranus plants land mines in your most comfortable ruts. Uranus takes Murphy's Law (the maximization of perversity) and enlarges it to encompass everything in your life. Uranus makes you feel like a mother hen who has hatched a clutch of ducklings. The mother hen knows that her babies will all drown if they get into the water. Uranus has you flapping and clucking in panic along the shoreline as your cherished beliefs, like the ducklings, go for a swim. So long as you don't get into the water to save the beliefs, thereby drowning, you can survive Uranus. You eventually may give in to the new, changed reality that Uranus leaves in its wake. You actually may decide you like the new you.

Variable: Conjunction (0°)

You'll certainly remember the year that transiting Uranus conjuncts your Sun, or your progressed Sun conjuncts natal and progressed Uranus.

Through a series of unexpected abrupt events, you'll change your whole view of yourself during this year. As the conjunction approaches, you may feel like a skier who is at the top of the mountain for the first time. You can't go back down the lift. It's too late to go back to the non-skiing person you used to be. You're scared, but at the same time, you're excited. You might as well get going, because you'll just catch cold hanging around the top of the slope.

Unless you panic and forget to use the things you've learned up to now in life, you'll make it back to the lodge. The you that gets to the lodge won't be the you who left the lodge, though. After skiing through the year of the conjunction, you will have a new grasp of all the things you actually can do when you *have* to do them. Change will never again scare you the way it did the first time.

Quite a few astrologers call Uranus a malefic because change, particularly the Uranus kind, which we cannot control or completely anticipate, finds all of us unprepared. Yet at the same time, no other planet can expand your awareness, encourage your independence, excite you about being alive the way Uranus can. You don't have to be arrogant, selfish, loud and obnoxious with the Sun-Uranus conjunction. You won't be able to be a quiet little mouse, but that doesn't mean you have to turn into a boor. It's up to you to use the conjunction for your own growth, rather than in mindless rebellion.

Tension: Semisextile (30°) and Inconjunct (150°)

These aspects usually indicate that you need to find some outlets for your creativity. You can't stifle your abilities indefinitely. The tension involved occurs when you inappropriately let your two-year-old side out. You have to let the inner kid go out to play every now and then, but you need to work out the appropriate time and place for this activity.

For some people, the tension aspects have very little to do with their internal children, but rather with a rigid concept of reality. Uranus, remember, is the exploder of rigidity, changer of reality. If this is happening to you, you'll find that the events in your life don't fit your ideas about what is real and what is not. You may find it hard to believe that what's happening to you is really happening. These aspects are not action-oriented, so you don't have to change anything or experience major disruptions in your life, but you may have a disorienting sense of unpredictability. It's a little like seeing a giraffe browsing on the foliage along the Appalachian Trail. If nobody else mentions the giraffe, and there are no news accounts of lost circus animals, you may conclude that you did not see a giraffe at all. But with the tension aspects present, you know you saw the giraffe. You can get very touchy about the whole thing, becoming furious if anyone teases you about it, or you can stop arguing about it and privately wonder why a giraffe was there. An event like this isn't likely to change your whole life, and neither is a tension aspect between the Sun and Uranus. You will be prepared for absolutely any kind of animal, even on the Appalachian Trail.

Stress/Action: Semisquare (45°), Square (90°), Sesquiquadrate (135°) and Opposition (180°)

Precipitate action is the biggest problem with these aspects. The dynamic interchange between the Sun and Uranus pushes you into taking action, but you may find yourself acting much too hastily. Even though the events are abrupt and spectacular, you have to stop and think or you can get yourself into a big mess.

The other side effect of this combination is a tendency to be careless of your own physical safety. If transiting Mars makes a stress/action aspect to your natal Sun while transiting Uranus is within a degree of the same type of aspect to your Sun, or during the time that your progressed Sun is within 15 minutes of a stress/action aspect to Uranus, you have a classic accident pattern. This means that you should stay away from high crime areas, be careful in your car, and in general behave as if you wanted your body to stay arranged exactly the way it was before the aspect started. You really don't have to be mugged to experience the changed view of yourself which comes through the hard aspects between the Sun and Uranus.

It may be very difficult to contain your temper during these aspects. Don't climb into your car and drive 110 miles per hour because you are angry. You'd be better off actually fighting with someone than doing that.

The stress/action aspects between the Sun and Uranus usually manifest in some obvious real way, like lightning striking a tree. Don't stand under any solitary trees during this thunderstorm, and you won't be permanently scarred by Sun-Uranus hard aspects.

Ease: Sextile (60°) and Trine (120°)

There is a playful quality to the ease aspects between the Sun and Uranus. You'll be able to see the unusual and wonderful sides of life, able to create a more exciting adventure out of the ordinary life you already have. If you are lucky enough to have some stress/action aspects from other progressions or outer planet transits, you'll have some push to start the ease aspects moving. Then you will find that no matter how impossible the situations around you seem, you'll discover a way around them.

The stress aspects don't have to be to your Sun, either. Suppose you have transiting Pluto square your MC, symbolizing a major, permanent change in career direction. If your progressed Sun is simultaneously sextile or trine your natal and progressed Uranus, or transiting Uranus is sextile or trine your Sun, you can take the lemons that Pluto is dishing out in career areas and distill them into a fantastic new superconductor for computers.

There are two necessary keys to using the ease aspects. First, you've got to get moving. We all tend to enjoy a sense of the unusual, but without some hard aspects to indicate action, you won't have any reason to change much. Second, if you do have some difficult aspects indicating a push towards doing something, you have to trust yourself and let yourself use the inventive side of Uranus. If the aspect is from the progressed Sun to natal and progressed Uranus, you have to concentrate on the present situation, for your progressed Sun is your current manifestation of your life energy. If you are busy living in the past, through your natal Sun position, you won't be able to use the energy of your progressed Sun. The ease cannot work through your natal self-expression. If you let go of the past, you can move right ahead with creative, inventive solutions to any and all of the events in your life.

SUN-NEPTUNE ASPECTS

Neptune, spinner of dreams, weaver of clouds, symphony of unreality, symbolizes both the hope of and the destruction of the ego. Neptune always dissolves the hard edges of reality. When combined with the

Sun, symbol of your manifestation of your inner self, Neptune blurs your ability to see yourself clearly.

When your progressed Sun is connected to your natal and progressed Neptune, or transiting Neptune connects to your natal or progressed Sun, you are dancing with the god of unreality. You may dance with the creative side of this god, writing poetry or playing music, but far more often you will dance with the seductive side of the god, losing your ability to objectify in your desire to escape the harsher sides of reality. Then Neptune becomes the deceiver, rationalizing all and any actions.

You cannot dance with only part of Neptune. To dance with the spiritual side, you must relinquish yourself, for you must realize that the ego structure is illusion. Yet you cannot survive on the Earth with no ego structure, for you must still do the things that maintain life in the body, the Saturn kinds of things like eating, drinking, staying warm and dry.

It is possible to dance so completely with the deceptive, rationalizing, sneaky side of Neptune that you virtually abandon the spiritual side. You don't have to choose to do that, but you can. You can pretend that you are sacrificing yourself for others while you are weaving webs of control around their lives. You can pretend you are taking drugs (or drinking) so that you can continue to support the people depending on you, while in reality you are destroying your ability to support anyone. You can lie and cheat and steal and pretend you still like yourself. Or, you can use the flip side of the Neptune coin and let other people do all of these things to you, while you pretend you have contributed nothing to the situation. Then you can be the one who enables your spouse to drink to oblivion and make the excuses that allow him or her to deny the alchohol problem.

Through all of this, Neptune silently shreds reality to tatters. Between the philosophy and the Beaujolais, transcendent, illuminating spiritual insights can and do occur. The problem with Neptune is that it may be difficult to be coherent enough to recognize these moments of illumination.

Variable: Conjunction (0°)

One of Ashleigh Brilliant's postcards says: "Having abandoned my search for truth, I am now looking for a good fantasy." When you have transiting Neptune conjunct your natal or progressed Sun, or your progressed Sun conjunct your natal and progressed Neptune, you look for that fantasy for about a year. Along the way, you may come across some profound spiritual insight into your own inner self. Unfortunately, for most of us the insights are often like the grand solutions to problems that we discover in our sleep. When you wake up, you know that you just had the answer, but you can't quite remember what it was. Life takes on a surrealistic hue when you have the Sun conjunct Neptune by transit or progression. You are aware that there is more than this concrete reality to life, but you are not quite sure what that involves.

It's very hard to deal directly with the effects of the conjunction, for it's rather like wrestling with a wraith. Part of you is not living in the real world at all. The alternate reality part of you inhabits may be a spiritual dimension or a fantasy dimension. If it is a criminal dimension, you do not pay any attention to the possible outcomes of your actions. You are sure you won't be caught. If it is a fantasy dimension, you may decide to cop out through insanity. You won't accept personal responsibility. If it is a spiritual dimension, you can gain tremendous insight.

After the conjunction separates, you will find out how much of each of these manifestations you chose to experience, for once you are out of the fog, you'll be able to see most of what went on during that period.

Tension: Semisextile (30°) and Inconjunct (150°)

You may feel like you are conducting a private war during these aspects between the Sun and Neptune. Your internal war is either between the psychic, intuitive side of yourself and the "real" manifestation of your-self, or perhaps between the honest, upright you and the larcenous, sneaky, lying side of you. Most of us wage the war on both fronts.

The tension of these aspects usually involves interpreting the reality of the world around you and your interaction with that world. The rigid side of these aspects points towards stamping out Neptune, but the need of the human spirit for wonder, mystery and hope is far too great to allow complete eradication of Neptune.

If you have a particularly strong natal Saturn, and are quite firmly entrenched in reality structures, you may manifest this aspect through another person. Then you have to cope with a space shot (if you're lucky) or a con artist or a crazy person (maybe drugs, maybe not) during the tension aspect. The Neptune person will make you see the Neptune parts of yourself.

Stress/Action: Semisquare (45°), Square (90°), Sesquiquadrate (135°) and Opposition (180°)

These are the symbols of the ultimate game of blind man's bluff. As originally played in England, this was not a nice game. The blindfolded person had a stick, and so did everyone else. The object of the game was to hit the one with the blindfold without getting hit back. If the blindfolded boy hit you with his stick, you were the next one blindfolded.

During the stress/action aspects between the Sun and Neptune, you have two objectives. First, you have to recognize that it is a game, and second, you have to try to take off the blindfold.

Somehow, during these aspects, life does you a dirty deed which tests all of your illusions or fantasies about what life is all about. If you react by flailing around with your stick, you have decided to participate in the game of blind man's bluff. Almost all of us respond this way. If you are lucky, you manage to hit someone fairly quickly, transferring the blindfold to the next guy in line. If you are not so lucky, life can deal you quite a few whacks during the stress/action aspects.

Some of us manage to figure out the game after the first blow. Then we can refuse to play. We can acknowledge our illusions, take off the blindfold, and let the others continue if they wish. This is the hardest response because the illusions we have to acknowledge are generally called "reality." When we recognize that this is a game, we recognize that life holds more than a physical reality. Once we lift our sights from the mundane to the spiritual, we have taken off the blindfold.

The stress/action aspects between Neptune and the Sun offer you the greatest opportunity for spiritual growth that you will experience in your lifetime. This opportunity is usually hidden in extremely difficult events. You can only gain the spiritual insight if you can let go of your reality structures.

Ease: Sextile (60°) and Trine (120°)

The notion that Neptune is a malefic doesn't hold up at all during the ease aspects between the progressed Sun and natal and progressed

Neptune. These aspects almost always provide a time of free-flowing imagination. You'll be able to visualize ideas much more quickly. Not only that, you'll find that you enjoy the beauty around you more completely, for you'll notice it more. You won't suddenly blossom into a musician or artist if these gifts were not already present, but you will appreciate all of the Neptunian sides of life much more completely.

Even if you are a dyed-in-the-wool realist, you'll be more tolerant of your encounters with people and ideas that you think are spacy. Whether or not you discover your own psychic side, you will be able to rely on your intuition a bit more.

If you already have a lot of Neptunian traits in your personality, you'll develop them more easily, or at least feel more comfortable with this part of yourself. You will be able to let go of the notion that everything can (or should) be explained. Although these aspects relax an overly intense Saturn (if you have one) they don't create chaos if your natal Saturn isn't a problem.

The ease aspects help you build castles in the air, but also let you know that they are fantasy. While neither of these aspects indicate that you'll do anything in a concrete sense, both the sextile and the trine provide avenues of escape that you can use for recovering if you are undergoing stress from other positions at this time.

SUN-PLUTO ASPECTS

Pluto, planet of death and rebirth, transformation and permanent change, symbolizes your will, your personal power. When the energy of Pluto is combined with your Sun, you are about to change your view of yourself.

There is one major difference between the changes which transiting Pluto symbolizes when it aspects your natal Sun and the changes symbolized when your progressed Sun aspects your natal and progressed Pluto. The progressed aspects are faster. Transiting Pluto can wander back and forth and stay in aspect for up to two years, while your progressed Sun moves along fairly regularly. Pluto crawls in a progressed chart, often managing to move only a minute a year, so your natal and progressed Pluto positions will not be very far apart. Most of you will be finished with both the aspects to the natal and progressed Pluto from your progressed Sun within a year at most.

There is a small problem with timing the events of the year, because the position of Pluto is not exact in the ephemeris. Of course, you've got the same problem with transiting Pluto. The maximum error for the position of Pluto in the more accurate ephemerides is 10 minutes of arc. Usually the position is closer, within a few minutes of arc of the observed position.

If you allow a fifteen minute approaching and separating orb for the progression (the diameter of the Sun), you may not center on the most intense time of the aspect. With Pluto, it's better to allow a slightly bigger orb (30 minutes approaching and separating), which pretty well insures that you'll catch the time that the aspect is really happening. Then ask questions. Any aspect between your progressed Sun and Pluto has such a profound effect on your current self-image that a few questions will settle whether or not it is in orb.

Since Pluto symbolizes both power and change, many people think that Pluto always smashes things to bits so that a new birth can occur. Indeed, the results of Pluto often do appear in this manner. However, Pluto can work subtly and tirelessly in the background to effect the changes needed. Pluto power is not merely the caveman or gangster stereotype, for Pluto power can manipulate when manipulation will achieve the results desired.

When your progressed Sun is approaching an aspect to your natal and progressed Pluto, or transiting Pluto is homing in on your Sun, you are symbolically approaching a time in your life during which you have to recognize and use your personal power. If you have been taught that power is bad or that you can't display dominance, or if you have decided that you are a pawn of the universe, you will have difficulty with all of the connections between your Sun and Pluto. Until you can own your Pluto, until you can recognize your power plays and needs for self-determination, you will have to get someone else to "do" Pluto on you. Then you are the victim. The Pluto victim isn't the self-sacrificing Neptune victim. Pluto victims use the manipulation inherent in Pluto to gain mastery over the people who have to play the Pluto part for them. Here appears the power of the weak, the power of Pluto. When you refuse to acknowledge the power you have inside yourself, and you play the Pluto victim, you won't want to admit that you completely dominate the lives of the people around you through your (apparent) weakness. Your Sun is soaking up all of the dominance symbolism, whether or not you feel that things are being done to you or by you.

Variable: Conjunction (0°)

The effects of the conjunction between Pluto and the Sun depend almost entirely upon your self-image for their manifestation. If you see yourself as a fairly competent, powerful person, you will be able to use this year to pursue your objectives with renewed depth and intensity. Your intensity may scare the wits out of some of the people around you, but you may not notice this. This combination of energy won't settle for less than the whole thing, so you can get very obsessive about the things you use to define your self-worth. If you judge your worth by the amount of money you earn, you may become obsessed with earning more. If you define your personal power by the number of people you have at your beck and call, you might collect serfs all year. If you define yourself in terms of recognition, you can work tirelessly towards greater fame. The conjunction forges a link between your manifestation of your life energy and your use of personal power. The transformation which then happens is the full acceptance of your abilities to get what you want.

If you have always had an image of yourself as a powerless, weak personality, it will be much harder to integrate your Pluto power with your manifestation of your life energy. You can't use this conjunction to get what you want out of life if your personal script calls for you to be a loser. If you want to, however, you can use the conjunction to change your script. Then, although you may not have vast outer changes during the year of the conjunction, the internal change will insure that you completely abandon the losing script. Contrary to much of the astrological lore, Pluto is not irresistible. If you have an awful lot invested in being a loser, and absolutely refuse to alter your script, the year of the conjunction somehow will validate your internal image. You will find some way to completely and utterly fail at everything. Even this can have its positive outcome, for all you can do for an encore is rise, phoenix-like, from the ashes. The devastation of Pluto will tell you about your inner self. Whether your personal phoenix flies or crawls from the ashes, it will emerge. You will be changed.

Tension: Semisextile (30°) and Inconjunct (150°)

These are about the most difficult aspects possible between the Sun and Pluto because they increase both the rigidity of Pluto and the tension between power and will. Since these are not action aspects, most of the tension is felt on an internal level. You are not comfortable with overt expressions of dominance, yet you cannot tolerate being dominated, pressured or forced into activities. With either of these aspects, it seems that you have to exert pressure or you will be pushed. The inherent lack of harmony between the signs involved in the semisextile or inconjunct aspects insures that you won't be any more comfortable with manipulation than you are with the "big stick" kind of Pluto. These aspects usually manifest through other people. Your boss or spouse or parents or kids pressure, wheedle, manipulate and somehow make you drag out your own Pluto. You will have to use your Pluto power to avoid being trampled to death. You aren't likely to be psychologically stomped into dust with this aspect, for the rigidity (which is one of the prime causes of internal tension) also refuses to lie down and be walked upon. After the aspect passes, you will be able to sort out who did what to whom. Then you can respect your own power to endure adversity.

Stress/Action: Semisquare (45°), Square (90°), Sesquiquadrate (135°) and Opposition (180°)

These aspects usually surface as events, so everyone around you can see them. Thus, lots of people believe that the stress/action aspects are more difficult than the tension aspects, but that is not accurate in the case of Pluto. The stress/action aspects bring you face to face with your power. You have to make choices, choices which involve changing your self-image. You can't sit around and wish it would go away—it won't. During these aspects you have to refuse to be bullied anymore. That's when you discover that the person pushing you around is impotent in the face of your refusal to be pushed. If you are the bully, you will get stopped during the hard aspects between the Sun and Pluto.

The stress/action aspects between the Sun and Pluto create a dynamic tension which forces you to balance your self-expression and your need for power. If you go over to complete Pluto, becoming ruthless in your obsession to have your own way, you will hit a brick wall. Your use of either manipulation or force will backfire, leaving you with a big mess on your hands. If you try to ignore Pluto and deny your needs for autonomy, you will be so stifled that you cannot grow at all.

None of the nastier Sun-Pluto symbolism has to happen to you. If you are afraid of being mugged or raped, take some courses in self-defense. The very process of learning how to defend yourself changes your self-image and allows you to develop a sense of power over your own destiny. This is a positive, useful way to develop the energy of the stress/action aspects.

Ease: Sextile (60°) and Trine (120°)

You need very little prodding from other aspects to start the ease lines between the Sun and Pluto working. You can literally get whatever you want during the ease aspects. This brings up the inherent problem of Pluto: be sure that you know what you want, because you are going to get it!

Difficult aspects from other progressed positions or transits simply seem to make the ease line function better. These aspects work on a principle similar to judo, for when others try to strong-arm you during these aspects, you allow them to use their own energies against themselves. Meanwhile, you sail along doing whatever it was that you wanted to do in the first place.

Since you are more likely to use persuasion during the ease aspects, you rarely get into situations where your new Pluto energy irritates others. Rather, others are usually swept up into the tide of helping you get where you want to be.

CHAPTER 6

Fluctuating Feelings: MOON ASPECTS

Since the Moon represents your yin response nature, the cycle of aspects between your progressed Moon and your natal Moon marks the stages of emotional growth. The Moon takes roughly twenty-eight days (equal to twenty-eight years in the secondary progression) to completely circle the zodiac. In *Secondary Progressions: Time to Remember*,[15] I delineated the aspects of the progressed Moon to the natal Moon. During the first cycle, you grow to adulthood, learning to separate yourself and your own unique emotional responses from the emotions and person of your mother.

As you let go of your adolescent issues with Mommy, you grow to adulthood, and your progressed Moon starts to focus on relating, on the need to give and receive nurturance. The progressed Moon is the most prominent planet in the secondary chart in timing events. For that reason, the delineation of all the aspects from the progressed Moon to the natal Moon was included in *Secondary Progressions: Time to Remember*, so I'm not writing it over again here.

---

[15]Hastings, *Secondary Progressions: Time to Remember*, pp. 13–27.

MOON-MERCURY ASPECTS

Aspects between the Moon and Mercury by progression connect your conscious thinking process to your emotional response patterns.[16] Most of us have an urge to analyze our responses during all of the aspects. The difference between the easy aspects and the difficult aspects involves *why* we want to think about our responses, not whether we want to think about them.

During easy aspects, you are more likely to approve of your response nature as well as your way of thinking. The more self-critical parts of the Mercury symbolism don't bother you as much when the aspect between the Moon and Mercury is easy. When the aspect between Mercury and the Moon is difficult, the side of Mercury that is exaggerated can be the other symbolism of Mercury: worry.

When the progressed Moon is aspecting natal or progressed Mercury, the aspects only last a few months, for the progressed Moon moves about 1 degree per month. When progressed Mercury is aspecting the natal Moon, the aspect duration is longer, for Mercury progresses at most about 70 minutes per year. You usually notice these aspects for the whole year involved, although the time that the aspect is exact is the critical period.

Sometimes Moon-Mercury aspects don't have anything to do with analyzing how you feel. Periods of negotiating, writing contracts or resumes often accompany connections between the Moon and Mercury by progression. Moon-Mercury contacts can indicate learning skills which require dexterity and attention, such as learning to type or use a word-processor, or even developing some mechanical skills. Taking standard exams, such as college boards or GREs, may accompany Moon-Mercury aspects, particularly if you feel that your future hinges upon the exam.

Variable: Conjunction(0°)

While these two planets are conjunct by progression, your thinking and feeling are one. You know quite well how you feel, and are unusually

---

[16]Transiting Mercury moves too fast to be a major influence in our lives. If Mercury makes a station within a degree of an aspect to a natal planet, it will work with essentially the same delineations as those given for the progressed aspects.

quick to recognize your response patterns. If the conjunction is in a sign in which the Moon is stronger, such as Cancer or Taurus, or in a sign where Mercury is weak, such as Pisces, Sagittarius or Leo, the Moon will dominate the conjunction. Then your combined thinking-feeling process tends towards more feeling, less thinking. This really means that you won't talk about your feelings as much as someone who has the conjunction in a sign in which Mercury is stronger. If the conjunction is in Gemini, Virgo or Aquarius, where Mercury is strong, or in Capricorn or Scorpio, where the Moon is weaker, Mercury will dominate. When Mercury rules or is exalted in the sign, you will communicate your feelings. When the Moon is in its fall or debility, you will analyze your own feelings, but may not choose to tell this to the people around you, for neither Capricorn nor Scorpio is particularly talkative.

Tension: Semisextile (30°) and Inconjunct (150°)

The tension aspects suggest arguments with women (or with Mom), but the underlying reason for the arguments rarely reaches your consciousness. These ties between the symbol of your essential inner feminine side and the symbol of conscious thought and expression indicate that you are not very comfortable with your responsive yin nature. Since neither of these aspects is an action aspect, usually you can't explain or understand why you feel uneasy about your responses. When you look at your responses through the lens of someone else (he or she is making you feel bad), you have some sort of explanation for why you feel uncomfortable. If you can figure out what it is that the other person is doing that rubs your feminine side the wrong way, you have a chance to gain some understanding of your own response nature. Most of us analyze the tension aspects after the fact. So long as you get to the analysis sometime or other, it's irrelevant whether you look at the "why" during or after. You'll only run into a problem with the tension aspects if you absolutely refuse to see any reflection of your own response nature in the tensions of the time.

Stress/Action: Semisquare (45°), Square (90°), Sesquiquadrate (135°) and Opposition (180°)

During these aspects, you are either analyzing your response nature so much that your thinking process scrambles your emotional response, or your emotional response is so strong that you have trouble thinking clearly. Sometimes you think very clearly but get so upset about the situation that you become temporarily tongue-tied when you try to say something about it. When Mercury is stronger by sign (or by angularity) the first difficulty (scrambled emotions) is the most common. When the Moon dominates, it's harder to spit out your thoughts. Regardless of which dominates, when any of these aspects is exact, you may face situations which demand that you respond and think at the same time.

I can just hear about one-fourth of you saying "Whew! I have my natal Moon in an air sign—no problem—I always do that anyway!" Horsefeathers. No matter where your natal Moon or natal Mercury is, you'll find that you have to rise to the occasion during the stress/action aspects. You may have to take a major exam, finish a complicated business deal, negotiate a contract while your relationships are falling apart, or your (insert the one that applies to you—Mom, Dad, kid, spouse, lover, pet) is sick and needs nurturing. Nobody has a natal set-up that is immune to these times of chaos.

The lessons of these aspects seem to involve balancing emotion and thinking so that you can walk the tightrope of living without giving up either thinking or feeling.

Ease: Sextile (60°) and Trine (120°)

In everyday life, these aspects are very hard to detect. You usually take your own competence for granted, noting only the times that you are not coping magnificently. Since you don't get flustered when you have to make decisions, you don't even notice that you're making decisions. There is a kind of inertia at work here which leads you to believe that since things are moving smoothly, they will always move smoothly.

If you have any difficult aspects from other progressions or outer planet transits, the ease aspects between your Moon and Mercury by progression assume much more significance. In these cases, you will be able to handle both the emotional and intellectual sides of whatever the other aspects symbolize with clarity and without undue worry. You can make excellent business decisions because you have a good balance between your mind and your response nature. You can put away mental gremlins, for you have the ability to analyze where your fear originates.

MOON-VENUS ASPECTS

Moon-Venus aspects by progression[17] seem to love a good time or a party, for they are often present when people get engaged, married or have children. Their presence doesn't guarantee nuptials, nor does their absence deny romance. Rather, they show up frequently when people have major pleasant changes in relationships.

Of course, as with every planetary combination, there is a darker side to the combination of these two energies. The negative side tends to show more readily with the ease lines than with the stress/action or tension lines, perhaps symbolizing too much of a good thing. Venus can be self-indulgent, and the Moon can be self-pitying. When you combine the difficult symbolism of both, you may become extremely self-centered. Then everything in your life revolves around YOUR comfort, YOUR pleasure, YOUR spoiled child within. Everybody has a spoiled child inside, so everybody has the ability to pull out the negative side of this combination. This combination can be very manipulative, for you'll use charm, emotion and anything else you can think of to get your own way.

Most of us do a little of both sides of Venus-Moon connections. We generally get into relationships because they bring physical and/or emotional pleasure.[18] If your Sun is under stress while the Moon-Venus aspect is present, you may have such a negative self-image that you can't get yourself together enough to form a relationship. The Moon-Venus connection then may function as a source of positive reinforcement, counteracting negative symbolism rather than bringing out a clear positive result of its own.

Variable: Conjunction (0°)

Something is going to happen in relationships when your Moon and Venus are conjunct by progression. Often, the conjunction means marriage or

---

[17]Transiting Venus moves too fast to be a major influence in our lives. If Venus makes a station within a degree of an aspect to a natal planet, it will work with essentially the same delineations as those given for the progressed aspects.

[18]I am aware of the fact that sadistic, brutal relationships exist. They are not often symbolized by Moon-Venus connections. In fact, the Moon-Venus connection usually marks a time during which these relationships are not quite so sick.

engagement. Sometimes it means separation (as it did in the example of Marjorie Singer, in my first book, *Secondary Progressions: Time to Remember*). Sometimes it means pregnancy. If you are a woman and don't want to be pregnant, be very careful when your Moon and Venus are conjunct by progression. Your body and your emotions really don't care what your rational Mercury wants. This conjunction can bring out that totally irrational desire to procreate which keeps the human race from extinction.

If you over-indulge in food, alchohol, drugs or spending money while these two are conjunct, you should seriously consider some kind of therapy. When the most negative parts of the Moon and Venus show up during the conjunction, it means you have a big problem accepting (and liking) your feminine side. Both men and women can have problems with their yin projection. If you are at all uncomfortable with your feminine side, it will show up during the conjunction.

Tension: Semisextile (30°) and Inconjunct (150°)

This aspect is like a small headache, one that isn't severe enough for you to take aspirin or acetaminophen, but enough to make you crabby. You tend to snap at loved ones or take sudden dislikes to your furniture, wardrobe or other possessions when these two planets are in the tension aspects. What you really are doing is wondering if you have any good taste at all in your choices about the things or people you love. You see, hear and feel selectively, instantly picking up on criticism, criticizing yourself constantly. Maybe it IS time to get rid of the fourteen-foot brass giraffe that you bought while your progressed Sun conjuncted your natal Venus in Leo a few years ago. So what. It isn't the end of the world. Just sell the darn thing and get on with your life.

During this season of discontent with your inner workings in areas of love or self-indulgence, it's a good idea to postpone either the marriage or the separation plans. If you wait about six months, you'll see everything a bit differently. Unless you're in a terribly destructive relationship, you probably can stand to wait out these aspects.

Stress/Action: Semisquare (45°), Square (90°), Sesquiquadrate (135°) and Opposition (180°)

Since I am an incurable romantic at heart (natal Venus in Pisces), these are some of my favorite aspects. I cheer up immediately when I see them in a client's chart. I can't wait until they are back in my chart. It takes a huge pile of negativity to make these aspects awful. You'll have to work incredibly hard at it to be miserable during these aspects. You may not become engaged or married (particularly if you already are married) but you'll have plenty of opportunity to do either or both, if you're interested.

That last phrase (if you're interested) is a key here. I had one client who kept telling me (over a period of five years) that she wanted to be married (she's divorced). She went to stay with her mother in an isolated spot of rural New England while her progressed Moon squared her natal Venus. Then, the next year, when her progressed Venus semisquared her natal Moon, she did the same thing. You would think that I would catch on by then, but sometimes I'm quite dense. When she did it a third time, and visited her Mom when her progressed Moon squared her progressed Venus, I finally got the picture. She really did not want to be married again—in fact, she was so scared of that possibility that she went to the extreme of visiting the one person who would insure that she didn't meet any eligible man. At this point, we talked about it, and she discovered that she really does love running her own life. Now that she sees this more clearly, she isn't so upset by the fact that she gets into "friendship" rather than "serious" relationships.

Most of my clients have had relationships start or change during hard aspects between the Moon and Venus by progression. Since both Venus and the Moon progress rather rapidly, you can have the stress/action aspects between your progressed Moon and natal or progressed Venus, or between progressed Venus and your natal Moon fairly frequently. You can have a few years in which (like the client I mentioned above) you have three of these aspects in quick succession. During these times, you'll have the opportunity to make quite a few choices about how you feel in and about love situations. If you don't seem to make any choices or meet anybody you want to love, you may be hiding (which is a real choice) like the woman I referred to above.

Ease: Sextile (60°) and Trine (120°)

I don't wander around humming love songs when I see the ease aspects between Venus and the Moon by progression. I start thinking loathingly about aerobics and diets, because most of us begin packing it on when these two energies combine in an easy manner. It's a good time to be pregnant, if you are female and want to be pregnant. All too often, you look back on the times when you had these easy aspects and see that you manipulated your loved ones rather ruthlessly. This combination could win awards for laying on the thickest guilt trip possible. The trouble is that you don't recognize the guilt you're strewing around in the pursuit of your own way until the aspect is long gone. All you have to do is say, "Honey, would you please . . ." and honey pops up and says "Sure, dear."

These aspects DO NOT show up often during marriage or engagement. That may be because those who are spiritually enlightened enough to use only the highest parts of both symbols did not have to incarnate. The best way to handle these pesky sextiles and trines is to attempt to regulate your intake of goodies on all levels. If you try, you can get through this period without a giant spoiled child inside or a giant waistline outside.

If you have some kind of stress/action aspects from Saturn, Uranus, Pluto, or between other progressed planets and natal or progressed positions, then the above description of the Moon-Venus ease aspects probably won't be completely accurate. The difficult aspects seem to be softened by the presence of the ease aspect between the Moon and Venus. This very softness can be quite deceptive, though, for when "Honey please get me . . ." involves dope or alchohol or chocolate bars, you have the set up for an extremely devastating combination of energies. Then your loved ones contribute to your spiral of self-indulgence, and the stress/action aspects work through the ease line of the Moon-Venus connection to make the slide into self-destruction quite pleasant.

MOON-MARS ASPECTS

Our society has a peculiar attraction/avoidance to Mars energy, which I'll discuss more fully in the section on Mars. Mars represents energy, action, anger, aggression, in fact all those things that help to keep you intact in your ego structure. Mars is a powerful yang symbol, representing the "I do" part inside of you. If you didn't have this symbol in your chart, you would never do a darn thing, because you simply wouldn't initiate anything. Since the Moon is the strongest yin symbol in the chart, this combination of energies produces a conflict, even when combined in the traditional "ease" aspects. The combination of Moon-Mars energy results in everything from strong, protective, nurturing responses to unreasoning emotional outbursts (temper tantrums).

One of the most common ways to express Moon-Mars energy is to drag out "mother" issues and have at them again. Whether you do this by arguing with your real Mom or a surrogate mother figure, or by getting testy about your own nurturing or mothering tendencies, you'll find a way to combine "doing" and "feeling" when the Moon and Mars are connected by progression or transit.

When the progressed Moon aspects natal or progressed Mars, the aspect lasts a few months, but the action happens in the week surrounding the time that the aspect is exact. When progressed Mars aspects the natal Moon, the aspect lasts for several months, surrounding the time that the aspect is exact. Transiting Mars zips by in a day or two, unless it is making a station.

Variable: Conjunction (0°)

You'll respond to emotional inputs and do something about them so fast during the conjunction that you may be reacting before you've got a handle on what you're reacting to. If the conjunction is in a sign in which Mars dominates (Aries, Scorpio, Capricorn) your feelings may take a back seat to your actions. In the worst case scenario, you've started to do something about the things going on before you really know what is involved. Then you can get yourself into hot water by leaping in on an assumption, staking out your ground, and becoming emotional about the position you've taken. If the conjunction is in a sign that the Moon dominates (Cancer, Taurus), you get just as upset, but you may either bury the anger or brood over it. Then you can become so involved in having hurt feelings that you explode on the slightest pretext.

From the above, it might seem that the conjunction of the Moon and Mars is nothing but bad news, but this isn't necessarily so. If you've been stuck in habit patterns (Moon rules habitual action) which don't get you anywhere, the conjunction helps you out of those ruts. The folks around you might not be pleased with the way you get out of those ruts, but the important thing for you is to get out any way you can.

Tension: Semisextile (30°) and Inconjunct (150°)

The tension aspects between Mars and the Moon put you between Scylla and Charybdis. It takes a steady hand and iron nerves to navigate this narrow passage. Mars, on one side, wants to act to deal with your feelings, while the Moon, on the other side, wants to respond completely, and give in to the emotional tugs.

To bring this concept out of the metaphor and into reality, you've got choices to make which involve action and response, choices fraught with guilt or anger. So your parent, or child, or spouse (or, in a pinch, your dog) needs your attention (read nurturance), but you need to get on with some project at work or in your own life. You won't be happy if you go to work, because you're guilty about the nurturing you are not doing, yet if you stay home and bring on the chicken soup, you're cross all day.

There are thousands of original, creative ways to manifest this tension. You can carry on an undeclared war with your emotions, keeping the whole thing internal, or you can import somebody else to make one of the two demands. If you import the Mars end, you've got to put up with somebody who is likely to batter your emotions unmercifully. Then you need to get your own Mars out and put a stop to the aggressive behavior. (You have to get into a fight.) You may prefer to import the Moon side, and latch on to somebody who backs up to your door with a twenty-ton load of guilt and dumps it on you. In theory, women are supposed to make the second choice and men the first, but my clients seem to do either or both without regard to whether they are male or female. Anyway, if you're pushing your way through the piles of guilt, you've got to get out your own Moon and separate your real responses from the ones that have been laid at your door.

These aren't action aspects, so whether you scream and holler (Mars) or mope and sulk (Moon) you won't be done with the tension until the aspect passes. If you can try to examine the basis for the difficulty—the underlying disparity between your own yin and yang sides—you've gotten the best possible understanding out of this combination.

Stress/Action: Semisquare (45°), Square (90°), Sesquiquadrate (135°) and Opposition (180°)

Watch these aspects between Mars and the Moon because the stress/ action lines mean that things are going to start popping. The cliché definition says that you'll argue with women. Maybe you will, but there are a lot more things you can do with the stress/action aspects. You don't have to find a new sister-in-law who reminds you of all the things your Mom did that you didn't like. Somewhere deep inside, you know that Mom would love this new sister-in-law who has never had an original thought in her life. The guilty side of you (the Moon) wants Mom to like you even though you don't do a single thing the way Mom did. The action side of you (Mars) wants to justify or at least argue about the way you do things. As soon as you can let go of your adolescent resentment toward the whole nurturing issue, you can branch out with the hard aspects between Mars and the Moon.

While most of us get roped into a least a little irritation and resentment of the feminine during the hard aspects, you don't have to stay in that angry spot. This combination of energy and emotion can propel you to achieve quite a bit. Think of it as a catapult, which has tremendous potential energy. If you put your current projects into that catapult, you'll be able to launch them with passion and energy. If you just load the catapult with the mud of your old emotional residues, it will spew mud all over everything in your life.

This is the time to start moving. Find something new and get involved in it. Create a reality which needs the energy you have all loaded and ready to go. Volunteer to spend a few hours a week helping battered women, men or kids. Become interested in getting rid of some of the negative things in the world, or in building some positive things into your surroundings. As soon as you latch on to something that needs both energy and emotion, you'll be aiming your action aspect in a way that will let you feel quite good about the events when they are completed.

Ease: Sextile (60°) and Trine (120°)

The ease aspects can turn all the other transiting or progressed aspects into something positive. When you have either a trine or a sextile between Mars and the Moon you can bring out the positive side of all kinds of influences, because your energy and your emotions are in harmony. For instance, do you have Pluto square your Sun? If you've also got progressed Mars trine your natal Moon, you'll let go of the self-images that aren't very useful to you, but keep your emotional world intact. Do you have Saturn opposed your natal Pluto? While progressed

Moon sextiles your natal Mars, you'll deal with that pressure cooker with your boss or some other power figure without dragging in a sense of emotional insecurity.

These aspects color the interpretation of everything else in the chart. Use them as background, primarily to tell you how the other aspects will work. If you trust your emotional side, you'll find that everything else falls into place fairly nicely during the ease aspects.

MOON-JUPITER ASPECTS

The ice cream truck is coming down the street and you've got the money to buy a goodie. That's Jupiter-Moon when you're eight years old. When you're forty-eight, the ice cream truck may come in other disguises, but the feeling is just the same. You're not going to worry about whether the ice cream will fall out of the cone, or whether you'll get a stomach-ache from eating it too quickly, or whether you'll spoil your dinner. Jupiter-Moon is too involved in great expectations to bother with "what-ifs."

The negative side of Jupiter-Moon connections usually doesn't show up until the aspect passes, for any kind of tie between these two energies brings a sense of luck and optimism before it shows you the other side. After the aspect separates, you could wake up to find that you just married someone you can't stand, or that you just promised the world you would deliver the evening star next Tuesday. Or you could wake up to discover that your guru just absconded with the proceeds from the sale of your house—and you have no recourse.

On the other hand, you could get through the aspect and learn that although the person you married isn't perfect, he or she is a darn sight better than anyone else around, or that although the business you started won't make the Fortune 500 this year, it can show a steady growth and profit.

There is a difference between progressed Jupiter aspecting natal Moon and progressed Moon aspecting natal Jupiter, although this difference diminishes as you get older. When you are young, the aspect from the progressed Moon to both natal and progressed Jupiter will only last a month or two, because progressed Jupiter moves about 16 degrees in sixty years. The aspect is in effect during the time that it takes the progressed Moon to get from the natal to the progressed position. The time between the aspect from the progressed Moon to the natal and then the progressed Jupiter (or vice versa if natal Jupiter is retrograde) increases as you get older. During this period, the aspect is intense when it is exact to the natal position, to the point exactly between the natal and progressed positions, and to the progressed position. Of those three, the aspect to the point between the natal and progressed positions is usually the most intense. When transiting Jupiter aspects your natal or progressed Moon, the aspect can last anywhere from a few weeks (Jupiter *not* making a station) to six months (Jupiter makes a station). Be sure to check the *duration* of the transit to determine the long-range effect of the aspect.

Variable: Conjunction (0°)

Jupiter makes things bigger. This concept provides the key to understanding the differing effects of Moon-Jupiter conjunctions. Jupiter doesn't really care whether you get into a wonderful buoyant time or a bigger mess. This particular conjunction has the potential to show you exactly what your own emotional stance is all about. If Jupiter brings a giant mess, you really do have a rather negative response pattern. If you go into a screaming funk over those last words and start running over all the outside things which lead you inevitably to your own response pattern, you have missed the point. Jupiter can enlarge a disagreeable emotional situation until you simply have to give up and start taking things one day—or even one hour—at a time. Your body and brain can only endure a certain amount of exaggerated emotional response before exhaustion sets in.

Jupiter doesn't always indicate an emotional mess. In fact, it can symbolize a rather wonderful time characterized by optimism, humor and a sense of adventure. The best guide to Jupiter is your own past history. You can use transiting Jupiter to figure this one out. Every twelve years transiting Jupiter conjuncts your Moon. What kinds of things came up during the last transit? Were they fun? The progression will be similar, but will last a lot longer. If you became involved in a mild infatuation or a fun relationship while transiting Jupiter conjuncted your natal Moon, you may get married or engaged with progressed Moon conjunct natal and/or progressed Jupiter. If you hatched a new idea or two under the transit, you could start a new business or have a baby with the progression.

Tension: Semisextile (30°) and Inconjunct (150°)

You may not notice much when the tension aspects occur between Jupiter and the Moon, unless you have fairly strong transits or progressions elsewhere in your chart. It's a time when you're more susceptible to worry or stress, feeling "out on a limb" emotionally. That feeling usually comes from your own increased tendency to take risks with your emotions, particularly when the semisextile or inconjunct is exact. If a difficult progression or transit is hitting your natal Sun simultaneously, you may jump from issue to issue, and respond in larger-than-life ways to each event.

The underlying symbolism of these tension aspects involves enlarging upon all nurturing issues. No molehill is too small to be noticed. On the other hand, if you really don't have much to enlarge upon in your own life, you can take on a huge rescue mission while you are in the midst of this aspect. You might find someone whose problems are truly insurmountable, and go to work on them. If that is what happens, you probably should look at why you feel a need to be the ultimate savior. However, if you don't want to look at this too closely, or if you're actually dealing with most of your stuff pretty well, I'd love to have you around if your tension aspect occurs while I'm in the midst of a crisis. You'll bring me chicken soup and hold my hand and generally share my load. You see, the aspects set you up for tension, but in fact may prompt you to relieve some of a friend's or relative's tension. During this process, you'll learn about times to help and times to let go.

Stress/Action: Semisquare (45°), Square (90°), Sesquiquadrate (135°) and Opposition (180°)

These are probably the best aspects you can have between the Moon and Jupiter. Sure you'll take some chances, but unless you have had Saturn surgically removed from your chart, you are not likely to get so far down the magical possibility trail that you can't bring out any positive results. The best combination in my mind (one that I want to be sure to ask for before I incarnate again) is having this progression during all difficult

Saturn transits. When the Moon and Jupiter are connected by the stress/ action aspects, you may be scared by the enormity of the next step, but you'll probably take it. If you've got a strong Saturn background, you'll investigate the options before you jump. Even without a tough Saturn, you'll have lots of choices during any of these combinations. If Neptune is crawling all over you—by transit or inner planet progressions to natal Neptune—you could have trouble with the stress/action aspects between the Moon and Jupiter by progression. This combination sets you up for pie-in-the-sky and swindlers. However, in the absence of a simultaneous confusing Neptune aspect, the stress/action connection between Moon and Jupiter is very positive. You could get married, get engaged, have kids, start a new job, move to a great new place, etc. House positions as well as what else is happening in your life really tell which of the above options is most likely for you.

Ease: Sextile (60°) and Trine (120°)

This signifies a marvelously buoyant, optimistic and expansive time. You will tend to ignore petty problems during this aspect. Of course, this may come back to haunt you later, but while the aspect is strong you simply won't feel much negativity. The ease aspects don't usually signify events, so you'll have to look elsewhere in the chart (transits and/or other progressions) to find out whether any major changes are likely to occur in your life. If you do have something else, like a tough Uranus transit, the trine or sextile will provide a solid and cheerful approach to the upcoming changes. Then the process becomes an adventure rather than a chore.

MOON-SATURN ASPECTS

Any combination of Moon and Saturn involves emotional control. When you are dealing with progressed Saturn aspecting your natal Moon, the aspect is probably there in your natal chart, since Saturn only progresses a maximum of 8 degrees in sixty-five years. The closer the aspect gets by progression, the stronger it becomes in your life. During the year in which the aspect is exact, all transits to your natal Moon will involve

Saturn symbolism in some fashion. Because Saturn progresses so slowly, even the square from progressed Saturn to your natal Moon won't directly symbolize an event. In contrast, when the progressed Moon is making the aspect to natal and progressed Saturn, or transiting Saturn is aspecting your Moon, a conjunction or hard aspect often indicates an event, an inconjunct or semisextile indicates tension, and the ease aspects signify increased emotional control.

Most of my clients don't like Saturn very much. Saturn demands that you fulfill all of your responsibilities. None of us really feels so perfect that we are sure we have completed absolutely everything that Saturn could require. When this nit-picking perfection symbol is connected to the Moon, you try to control the ultimately uncontrollable, messy, unconscious side of reality called emotions. It's like trying to make a mud pie neat. There is only so much you can do before you've washed away the whole mud pie, though some of us do try to sterilize the mud pie of emotions while we have Moon-Saturn connections. Other people whisper behind your back about how you've grown cold. You actually are afraid of being rejected, or are in the midst of licking your wounds following a rejection, or simply are trying to get a handle on how to be in charge of your response nature.

If you are involved in the business world, any aspect between the Moon and Saturn can indicate a fine time for real gains in your business. If you can separate your business from your personal life, you can set yourself up to manifest the major positive meaning of this connection, which is in business. You will see the reality of every situation, and you will be able to eliminate (or control) your emotions so that they don't interfere with whatever professional decisions you have to make. This is also a good time to invest in the stock market, for your investment will be prompted by practicality and common sense, not emotion.

Variable: Conjunction (0°)

When Saturn and the Moon are conjunct by progression or transit, your internal version of Mommy and Daddy get together and bring up your issues about parenting. The underlying theme of this conjunction is who will be the boss—your critical parent or your nurturing parent. Both of these are inside you by the time you become an adult, so it's no use blaming your outside Mommy and Daddy. You can try parent-bashing, but even if you had the worst parents in the world and are lucky to have survived their torture, you still are responsible for your own adult nature. This means that during the conjunction, you won't accomplish anything unless you quit whining about your parents and start looking at the restrictions you put on yourself. You are not your parents. If you are determined to avoid confronting yourself, you can choose to become emotionally involved with a total rat during this conjunction. Then that rat will run your life, stomp all over your feelings and make you miserable. An alternative to this choice, which still lets you survive the conjunction without looking at your parenting issues, is to work so hard that you simply don't have time for personal relationships. Some decent results could come from this choice, for you may prepare yourself for a great deal of success in the real world. If you've already mucked around in your own parenting issues until you think your brain is shriveling up like your hands do after an hour in soapy water, this second choice probably will be the most rewarding one for you. After the aspect passes you can let go of some of the fear that has held you hostage to your work.

Tension: Semisextile (30°) and Inconjunct (150°)

This connection between the Moon and Saturn brings you face to face with the difference between reality and feeling. The tension here revolves around being able to express your emotions perfectly, regardless of the situation. Very few other connections have the stress potential that these aspects (particularly the inconjunct) contain. Who decides what you should feel, or how you should react in any given situation? Your internal critical parent, that's who! This part of you never likes anything you do anyway, so you're already on the wrong side before you even start. During this aspect it is very important to sort through things to determine which ones are worthy of the time and bother. Take your B vitamins before, during, and after the stress situation, get a physical exam so that you don't discover you've got high blood pressure the accidental way, and remind yourself that perfection is on a sliding scale, measured when you are done.

Sometimes the inconjunct between the Moon and Saturn does not symbolize internal events at all. Someone close to you, either your mother or a mothering figure in your life, may become ill or move away. In this instance, you will deal with the possibility of separation from or loss of this nurturing person. The inconjunct alone does not indicate that either of the above events will happen. The inconjunct symbolizes your fears about loss or separation.

Stress/Action: Semisquare (45°), Square (90°), Sesquiquadrate (135°) and Opposition (180°)

The things that happen during the stress/action aspects between the Moon and Saturn usually leave you feeling somewhat rejected, dejected and not too good about yourself. You'll have some hard work to do and you're going to have to put your feelings aside for the moment in order to get that work done. Sometimes people do things like get married during a hard aspect between the Moon and Saturn. If this happens, you'll find some wonderful aspects by progression between the Sun and Venus, or between the Sun and Jupiter. Then the tough aspect between Saturn and the Moon simply provides structure within which the easier aspects can work. This marriage may or may not be made in heaven, but it will last a lifetime. When people are determined to get married when a stress/action aspect between the Moon and Saturn is approaching, I usually counsel them to set the marriage date at least a week after the aspect is exact. That way, the peak of the aspect occurs when they can still back out. The presence of a separating stress/action aspect at the time of marriage works like perma-set glue, creating a marriage that will last a long time, whether the two people involved like it or not.

There are numerous other ways to manifest this set of aspects. Build a house. Plan to start a business (but wait a while to incorporate it)! Write a book. Landscape the yard. In other words, do something that requires considerable concentration and effort but does not give you instant gratification. You will have to provide your own emotional strokes during this aspect, because no one else seems interested in providing them for you. Cheer up—it won't last forever, and you'll end up much stronger in the long run. If you have done the hard work the aspect demands, you'll be physically and financially ahead of the game after the aspect passes.

Ease: Sextile (60°) and Trine (120°)

The ease aspects between Saturn and the Moon are not exactly fun. They don't feel as tough as the stress or tension aspects, but they are no stroll through the park, either. Here you are developing complete control over your own responses to nearly everything, and life seems to want to test this control by sending you a few little nasties. Since these are not action aspects, none of the events occurring are really symbolized by the trine itself. It's just that the rest of the chart tosses things out that seem to need action and a steady hand during the sextile and sometimes during the trine. You are quite capable of doing what needs to be done, but you may get tired of what needs to be done. You can lose your sense of humor while this aspect is exact, not because you don't want the humor, but because everything seems so darned serious. The best way to make it through this is to get a firm hold on your natal Jupiter and an equally firm hold on the concept that nothing lasts forever. Armed with these two concepts, you can sail right through, taking care of everything without getting totally wiped out.

MOON-URANUS ASPECTS

Connections between the Moon and Uranus are never dull! They bring together such different energies that you'll be aware of the restructuring going on even with the trine. Uranus progresses so slowly that any aspect from progressed Uranus to the natal Moon is simply a perfection of a natal aspect. It won't mean a thing until it is exact to the minute, and even then it won't bring up anything radically new in your emotional life. During the year(s) that the aspect is as exact as it can get, you'll find that this connection tends to dominate your emotional life, particularly during transits or other progressions to either natal Moon or your natal and progressed Uranus. But you've spent a while getting used to this energy combination, for it takes years and years for Uranus to progress even 1 degree. Thus, in spite of its reputation for the unusual, which Uranus so richly deserves, the progression of Uranus to exact aspect to your Moon just brings you more of the same stuff you've always handled.

When your progressed Moon aspects your natal and progressed Uranus, or transiting Uranus aspects your Moon, things are different. If you have any sort of natal aspect between the Moon and Uranus, no matter what the aspect is, you will find the progression or transit much easier to deal with than if you have no aspect between the two. Even a minor aspect such as a quintile or novile or decile will do. Any natal connection between the two energies indicates that you have some idea of what to expect from a connection between the Moon and Uranus. If there is no connection in your natal chart, all of the aspects formed by progression or transit between the Moon and Uranus will have an element of surprise for you. When you read the following sections concerning the aspects, think of your own chart. If you have a natal aspect, you won't experience as much upheaval as may be described, but if you have no natal aspect, there may be even more change in store for you.

Variable: Conjunction (0°)

When you see your progressed Moon approaching a conjunction to your natal and progressed Uranus, or transiting Uranus closing in on your Moon, get ready for an adventure. If you decide that you won't be in charge of anything emotional while the conjunction is present, you'll have fun during the conjunction. If you dread change, prefer to hang on to your feelings until you really understand them, or sort of like your terrific self-control, this won't be one of your favorite combinations. This conjunction is like riding a spirited horse. You and the horse will get along best if you exercise minimal control. If you are sitting loose in the saddle, you can sway with the motion and stay on top. If you get stiff and scared, you will pull hard to rein in the beast, the horse will become more nervous, and perhaps buck. If you give the horse a freer rein, guiding rather than controlling, you may go over a few more jumps or run a little faster than you might have wished, but you'll both stay intact. Most of us are not used to horses. We drive cars, and the car has to be completely under our control. We think nice things about people who seem to have their emotional lives as controlled as their cars. A Moon-Uranus conjunction is jumpy, self-willed, subject to change without notice. When you start to tense up, pull out your favorite mantra or relaxing music, or get in the bathtub and remind yourself that this aspect won't be there very long. Loosen up and ride it out. You may find yourself remembering this particular ride with affection some years down the line!

Tension: Semisextile (30°) and Inconjunct (150°)

The semisextile or inconjunct aspect between the Moon and Uranus indicates that you really don't want to deal with emotional change or upheaval right now. These aspects are not action-oriented, but instead indicate a background that fears change. Somehow events bring you inevitably to the fact of change in your life. Your emotional status (your Moon) requires that you face your inner rebellious child (Uranus) and let go of some concept or symbol that you have used to characterize your independence. You may get a new job with a company which absolutely demands punctuality. You love the job and the pay is great, but you want to come in at 9:30 A.M. and leave at 6:00 P.M., even though everyone else has to be there from 8:30 to 4:30. You won't be able to keep both your Uranus independence and your new job.

Stress/Action: Semisquare (45°), Square (90°), Sesquiquadrate (135°) and Opposition (180°)

When you have stress/action aspects between the Moon and Uranus, you're on an emotional roller-coaster. Your feelings change constantly as people seem to pop into and out of your life. Your attitudes towards your emotional needs (particularly for nurturing) are at odds with your desire for independence. It's difficult to be vulnerable, but equally hard to be completely self-sufficient. The emotional situation can resemble my mother's description of riding her bicycle home during the great hurricane of 1938 in Massachusetts. She had no idea what was happening. There had been no warning; there had been no hurricane in Massachusetts for nearly one hundred years. Though the wind was fierce and the falling branches scared her, it simply did not occur to her that she was in any great danger. It is often hard to keep pedaling through these aspects, but you really can see the flying branches long before they hit you. You'll probably be in more trouble if you try to pick a nice big "safe" tree to stand near. Keep moving, stay flexible, and forget about the "right" way to respond to situations. Nobody has come up with a perfect solution for any emotional storm. You can change your mind, you can alter your course, you can back up and apologize. Furthermore, neither the 1938 hurricane nor the aspect between the Moon and Uranus can last forever.

MOON-NEPTUNE ASPECTS

Whenever transiting Neptune aspects your natal Moon or your progressed Moon aspects your natal and progressed Neptune, you've got a tie between your emotional side and the vague, unreliable, creative, possibly spiritual side of yourself. Often we simply refuse to see anything we don't want to see during these aspects. (This is the ostrich syndrome, peculiar to Neptune.) Aspects from transiting Neptune to your natal Moon usually last a lot longer than aspects from your progressed Moon to natal and progressed Neptune, which rarely are there for more than a month or two. Thus, most of us find the progressed aspect easier. With either combination, it is hard to be objective about feelings. To be blunt, we are rarely honest about our feelings during Neptune-Moon connections. Sometimes the dishonesty comes from others, but since we would rather not look too closely, we don't notice. We can be hopelessly romantic during Neptune-Moon periods, for our loved ones seem pretty marvelous. By itself, a Moon-Neptune connection usually doesn't bring major life changes or crises. The tendency to obscure responses usually alters the meaning of whatever else is going on in your life. Moon-Neptune can combine with difficult Saturn aspects very positively, as Saturn grounds Neptune and Neptune prevents Saturn from becoming rigid. Moon-Neptune does not combine as well with Jupiter, for the two exaggerate each other.

Variable: Conjunction (0°)

I've heard a lot of positive stuff about the spiritual side of this conjunction, and you probably have, too. I've had a couple of clients who did have a spiritual awakening of sorts during this conjunction. However, they had a couple of other things going on simultaneously, like transiting Pluto sextile the natal Moon while Neptune conjuncted it or the progressed Moon sextile natal Pluto while conjunct natal Neptune. Those of us born after Neptune and Pluto moved into the sextile position can't have the conjunction without the sextile occurring around the same time. None of us will experience the conjunction of transiting Neptune to our natal Moon without the sextile from transiting Pluto. My clients who have the semisquare between Neptune and Pluto natally don't find the conjunction so blissful. All of this makes it more difficult to sort out the meaning of the conjunction by itself. You'll have to try to keep your wits about you, for in your search for a spiritual base for emotional response, you may find a few false prophets. Unless you have a strong connection to reality, the glow disappears as the aspect passes. Do not marry the "wonder" you find until the conjunction is past history. Don't sell your house and donate the proceeds to the minister/teacher/guru you've found while the aspect is in effect. If you are a singer, songwriter, artist or writer you will find the magic muse at your side. If you stay away from the drug scene, this probably will be one of the most highly creative periods of your life.

Tension: Semisextile (30°) and Inconjunct (150°)

It's hard to answer the question "What's bothering you?" during tension aspects between the Moon and Neptune, because you really don't know. You've got a vague uncomfortable feeling about your response nature. You can't tell if it is God talking or the radiator pipes banging. Your spiritual quest may be stalled and your friend's new teacher leaves you confused. You wonder just who is out of step, you or the rest of your crowd. If you do hear a different drummer, that drummer has decided to do a jazz riff. The worst of this is NOTHING HAPPENS. Nothing good, nothing bad, nothing at all that can't be seen much more clearly through other aspects. Events indicated by other aspects get a dose of undefined aggravation added. This combination simply seems to sprinkle a divine discontent on the way you respond to all the other areas of your life.

Stress/Action: Semisquare (45°), Square (90°), Sesquiquadrate (135°) and Opposition (180°)

This combination of Neptune and the Moon is like the Heisenberg Uncertainty Principle of emotion. If you know what it feels like, you don't know where it came from. If you know where it came from, you don't know what it feels like. Are you the deceiver or the deceived? Chances are, you are a bit of both. If you've got a body, you've got parts of yourself that are not completely honest. Oh, you may never actually do anything that is really dishonest, but everyone has parts that evade the truth, shade the story, color the outcome. During this combination between Neptune and the Moon, these not-so-wonderful feelings add an element of chaos to every issue. If you have a lot invested in being perfect, you may want to run away from home, because no other combination can make you so confused about what actually constitutes emotional honesty. You won't be able to control your feelings any more than you can control the weather. You may be a sucker for a sob story now. You can play the martyr with enormous feeling. These aspects symbolize events, but unless you are a musician or an artist, Neptune events don't have clear beginnings or clear endings. Instead, they seem to materialize out of the mist without ever coming completely clear, then dissolve again without ever letting you know exactly how real they were.

Ease: Sextile (60°) and Trine (120°)

Marvelous maidens and handsome princes ride out of the morning and charm you. Flowers bloom, birds sing, and romance awakens with the ease aspects between the Moon and Neptune. Musicians and artists have a wonderfully creative period, and if a transit or progression simultaneously kicks off Saturn they may capture this creativity in a major work. Drunks and druggies get their fixes or their drinks and feel just fine. This combination usually gives a sense of attunement on an emotional level. Thus, you can handle all sorts of otherwise disagreeable events without undue trauma. You have access to a peaceful part of your emotional makeup. It's irrelevant whether this sense of wonder stems from a real ability to know your own feelings or an ability to ignore the uncomfortable parts of your responses. Enjoy the serenity. If you learn meditation or other means of centering, you are using this aspect in a way which can bring you closer to understanding that you contain the answer to harmony within yourself.

MOON-PLUTO ASPECTS

You want what you want and you want it NOW! You are probably applying emotional pressure to others, but if you are like most of us, you feel that the reverse is true. Your feelings seem to be locked in a vise that someone else is twisting shut. Obsessive behavior peaks now. If you don't have a natal aspect between the Moon and Pluto, the connection between emotion and power will astound you. If you have spent your life denying or giving away your power, you will find someone else to play Pluto for you.

When the aspect is from your progressed Moon to your natal and progressed Pluto, it will last a month or so. You'll have a chance to go inside and find the center of your own strength. Then you can dust off the warrior inside and make it work for you. If the aspect is from transiting Pluto to your natal Moon, you'll have to go inside yourself to find your own power because somebody out there is applying a lot of pressure. The transit can last a couple of years, so you have plenty of time to try out the "helpless, hopeless" or "I don't own Pluto" if you want to. During the time you refuse to get out your Pluto someone else will dominate your emotional life. You can hook up with a total rat, or your kid might turn into Dracula. If you've got a pretty strong natal Pluto and you're willing to use it, you can become obsessive about emotional rights. Your attitudes about power and emotion will change permanently after any major aspect connecting the Moon and Pluto.

Variable: Conjunction (0°)

Welcome to the obsession express! Everything is intense when the Moon and Pluto are conjunct. You won't have trivial feelings now. If the connection is between the progressed Moon and your natal and progressed Pluto, you're obsessing about attributes of your own power. You want to get moving to change the things that don't feel particularly good in your life. If the aspect is transiting Pluto conjunct your natal Moon, you're obsessing about the intensity of your own emotional response pattern. The presence of this aspect doesn't tell us whether you are applying pressure or are the one being pressured. Either way, people will try to influence your decisions. Unless you pay attention to what's really happening, you may wind up feeling that you have been dominated or forced into decisions, regardless of which end you started from.

During the conjunction it rarely occurs to anyone to simply leave the issue alone until it becomes clearer. You lock into the idea that if you don't make a decision instantly you have somehow lost out, given in, retreated (given up your power!). When you are really involved in making sure you do unto others before they get a chance, this conjunction can be very, very difficult. You have to let go before you can reassemble the emotional stability that was possible before the conjunction.

Tension: Semisextile (30°) and Inconjunct (150°)

The tension of these aspects involves letting go of emotional manipulation. Whether you are the manipulator or the manipulated, you can't ignore the power plays in the emotional arena now. If you try to slide through with no change in your feelings, this aspect may manifest through your body. Then you get sick. Sometimes it is easier to deal with illness than it is to deal with emotional manipulation. Some of you recognize how you take things out on yourself, so you don't get sick. Instead, you try to give the power part of this mess to someone else. Whenever you give away Pluto, you get that negative side of Pluto right back. Since this aspect involves the Moon, not the Sun, you can be emotionally battered during the semisextile or inconjunct. But you do not have to get sick or beaten up (emotionally or physically) to quit allowing yourself to get sucked into manipulation games. When you know this aspect is coming up, watch your own responses. If there are human beings who never have applied a little guilt or a little pressure to get things to go their way, I've never met them. Forgive yourself for being human, but do monitor to make sure the guilt games don't end up taking over your entire response pattern.

Ease: Sextile (60°) and Trine (120°)

You can persuade people that the best way to do things is the way you would like them to be done. Thus, do whatever you want to do now, because it will work. The potential problem is inertia (worse with the trine), which means that you may not do anything. Unless some other combination is pushing you towards action, Moon sextile or trine Pluto usually does not symbolize any direct action.

Most of us bask in feeling fine now, and don't get involved in many new things. If you use this period to push people around (sweetly, though—it is an ease combination), you could have some nasty repercussions after the aspect separates. Then your willing workers may start to wonder just what possessed them to let you run their lives.

Some of us have found that the progressed Moon gives us a wonderful toy every four or five years. Guilt games work, power plays succeed, you can do no wrong. Then after two or three weeks of gorging yourself on power politics, the kids say no, your spouse tells you to go to hell, your roommate dumps the trash at your doorstep. It should only take a couple of these passes (for many people, these learning experiences are completed in adolescence) before you temper the human tendency to grab the power and run. When the aspect is from transiting Pluto to the natal Moon, you have a harder time avoiding the easy manipulation, because the aspect is there for a year or so. Since transiting Neptune stays in its sextile to transiting Pluto for quite a while, it's a little silly to try to determine exactly what you're doing during this aspect. Better to enjoy the easy parts of the symbolism while trying to keep your fingers out of too many other lives.

Stress/Action: Semisquare (45°), Square (90°), Sesquiquadrate (135°) and Opposition (180°)

Change is coming, and it won't ask whether you want any or not. All of the changes symbolized here have the underlying connection of emotional power. You may find dominance games, power plays, irritations both major and minor in most of your exchanges with the world. It may be nearly impossible to get your own way. The ice cream store is out of your favorite flavor and your lover is out of human kindness. Your emotional life keeps taking unexpected detours. You simply cannot force this combination to work. The harder you try to make it come out perfectly, the more involved and impossible the situation becomes until you have to do what Pluto requires. You have to let go. You simply can't run everything, but right now you want to. So life rains on your picnic, it hails on your car, it delays your flight and the garbage men go on strike. Once you stop trying to influence the outcome and start looking for the humor, chances are the aspect is leaving and you've learned its lesson.

CHAPTER 7

Thinking About Thinking: MERCURY ASPECTS

Mercury moves much too fast for the transits to have a very large effect on us. When Mercury is stationary retrograde or stationary direct within a degree of a major aspect to something in your chart, you'll probably notice that particular retrograde period more than you usually would. Tracking transiting Mercury is fun when you have just begun studying astrology, for you can see the little changes on a daily basis as it moves into and out of aspects in your chart and the charts of your family members. Transiting Mercury can trigger outer planet aspects or progressed aspects. If you are reading this section and looking at transiting Mercury, please consider that the effects are usually minor.

Progressed Mercury, on the other hand, is a BIG DEAL. Progressed Mercury symbolizes how your mind works right now. What kinds of things are you thinking (and worrying) about? How are you approaching reason and logic? What areas of your life are requiring more thought? Look at both the position and aspects of your progressed Mercury for answers to these questions.

MERCURY-MERCURY ASPECTS

The major aspects possible from progressed to natal Mercury are the conjunction, semisextile, semisquare, sextile and square. Each of these aspects brings a mental re-evaluation, albeit of a different kind depending on the nature of the aspect. The connecting link with the different aspects is mind games. During the easier combinations, the mind games are fun; during the harder combinations the mind games may bother you. If you can remember that both of these symbols are YOU, you'll realize that the one playing around in your head is you. You'll get a chance to see the differences between how you think about things now and how you used to think about things. You'll be able to make some choices about which method works better. You don't have to stick with one or the other. You can use your natal symbolism when it is more appropriate, your progressed symbolism when that fits the situation. You will be straddling a couple of different signs, so you can combine cardinal and fixed or fixed and mutable; you can put together yin and yang, or the different elements. All of the aspects increase your mental flexibility while they are within 10 minutes of arc.

Variable: Conjunction (0°)

The conjunction of progressed Mercury to its natal position is a wonderful time of change for most folks. You had Mercury retrograde at birth or it went retrograde shortly after you were born. If your natal Mercury was retrograde, your progressed Mercury will conjunct your natal position once. If Mercury went retrograde shortly after you were born, it will conjunct your natal Mercury twice. Although my clients have shown me the wonderful diversity of the outer things that change when progressed Mercury conjuncts its natal position, they have also shown me the fundamental attitude changes they have in common. While the outer effects range from moving to another country and learning a different language to making a major career change, the real difference between before and after the conjunction involved their attitudes toward what they could learn or assimilate. You could alter your entire philosophy of life, or simply discover that you can learn math. Some parents reported changes from couch potatoes to students (and one went the other way, sorry to say). All of the parents noticed changes in the goals their kids set for themselves. Any transits to this progressed conjunction do double duty—and consequently seem twice as important while the conjunction is there.

Tension: Semisextile (30°)

That little voice in your head that tells you how stupid you just were becomes a screaming nag during this aspect. You can't possibly please that rotten voice now, no matter what you think or say. You'll think of the right way to handle every situation a few hours after you've yelled yourself hoarse. You'll decide what you could have said about ten minutes after the other person leaves. Now some of you may think you've had this aspect permanently, but the difference is that during the aspect you take yourself to task about this. You may be able to chuckle about it while progressed Mercury is not semisextile natal, but you cannot find anything humorous during the aspect. Guilt gets out of hand here. Because of the mixture of the aspects from anything else (a nice transiting aspect to one of the two positions is lousy to the other; the only exception is two lousy aspects: the opposition and inconjunct), you can and will aggravate yourself regardless of the choice you make in any situation. Fortunately, the semisextile does not indicate events. Thus, you can try first one, then the other thought pattern, drive yourself batty, and wait until the aspect goes away. Let yourself use the line of least resistance here. When you do that, you actually discover the strengths of each method of thought. Then when the aspect passes you are a seasoned veteran of the mental switch-hitting league. And that voice shuts up.

Stress/Action: Semisquare (45°) and Square (90°)

This aspect pattern between progressed and natal Mercury requires a fundamental change in concept. Something you always thought or believed to be true has changed. You always hated (fill in the blank— dogs, lawyers, spinach) and now you discover (fill in again— you own one, you are one, it tastes good). You always prided yourself on your liberal attitudes and now you discover you are profoundly uneasy when your taxes go up so that they can build low-income housing in the cornfield across the street. Most of us talk a lot about the stress involved. In fact, you may drive everyone else nuts because that is *all* you talk about. During the talking, try to do something about whatever is causing the mind-snap. Very often the mind-snap involves prejudice. The sharp aspects make you reconsider patterns of thought. The presence of this aspect does not mean that you will abandon prejudice. It simply means your own prejudices will become less comfortable. There is no guarantee that you'll end up more liberated after the aspect. You simply may ignore it as an aberration. But during the aspect, you will have to think about it.

Ease: Sextile (60°)

Even if you don't wake up singing, you do feel good during this aspect. You can see clearly now, your jokes are funnier, your communications easier, your friends closer. You are feeling more at home inside your own head now. You won't nag yourself as much, and you'll try things you always thought you would like to do. There isn't a lot of staying power to the sextile alone, so don't expect to write a great novel unless you have quite a few other aspects happening simultaneously. Do consider going back to school or learning something new. Investigate all sorts of mental or craft areas, for your creative and mechanical ability is enhanced. This aspect can ease all sorts of other difficult ones, for you have a stable thought pattern during the sextile.

MERCURY-VENUS

Connections between Mercury and Venus by transit usually pass much too fast to signify events. These two planets are weak triggers. If you have outer planet aspects and progressed aspects to Mercury or Venus occurring within a week or two of each other, an aspect between transiting Mercury or Venus to natal Mercury or Venus can trigger an event. The event itself will bear the flavor of the other aspects, however, not the imprint of the Mercury-Venus combination.

The picture changes completely when you are looking at an aspect from progressed Venus to natal or progressed Mercury, or from progressed Mercury to natal or progressed Venus. When either of these planets is progressing rapidly they can move at a rate of about 90 minutes per year. Only the Moon progresses faster. The week during which the aspect is exact indicates a maximum effect of the aspect, but any other major outer planet or progressed moon aspect occurring within two weeks of the exact aspect between these two can be used better to time events.

The combination of Mercury and Venus appears fairly plastic, in that it certainly colors other aspects, but often does not appear to take precedence in the timing of events. By itself, this combination is more likely to indicate a change in attitude or thought pattern than an outer event. When you have a combination of these two planets, you are more likely to change your mind about whether or not you want to be in a relationship than to actually start a relationship. You'll decide you do have a romantic interest in someone who may have been a friend. You may determine that you really prefer country French furniture to colonial. Some of the decisions involve people, some involve things. When you change your mind about these things, or become comfortable with your inner choices, you've set the stage for events to follow. If you really think that men (or women) are basically rats, you can't very well set up a long-term relationship. If you change your thinking about the relative attractiveness (honesty, ability to love) of the opposite sex, you've made the first major step towards a relationship.

Variable: Conjunction (0°)

This combination of Venus and Mercury brings a reassessment of how, who, what and why you love. For some of us, the conjunction isn't a lot of fun, because we get stuck in the worry end of Mercury and become frantic about how we look (too fat, too thin, too big, too small). You are positive that nobody who had half a brain would ever look at you anyway, so you either starve yourself half to death (not very common) or pig out constantly (much more common). If you've got money and a lousy self-image, you can buy yourself lots of presents now. But there is a better alternative with this conjunction, one that you only have to accept to have happen. If you can allow that simply because of your existence, you are intrinsically loveable, you can accept compliments, gifts and friendship from others. Whether or not you want to accept these things, they will be available during the conjunction. If you are concentrating on looking only at your own reactions and at yourself, you won't notice these things. That's when you have to give them to yourself or stuff yourself with food. If you can love yourself enough to take that same old lumpy body and those same old boring clothes out to a club or a dance or a social gathering, and while at that gathering can look around at the other people and give them some of that Venus-Mercury conjunction, you'll find all the neat possibilities of the conjunction. Go out and play—this conjunction was made for fun!

Tension: Semisextile (30°) and Inconjunct (150°)

The tension aspects between Mercury and Venus by progression bring up nagging ways you can worry about the things you like to do, the people you enjoy, the stuff you want to have. You can bother yourself about your materialistic side (even the guru has this side) or about your inherent ability to love or accept love. For many of us, this tension spills out into our interactions with the ones we love, and we become sarcastic or we put on a condescending tone of voice with those close to us. This sets up a ping-pong game with words as the ball. "Jealousy and Fear of Loss" is the name of the game. The trouble with this game is when you win you lose, because the only way to win is to find out that your fear or jealousy was well founded. Then you kill the relationship, and there you are. To get out of the game, watch your own responses. Before you assume that he or she never loved you and is in the midst of a torrid affair with someone else, back off and look at what you are doing to yourself. Unless there are some other pretty major aspects going on, your fears in relationships may be unfounded. If you've got some sort of natal pattern that indicates a fear of abandonment (Saturn in hard aspect to your Sun or Moon, for example) the tension aspect between Mercury and Venus by progression can be quite difficult. If this isn't a primary fear of yours, you may not find the progression more than mildly uncomfortable.

Stress/Action: Semisquare (45°), Square (90°), Sesquiquadrate (135°) and Opposition (180°)

If you're looking for a relationship, these are the aspects that can get you in the right frame of mind to go for it! You'll be teasing, testing, changing your ideas about what (and possibly whom) you like. Watch out for sarcasm—words can wound. Most of you find these aspects fun, but it is possible to get so absorbed in self-interest that you shut out others. Then you'll eat the refrigerator and wonder why nobody loves you.

The stress/action aspects between Venus and Mercury by progression usually appear attractive to other people. You'll have to work at staying depressed now, because funny incidents keep popping up in the most unlikely places. Unless you have amputated your sense of humor, you can see the silly sides of most incidents during this combination. You're just more fun to be around when you can laugh instead of fuss while the ice cream drips down your chin.

One of these aspects often precedes engagement or marriage, but it usually doesn't show up when you meet the fantastic love of your life or when you actually tie the knot. It shows up sometime between the meeting and the engagement, or just before the meeting. Maybe this one works like the cup of water you need to prime a hand pump. Once it is in place, the water can start to flow.

Ease: Sextile (60°) and Trine (120°)

These are days of candlelight and roses. The easy flow between what you think and what you like lets you project an easy sensuality which delights those around you. You won't turn into a femme fatale or a Don Juan unless you already were one, but you'll probably relax about harmless flirting with the busboy or waitress. You can tell others what you like now. That is quite definitely a plus, because unless you've hooked up with an extraordinary psychic, your partner can't tell by osmosis what you want. If carnations make you sneeze or wool makes you itch, you can express this before your lover presents you with a gift of forty dozen carnations or an exquisitely expensive English wool sweater. We are not usually aware of exactly why others like to give us things during the ease aspects between Venus and Mercury. It is fun to give someone something when the recipient purrs and strokes the article, saying, "Thank you very much." If you are the one with the aspect, you probably don't notice yourself glowing and gloating over the little things others give you. But the givers notice and like it.

MERCURY-MARS ASPECTS

Whenever you combine energy and thought, the most likely result is words. Transiting Mercury usually moves much too fast to bring about any major incident, but transiting Mars symbolizes the frequent changes in daily communication. The difficult combinations are irritating, the easy combinations somewhat stimulating. Unless there are background aspects (outer planet transits or progressed aspects) rounding out the Mercury symbolism, the transiting Mars events are things you forget in a week or so.

In contrast, connections between these two symbols by progression last at least a month, with the maximum impact during the week surrounding the exact aspect. Mercury and Mars often progress at about the same rate. The two may travel together, maintaining their aspect within 5 minutes of arc for years. Whether you've got a progression to a natal position, or the two progressed planets aspecting each other, you'll have time to build up quite a head of steam. While a tough transit of Mars to Mercury can be satisfied by an irritating encounter with a sarcastic bellboy, it is self-destructive to stay cross for the duration of the progression. Easy progressions give you lots of time to translate words into action and/or action into words. Difficult combinations teach you what you can and cannot do with your own aggressive instincts.

Variable: Conjunction (0°)

This often feels like someone turned up the volume in life. Your brain is working overtime; it may be hard to sleep. The sudden intensity of your thoughts may startle you. You may be more aggressive in the way you talk and think during the conjunction. Your mouth is in motion before you get your brain in gear. If your natal chart is already pretty aggressive, you may drive people away from you as you charge into one project after another or keep climbing up on soapboxes. If you turn anger against yourself while giving in to the demands of others, this conjunction provides the opportunity to discover the positive sides of your own energy. No matter how you've tried to delete Mars from your life, once you have a conjunction of Mars and Mercury by progression (or a station of transiting Mars conjunct your natal Mercury) you simply have to stand up and be recognized. The transit usually brings this about through the aggression of others. If Mars is zipping by in a fast transit, you've got a day when everyone interrupts you or cuts you off in traffic (drivers in Boston and Montreal must have these two permanently conjunct). When the conjunction is going to be there for a while, you have time to think about the whole concept of aggression. The conjunction can be exhilarating, because you can discover that the world won't collapse if you raise your voice. If you can direct this energy, you can get a prodigious amount accomplished during the conjunction.

Tension: Semisextile (30°) and Inconjunct (150°)

Tension aspects between Mercury and Mars symbolize the need to let go of certain patterns of thinking or displaying aggression which you have outgrown. Problems arise because you've grown used to your old patterns, and it feels like you're watching part of yourself die. This inner tension spills out into your outer interactions through sarcasm, which you can give as well as get now. This combination is great for second-guessing and guilt. You assure yourself that you won't let someone or something get to you anymore, and then it happens again and you're upset again. You are stuck in traffic, with the temperature gauge rising in the car, the headache gauge rising in your brain, forgetting all about the mantra you learned to disengage yourself from the situation. If you add a load of guilt, you can get your blood boiling.

You really don't have to drive yourself into a stroke or migraine now. Don't waste energy with indiscriminate worry, particularly during the inconjunct. A progression between Mercury and Mars or a station of transiting Mars inconjunct natal Mercury will be there for at least a week, probably longer. While the aspect is approaching, sort out the things you can change through your attention. Ignore the rest. Schedule lots of R & R time, so that just in case this manifests through the people around you, it won't drive you nuts.

Stress/Action: Semisquare (45°), Square (90°), Sesquiquadrate (135°) and Opposition (180°)

Until the day that someone invents a time machine, people will probably have trouble with the stress/action aspects between Mars and Mercury. You think of something and want to do it yesterday. Needless to say, tempers become frayed. Everyone without this aspect will tell you to slow down and think things out. People who have this aspect in their natal chart can offer some insight, but they have learned to live with it and don't understand why it is making you crazy. When transiting Mars is in direct motion, it hits you with one of these aspects about every six weeks. Unless there are major outer planet transits or progressions kicking off your natal Mercury, this transit indicates nothing more than minor frustration or irritation. Most people don't wonder why they have to do things during this aspect. You fix the flat tires, change the blown fuses, separate the squabbling kids. When the aspect is by progression or from a station of transiting Mars, it indicates a series of events which may cause you to look at why these things are happening. You can pick up the nails in the driveway, track down the appliance that keeps blowing fuses, refuse to be drawn in to the children's fights. If you really get down to the "whys" now, you'll finish this aspect with a new respect for your own ability to direct your energy profitably.

Ease: Sextile (60°) and Trine (120°)

Your wit is sharper, your mental activity increases. You can make decisions and implement them with ease. Transiting Mars brings you a day to schedule almost anything you want, because everything flows more easily. Most of us are basically lazy. During progressed sextiles or trines between Mercury and Mars, nothing aggravates you enough to make you want to do anything about it. This often results in a time during which things simply go the way you expect them to go. As a driven type A or cardinal personality, I find myself wishing that I had accomplished more during the ease aspect. I suspect that trying to force yourself into all sorts of new areas is the only way to ruin an otherwise nice period in your life. This connection deserves four or five stars because it can and will soften all kinds of other nasty aspect patterns occurring simultaneously.

MERCURY-JUPITER ASPECTS

Transiting Jupiter goes completely around the zodiac in twelve years. Take your ephemeris out and check the times that transiting Jupiter made each of the different aspects to your natal Mercury. Now you can tell whether you respond well to Jupiter or whether Jupiter tends to unhinge you. For all the wonderful things written about Jupiter, I have found a large minority of my clients who don't have wonderful things happen during Jupiter aspects. If you've gone back over the past twelve years and discovered that you were uncomfortable during Jupiter transits, take a look at your own natal chart. Most of my clients who have difficulty with Jupiter have some problems with taking risks. Very often Jupiter requires a leap of faith. Those of us blessed with very powerful Saturn symbolism in our natal charts don't like to do anything on faith. We want to be able to run everything. If that isn't possible, we want to have a good idea about what will happen next. But Jupiter-Mercury aspects bring grand ideas without necessarily including any way to implement those ideas. The easy aspects let you wander into a rut of righteousness. The hard aspects make that rut very uncomfortable, as current events upset lots of your notions about how you really think. The hardest outcome of this connection by transit or progression happens when you decide against taking the risk, then watch your friend do it in spite of the chances involved and your friend makes a million dollars on the idea you wouldn't give up your $20,000-a-year job to try. Happy Jupiter, the great benefic!

Variable: Conjunction (0°)

Jupiter conjuncts your natal Mercury every twelve years by transit. You may never have the conjunction in your progressed chart, or you could have a few of them as progressed Jupiter can conjunct natal Mercury or progressed Mercury can conjunct both natal and progressed Jupiter. If Jupiter is making the conjunction in the progressed chart, the aspect lasts nearly a year. Even if you generally hate Jupiter, your sense of humor gets a boost during the conjunction. Humming or smiling sneaks up on you. You can stay inside, but you know the sun is shining outside. Spring fever gets you in the dead of winter. It is really hard to dislike the conjunction while it is in your very own chart, though it is quite easy to dislike the conjunction when it is happening in someone else's chart. You'll probably talk a lot more, laugh a lot more, tell quite a few tall tales. It is wonderful for salespeople or politicians. If you abandon your natal Saturn completely you can climb pretty far out on a limb now. You'll probably do better in the long run if you at least consider the facts before making decisions during the conjunction. So far none of my clients has gone off the deep end as a direct consequence of decisions made during the conjunction. Two of them are still happily married to the partners they married during the conjunction.

Tension: Semisextile (30°) and Inconjunct (150°)

You're vacillating between believing you can do anything and everything and worrying about finishing what you know you have to do. Procrastination is a means of avoiding the whole mess, but it won't last for the duration of the aspect unless the aspect is a one-time-only pass of transiting Jupiter. With the other combinations lasting up to a year, you will have to get down to brass tacks sooner or later. Are you going to take a chance and try something new or are you going to sit in your scared safety worrying about maintaining the status quo? Maybe those folks who moved in next door and belong to a different racial or religious or ethnic group are not awful. Maybe they won't throw their garbage out the window, have wild drunken orgies, kill your cat and burn down the neighborhood. Your prejudices (Jupiter) are being challenged on a mental (Mercury) level. Are you going to sit inside worrying or go over and meet them? How important are the things you've always believed to be true? How true are they? These are the tensions surfacing now.

Stress/Action: Semisquare (45°), Square (90°), Sesquiquadrate (135°) and Opposition (180°)

The majority of my clients enjoy the hard aspects between Jupiter and Mercury, because they like new friends, new places, new hobbies. "Good causes" proliferate, and those of us who make the time to volunteer to work for the local public broadcasting station, the local hospital, or the current political race find the hard aspects introduce us to many new faces. The times when you refuse to be bothered with something that won't directly benefit you seem to be the times when you have trouble with the stress/action aspects between Mercury and Jupiter. During these aspects you have barely enough time to catch your breath between the things you've got to do. If you didn't want to get involved, if all your thinking concerns yourself, plenty will go wrong in your life to bring out the ceaseless mental activity the connection really signifies. This kind of thinking is usually called worrying. If you don't like the way the last transit of Jupiter touched off your Mercury, plan a few outside involvements for the next one. If you've got a progression coming up between the two, get yourself into whatever "cause" appeals to your personal sense of what is right and good. Then you, too, may be able to get Jupiter to work for you.

Ease: Sextile (60°) and Trine (120°)

You are fun to be with during these aspects. You have a great sense of humor and things just flow along easily. Be careful what you wish for, because with this aspect you're likely to get it. It is hard to put the words "mental" and "effort" next to each other now, because there seems to be no effort required in any mental areas. You could be thinking very clearly, or you could be not thinking at all. What you are not likely to be doing is worrying. By itself, a sextile or trine between Mercury and Jupiter doesn't do anything. The aspect improves every other aspect occurring around the same time. Your loose, optimistic attitude enables you to capitalize on every setback. I wonder if it is possible to sit down between lives and plan your next life so that you have some sort of trine or sextile between Jupiter and Mercury every time there is a really rotten aspect from Saturn, Uranus or Pluto. Then, when Pluto pushes you down and makes you let go of the bundles you're carrying, your hand will close over the world's largest diamond. When Uranus sweeps you away in a tornado, you'll find Oz. When Saturn steps all over you with shoulds and oughts and you go out to dig that ditch, you'll invent a new way to dig ditches and retire wealthy.

MERCURY-SATURN ASPECTS

The Puritans elevated Mercury-Saturn aspects to godly virtue. During the late 1960s and 1970s, Mercury-Saturn thinking was out of style, but a few people still believed in Our Lord of Perpetual Responsibility. During the 1980s, the yuppies brought Mercury-Saturn out of the closet, dusted it off, and now tout it as a means to have Venus-Jupiter. If you and your spouse work ninety to one hundred hours a week, you can buy cars, boats and houses, which you only have time to use about once a year.

When life hands you a connection between Mercury and Saturn by transit or progression, you have received the Puritan work ethic. The longer the aspect lasts, the more you find yourself working hard, concentrating more, taking control of your thinking process. If you have a natal connection and Saturn progresses to perfect the natal aspect, the closer progressed Saturn gets, the stronger the symbolism is in your life. Saturn progresses so slowly that you usually don't notice yourself becoming more and more controlled. When the aspect is from progressed Mercury (unless progressed Mercury is making a station), the aspect forms and separates within a year. You do notice that year, because everything seems so much more important. Transiting Saturn can zip through only making one aspect, but most of the time it takes about a year, going back and forth until your natal Mercury is properly chastised. You'll only notice a Mercury transit if Mercury is making a station within a degree of an aspect to your natal Saturn.

Variable: Conjunction (0°)

When Saturn conjuncts your Mercury by transit or progression, it brings a weight of "shoulds" and "oughts" to your thinking process. The progression of Saturn probably is intensifying a natal aspect, so it's been creeping up on you for a long, long time. If you've tried hard to shift the blame, seeking a way to get through life with minimum effort and minimum responsibility, Saturn brings your Mercury up short. Saturn often can manifest as a rotten boss who demands your best effort. If you've devoted your life to begging quarters on the pier at Santa Monica, Saturn appears as a new effort of the local police to round up the beach bums. Then someone else tells you what to do and where to go and how to think. If your progressed Mercury conjuncts your natal and progressed Saturn, the ghosts of Christmas past, opportunities missed, work escaped come to haunt you. Saturn never brings you a thing you didn't deserve. Small comfort. I have not yet met anyone perfect enough to have done absolutely everything he or she could have done at any time in life. You have to decide what is really your responsibility when you have this conjunction. If you already have an overactive Saturn in your life, you could wind up responsible for absolutely everything. You have to back away enough to honestly evaluate the limits of responsibility, then get to work on whatever you really must get done.

Tension: Semisextile (30°) and Inconjunct (150°)

This connection between Mercury and Saturn is often like a month of rain. You have to check your brain for mildew. Pessimism becomes an occupational hazard during the tension aspects. You worry about the things you ought to be doing, and worry about the things you can't possibly do, and then add a dollop of worry about what everyone else should do. While you're at work you can devote the corners of your brain to gloom about the situation at home, while at home you can fret over whether or not you'll be laid off. Try to ease up on this guilt mania, for you can drive yourself straight to the hospital with unrelieved stress. You won't get any relief while in the sick bed either, because you'll torment yourself by fixating on the expense. Relax! There is a rumor that even during the tension aspects between Mercury and Saturn you are not responsible for absolutely everything. You can't do anything about the things bothering you because the tension aspects don't indicate action. Sometimes this period is like having several hundred pounds of books to carry up three flights of stairs. You can give yourself a hernia trying to hoist a hundred pounds at once, or you can open up the cases and take ten books at a time. You get no awards for ruptured disks or strained muscles now.

Stress/Action: Semisquare (45°), Square (90°), Sesquiquadrate (135°) and Opposition (180°)

These are the aspects you'd rather have exact before the exams, before promotion time, before the crisis, because they instill such a fear of failure in you that you'd be better off struggling with them while you can still do the work. These connections between Mercury and Saturn demand effort. The toil and trouble don't guarantee any immediate reward. These are the things that pop up in life and are eventually "good for you." They offer "great learning experiences." At least they usually don't go along with physical harm to your body. These are the unbearable, picky English teachers of life who won't give you a passing grade until you learn where to put the commas. They don't care how James Joyce wrote; in their assignments they want sentences. Mercury-Saturn makes you play the game, follow the rules, defer your own desires. If you recognize a longer-term goal, you can use these times to develop an expertise which later can be useful. If you fret and chafe and try to rebel, you will have unlimited possibilities for frustration during the stress/action aspects. There is always a way through these connections, but the way through always involves hard work.

Ease: Sextile (60°) and Trine (120°)

These aspects between Mercury and Saturn indicate that you can concentrate better. Since your thinking process is grounded, you can apply logic to nearly every situation. The ease aspects put you in charge. These connections provide a background that pulls together any hard outer planet or progressed positions. This means that while you have a sextile or trine by progression between Mercury and Saturn, or transiting Saturn sextile or trine natal Mercury, you can use something like Uranus opposed your Sun to make a logical (albeit quick) change in your life.

Since the ease aspects don't usually signify action, you'll have to look at other transiting and/or progressed aspects to determine the kinds of things that are likely to occur. With a sextile or trine between Mercury and Saturn you can expect clarity and logic at the very least. You may find older people particularly helpful now. If you think you have a raise or promotion due, try to talk to your boss as close to the exact aspect as possible. In fact, any business dealings which you schedule during the time that the aspect is within a few minutes of arc should proceed smoothly. If you have no truly terrible hard aspects happening near that time, you may be too lazy to go after the very things that can guarantee a long-term result from the sextile or trine.

MERCURY-URANUS ASPECTS

Always stimulating, sometimes bizarre, bordering on crazy, life won't be dull during Mercury-Uranus aspects. Uranus is the *bête noire* of the predictive astrologer because it is usually unpredictable. The following section is about progressed Mercury aspects to natal and progressed Uranus, and transiting Uranus to natal and progressed Mercury. Transiting Mercury moves too fast to have any long-term effect, and progressed Uranus moves too slowly to do more than indicate a time during which a natal aspect is more prominent.

Creativity seems to peak during Mercury-Uranus connections. The more flexible you are, the better you will fare during any connection between these two planets. The ability to jump from one idea to another seems to develop naturally during ease aspects between the two planets. During the hard aspects between the two, you'll be busy keeping afloat. Sometimes every mechanical thing you own or use goes haywire. No matter how you feel about your mechanical ability, you'll learn more about refrigerators, alternators, computers and the insides of telephones than you ever wanted to know. I've had a couple of clients who got roped into doing computer stuff during Mercury-Uranus. It's amazing how angry you can get at a machine.

Variable: Conjunction (0°)

This can be one of the most exciting times in your life, for you are wide open to new ideas. If you have spent a long time solidifying your patterns of thought, you'll get blasted right out of complacency now. This is the time to become involved with computers, astrology, tarot, Kaballah, any of the weird and wonderful mental avenues symbolized by Uranus. You might be dragged in kicking and screaming (your company buys a whole fleet of computers and it's learn or be fired), or you can set up some appropriate symbolism on your own. If you plan ahead and jump into a field that seems odd enough to be attached to Uranus, be prepared to have the journey take you in unexpected directions.

If you are starting school or changing jobs around the time of this conjunction, your new studies or your new job will not be quite what you expected. You may discover that instead of majoring in electrical engineering, you'd really rather take philosophy or English. Or, you might find the reverse true. You may take a new job only to discover a huge difference between the job description and the day-to-day reality of the job. When the aspect is from transiting Uranus it's wise to reserve judgment until the last pass. At that time, the changes will be obvious. The first conjunction will get you ready, the second gets you set, use the third to go.

Tension: Semisextile (30°) and Inconjunct (150°)

These aspects are among the most difficult you can have between Mercury and Uranus. When transiting Uranus aspects natal Mercury, you are reluctant to change your way of thinking, yet new information indicates a flaw in your thinking patterns. If progressed Mercury is aspecting natal and progressed Uranus, you need to deal with the results of your own particular brand of self-willed determination. The semisextile is not usually as troublesome as the inconjunct, but the tension is similar. If progressed Mercury is aspecting natal and progressed Uranus, your two-year-old self is clamoring for attention. That part of yourself wants things this way, not that way, and wants them now. Most of all, that inner child wants to be recognized. If you have kept that kid in the closet for a long time, you may find that you are not particularly rational during the inconjunct or semisextile. If you have absolutely perfect self-control, you can shove this out into the universe and get back someone who sets mental mine fields all around you.

If the aspect is from transiting Uranus to natal Mercury, your mental reality sets will be subtly challenged. If you believe reality consists of what can be measured by a machine, you may see a ghost or a UFO. If you can deal with psi phenomona just fine, something happens to bend your philosophy out of shape. You may get hay fever or something that can only be cured by the (shudder) allopathic medical community.

Stress/Action: Semisquare (45°), Square (90°), Sesquiquadrate (135°) and Opposition (180°)

When this is the only difficult aspect going on, the challenge of the stress/action aspect is nearly always positive.[19] It's a bit like working a puzzle. You have to find where the various new ideas fit into your framework. Sometimes you wind up with a whole new way of looking at things. The more you resist, the harder the changes will be. The semisquare and sesquiquadrate are the only two aspects in this group that have the slightest trace of subtlety about them. Either of them can sneak up on you, bringing about change before you have time to think about it. The open aspects (square, opposition) are almost always as plain as the nose on your face (at least after the fact!). Kids grow up and leave home. You can count on it. But, just as you can read all about post-partum depression and still be amazed when you get depressed, you can intellectualize all about the changes occurring during the square or opposition from progressed Mercury to natal and progressed Uranus, or during the square or opposition from transiting Uranus to natal Mercury, and still be shocked when it really happens. You know perfectly well that living in the big city

---

[19]Transiting Uranus semisquared transiting Pluto for several years, adding a stress/action aspect from transiting Pluto. This particular combination of transits was not a lot of fun for folks with natal Mercury between 2 degrees and 8 degrees fixed or between 17 degrees and 23 degrees mutable.

won't be like living in the country. But you won't be prepared for *how* different until you get there and can't get to sleep at night.

Ease: Sextile (60°) and Trine (120°)

These aspects fall in the top ten for fun. Even if you don't do a single thing constructive, you'll have a good time at it. If you can combine these with a little action, you can turn yourself into an idea-generator now. Although Jupiter is connected to humor more often than Uranus, the combination of Mercury and Uranus through a sextile or trine lets you see the unusual. It isn't a big jump from the unusual to the ridiculous. Progressed Mercury sextile or trine natal and progressed Uranus brings up the better side of your inner child. If you can put this together with some current events in your life, you can forge an alliance between how you think right now and your inner creativity. Somewhere in each of us is a curious kid. This combination lets that naïve, alive part go out to play.

When transiting Uranus sextiles or trines natal or progressed Mercury, you are ready to absorb new ideas. You've got the ability to pick out the areas which stimulate your most creative thoughts. You can find creative solutions to any problems arising during these aspects. These times are perfect for making new friends, taking unusual courses, moving—in fact, implementing any type of change at all. You're simply in the mood to stretch your mind out, so try to give yourself as many opportunities as possible.

MERCURY-NEPTUNE ASPECTS

A gentle fog envelops your brain when these two get together. The aspects I'll be discussing in this section are those from progressed Mercury to natal and progressed Neptune, and from transiting Neptune to natal or progressed Mercury. Transiting Mercury moves too fast to have much effect, while Neptune progresses far too slowly to do more than intensify a natal aspect.

Progressed Mercury will aspect both natal and progressed Neptune within a six-month period unless progressed Mercury is making a station.

In contrast, transiting Neptune hangs around for at least a year. Since Neptune is now (in 1989) the planet farthest away from us, it can transit a particular degree and minute for two years. Thus, the transit often has a more pronounced effect on our lives than the progression. Neptune and Pluto have been sextile each other for quite a few years. You won't have any major aspect other than the semisquare or sesquiquadrate that involves transiting Neptune and doesn't involve transiting Pluto. This becomes particularly difficult when you are looking at the semisextile or the inconjunct, for you may have a powerful midpoint configuration. In the inconjunct the pattern is called a yod.

Variable: Conjunction (0°)

When progressed Mercury conjuncts natal and progressed Neptune, the conjunction seldom lasts more than six months. You get a look at the spiritual underpinnings of your belief system. If you have no interest in the spiritual side of life, you can become quite paranoid, unsure of who is telling the truth in any situation. You may not even be able to sort out whether or not *you* are telling the truth. You can work on your swimming or sailing technique, start painting or singing, slip into serious escape mode through drugs (alcohol is the usual choice in the USA), or take a religious escape route through a group that relieves you of your money and tells you what to believe. The alchohol route usually involves some simultaneous aspects to self-indulgent Venus. The religion route requires some sort of Jupiter influence.

When transiting Neptune conjuncts natal or progressed Mercury confusion peaks. If Mercury has any connection to your third house, your car(s) may all develop simultaneous mysterious ailments. The more you pride yourself on some sort of order in your thinking process, the harder this conjunction will be. Neptune symbolizes the unreality of the situation called life. It is a very poor time to make investments (particularly in the stock market) for your thinking process is not at all clear. Lock your investments into some sort of fairly safe fund, and use the conjunction to develop the artistic or spiritual side of yourself.

Tension: Semisextile (30°) and Inconjunct (150°)

Progressed Mercury semisextile or inconjunct natal and progressed Neptune prompts you to question your inner concepts of reality. You may find the tension centering on truth, or on whether you can trust your own current thought patterns. Unfortunately, the deceptive lower side of Neptune does seem to surface regularly during the tension aspects. Keep testing and questioning your own motivations as well as the motivations of those around you. You don't have to be the victim or the victimizer during the tension aspects.

The tension aspects from transiting Neptune pull in transiting Pluto since the two are sextile in the sky. If Neptune is semisextile your Mercury, Pluto is either semisextile or square your Mercury. Either situation intensifies the tension of the usually mild semisextile. If transiting Neptune is inconjunct your Mercury, Pluto is either inconjunct or square your Mercury. The inconjunct-square situation is a little easier to confront, because the need to change (Pluto) is out in the open. It isn't any easier to live through, but at least you can see what you are working with. When both Pluto and Neptune are inconjunct your natal or progressed Mercury, you feel like your brain is in a cosmic vise and someone is tightening the screw. Inconjuncts symbolize a need to adjust, a need to compromise, but also indicate a fear of change. The yod pattern is often referred to as the "finger of God." It is not a pattern you can slide around or soft-soap.

The transiting sextile goes with a generation that is aware of the need for spiritual transformation. When this sextile focuses your Mercury, the need for spiritual change becomes very personal. The events in your life will underline your need for a firm spiritual base. This base may not include the religion (Jupiter rules religion) you were taught as a child. Although organized religion does not have to exclude spirituality, it often does. If your religion does not address your spiritual needs, you may find that it is quite empty while you are experiencing the transiting yod.

Stress/Action: Semisquare (45°), Square (90°), Sesquiquadrate (135°) and Opposition (180°)

Although action and Neptune may seem like a contradiction in terms, it really isn't. Here you combine the concept of alternate realities and the concept of mind. Sometimes it's hard to tell whether you are having a spiritual awakening or a bad case of mental indigestion, but the stress/action aspects let you know that something is going on. When progressed Mercury aspects natal and progressed Neptune, you are much more open to possibilities of other levels of reality. If you are busy working in a mechanistic framework, your reality may only allow the addition of an alcoholic or two into your circle of awareness. If you marry the alcoholic, you'll have some long-term results from this six-month period. This is a good time to observe and proceed with caution.

You may find yourself slipping into and out of various types of credulity during the stress/action aspects from transiting Neptune to natal or progressed Mercury. Try to avoid giving your house to your current guru. Watch out for spectacularly bad investments; your head is not completely clear in the area of thinking. Do work at music, art or water sports, for these provide a wonderful external manifestation for Neptune. By all means investigate spiritual development, but don't throw away a perfectly satisfactory life because you are not sure of its ultimate meaning.

Ease: Sextile (60°) and Trine (120°)

This combination brings a sense of ease, a joy of thinking. Your intuition is unusually reliable; if you'll flow with it you will find all sorts of nice people floating into your circle of friends. You may suspend your judgment to the extent that you ignore the reality just in front of your nose, but most of us don't completely unhinge our discriminatory faculties during the sextile or trine. If you have a difficult aspect between Mercury and Neptune natally, the progression of Mercury to an ease aspect can let you see just what you are perennially struggling with in your natal dilemma. Alternately, it can side step the natal issue, providing a time during which the natal conflict becomes background.

The trine from transiting Neptune may involve an opposition from transiting Pluto, while the sextile may involve a conjunction from transiting Pluto. This combination seems to provide an easing of the strain indicated by Pluto. When Neptune actually makes the trine or sextile, you have a period during which you can function more or less normally in spite of the rather major changes going on in your way of thinking. Here Neptune seems to provide a sort of autopilot which enables you to let go of the strain for a little while.

MERCURY-PLUTO ASPECTS

Connections between Mercury and Pluto usually involve transformation of thought process. This change in the way you think can occur smoothly, with the trine or sextile, or under pressure with the more difficult aspects. You may find that you have to assert yourself (claim your power, own your Pluto) in order to reap the benefits indicated by the change. Sometimes it feels as if you have absolutely no choice about the changes, that you are a pawn in the hands of an inscrutable universe. If this is your experience, you have to dig around and find your own Pluto.

Progressed Mercury aspects to natal and progressed Pluto throw you into your own arena of personal power. Pluto manipulates, maneuvers, and may drag out a big stick. If you cannot allow yourself to manifest any of these options, someone else may express your Pluto for you. Then, even though your progressed Mercury is making the aspect, someone else is manipulating, forcing, pressuring you to change the way you think. If you can grab your own Pluto, you might become obsessed with an idea. This may not be negative in the long run, because if your obsession involves a business idea, a book, or is connected to things instead of people, you may run with it long enough to extract all that is possible in the process.

Variable: Conjunction (0°)

There is nothing quite like the conjunction of progressed Mercury with natal and progressed Pluto to absorb you completely in your pet passion. You'll single-mindedly forge ahead in one direction, oblivious to obstacles. In the process you probably will change your estimation of what you can and cannot think or do. The conjunction itself does not indicate whether you are consumed with developing the perfect strain of roses or the ultimate method for demolishing old buildings. It's a good thing this conjunction only lasts about six months, for you could burn out if it lasted any longer.

The conjunction of transiting Pluto to natal or progressed Mercury lasts too long to allow you to be consumed by an intellectual passion. Fortunately, most of us will have transiting Neptune sextile anything that Pluto conjuncts in the near future. Neptune provides an escape hatch for the intensity of Pluto. Buy yourself a nice set of earphones and some soothing tapes to smooth off the rougher edges of the changes coming. Trust your intuition; Neptune is giving you an edge here. You don't have to let others project their power plays on you. However, you may have to reassess some of your ideas about the things nice people do or don't do to themselves and others.

Tension: Semisextile (30°) and Inconjunct (150°)

When progressed Mercury forms the tension aspects to natal and progressed Pluto, you'll experience a nagging suspicion that you are either letting people walk on you or are alienating others through your own use of power. The aspect itself won't tell you who is engaging in the power maneuvers; it only says they are being done. Most of us vacillate between being done unto and doing unto others during this connection. The inconjunct requires particular attention, for the stress of adjusting to the mental power indicated may result in physical problems. If you have this one coming up, make sure you get a good physical exam, for if you do have high blood pressure, the strain of adjusting to subtle power plays can elevate internal pressures.

Transiting Pluto tension aspects currently involve transiting Neptune, since the two planets are sextile each other.[20] If the transiting Pluto tension aspect involves a simultaneous square from transiting Neptune, you will find it very difficult to sort out exactly how power fits into the events occurring. This combination seems to multiply the confusion of the Neptune transit, for there is a definite undercurrent indicating a need to change your thinking process. The necessary adjustments include taking a look at whatever you are lugging around in your martyr bag. All of us have a martyr bag. What's in yours?

Stress/Action: Semisquare (45°), Square (90°), Sesquiquadrate (135°) and Opposition (180°)

It may be slightly more difficult to ascertain exactly what you want out of your life with the sesquiquadrate or semisquare, but you will find out and root this out the same way you will with the more open aspects: the square or opposition. Be aware that this is like Humpty Dumpty, for you won't be able to reassemble the pieces later. Permanent, complete change in attitude is the outcome of stress/action aspects between Mercury and Pluto. Progressed Mercury aspecting natal and progressed Pluto implies change in your perception of your own power. If it feels like someone else is pushing you around, grab your power and turn it around.

---

[20]The yod and semisextile midpoint to natal or progressed Mercury from transiting Neptune sextile Pluto are discussed in the MERCURY-NEPTUNE section.

Transiting Pluto stress/action aspects to natal or progressed Mercury usually feel like others are applying the pressure. The changes you have to make in your thinking involve how you choose to respond to this pressure. You don't have to fold up your tent and slink away. The aspect will be around for a year or more, so you will have a hard time avoiding any expression of what you really think. If you get obsessive about maintaining a previous idea, you may be faced with a rather spectacular flop. If you can somehow be flexible (or, better still, develop an ability to discard ideas which simply don't work) you will generate new ideas. You then can come out the other end of the stress/action aspects with a heightened awareness of your own inner strength.

Ease: Sextile (60°) and Trine (120°)

If you think you want something, you can figure out how to circumvent the obstacles in the way to getting it during the ease aspects between these two planets. When progressed Mercury sextiles or trines your natal Pluto you can convince anyone to do nearly anything you want. It isn't usually an underhanded thing, for you simply present the reasons that your way will benefit everyone. If you have a lot of other nasty things in your chart, I suppose you could get into some heavy-duty power things now, but I haven't seen many people playing these games during ease aspects.

When transiting Pluto sextiles or trines your natal or progressed Mercury, you'll also have transiting Neptune conjunct, opposed or sextile Mercury. If transiting Neptune is sextile while Pluto is trine, everything seems fantastic. Have fun. In the other two cases, a strange phenomenon seems to occur. You don't know what is going on, but any time you catch a glimpse through the Neptune fog, you manage to get what you thought you wanted. Somehow, at the last possible moment, something comes through for you. The Pluto component is the ability to persuade. Changes that you make now feel right. You're ready to get on with figuring out what you want to be when you grow up.

CHAPTER 8

All I Want
Are . . . .
VENUS ASPECTS

Transits of Venus move so quickly that most of us don't notice them.
You will notice progressed or solar arc aspects from Venus, for either
of these last a month or so, focusing on the week when the aspect is
exact. Most of us prefer the love symbolism of Venus over all other
possible manifestations. We would rather think about wonderful relation-
ships, engagement, marriage, children and celebrations with loved ones.
These are all common events connected to progressed or solar arc aspects
of Venus. If none of these are possible, then perhaps Venus will bring
money, ease and comfort. All of us can fantasize about the soft side of
benign Venus.

Venus symbolizes the things and people we love. Venus involves
all the pleasure principles of your life. Venus can prompt you to wear
out the printing on your charge cards. You'll need an extra dose of
Saturn to keep from incurring debt during the "nicer" Venus connec-
tions. Venus almost always feels good, but isn't always connected to
things which are good for you. Too much of a good thing often
results in physical or emotional pain. Thus, if you overindulge in the
good food parts of Venus, you won't fit into the fine clothes parts
of Venus. If you seek the physical comfort parts of Venus through
drugs or alchohol, you may find yourself with a rather nasty addiction.
In my work, I have found Venus symbolism occurring more frequently
during times of active alcoholism or active drug abuse than I have
found any other planet. You see, during times of active alchohol or

drug abuse, the abuser/addict feels fine. Only the people around the abuser/addict suffer during the aspect.

VENUS-VENUS ASPECTS

Transiting Venus moves so quickly that the effect of any aspect is slight. However, if transiting Venus is making a station within a degree of an aspect to natal Venus, you may notice it, particularly if it is triggering an outer planet transit or a progression to natal Venus. This is a most pleasant trigger, for it usually brings you what you want. If you have not thought out the long-term consequences of your wants, it might be a problem. Venus can bring excesses of self-indulgence. In my work with clients, I've seen a Venus connection in pleasurable, addictive behavior more often than I've seen Neptune. While the Venus influence is present, you won't have to pay the piper.

If Venus is retrograde at birth or goes retrograde shortly after your birth, Venus can progress to conjunct the natal position. It can form the semisextile, semisquare, sextile and square to its natal positon by secondary progression. The following delineations are primarily directed at analyzing the progressed to natal aspects of Venus.

Variable: Conjunction (0°)

Just how do you go about giving and receiving affection? How important are your possessions? Are you basically loveable, or are you a cad, who didn't deserve to be here in the first place? When you have progressed Venus conjunct your natal position, you get to reassess all these questions. Sometimes the reassessment happens with lightning speed as you send out announcements of a wedding or the birth of a child. More often, the thought process is a bit more involved, for you've got a few years of behavior to look at. This can be a very "lucky" combination—you may have to do the reassessment of your materialistic urges from the position of having money. Then you simply have to decide whether you deserved to inherit or win money. I wouldn't advise a major gambling spree based on this single aspect. However, I'd probably suggest buying a lottery ticket or two on the day before, day of and day after the aspect—maybe seven dollars worth to cover the week of the aspect.

If you find your waistline expanding as the aspect gets closer, talk to a counselor about why you feel unloveable. You're feeding your face instead of your desire for solid relationships.

Tension: Semisextile (30°) and Inconjunct (150°)

Only the semisextile is possible by secondary progression from Venus to Venus. During the semisextile you may nag yourself about your secret materialism (or your lack of concern about things). The tension really revolves around the idea of deserving. How many of life's goodies do you really deserve? If you have struggled with poverty consciousness, you'll find this surfacing to interfere with things you might otherwise get and enjoy. Whether this is a big deal or a slight conscience attack depends more on what you have going on in your natal chart with your Sun and Saturn than on any other single factor. If you truly feel that you should be struggling to keep your head above water, you'll get into terrific guilt about your relative ease. There is always somebody, somewhere worse off than you are, so you can be guilty about your ease even if you are barely one jump ahead of the bill collectors.

Stress/Action: Semisquare (45°), Square (90°), Sesquiquadrate (135°) and Opposition (180°)

The most common stress/action aspect beween progressed Venus and natal Venus is the semisquare. This is usually a pretty neat aspect, for somehow it seems to bring things in its wake. The action almost always involves getting strokes. If you are dedicated to wrecking your own life, however, you can become active with drugs or alcohol during the semisquare. You'll be telling yourself and everyone else that you can handle it, you won't get addicted, and you feel just fine. Watch out for this pattern. It is the only negative one I've found with the stress/action combination. People who don't do drug-indulgence during the aspect can get into acquiring possessions. If you rack up some serious debt buying things, you'll have to declare bankruptcy after the aspect leaves.

If you still have a minimally functional Saturn, the above decisions won't be the ones you make. You can fall in love, get married, set up a new home, make a pile of money, design some fun things. You are attractive to others and will tend to attract people who are pleasant. Go out and play; just take it easy with the recreational drugs now.

Ease: Sextile (60°) and Trine (120°)

Your charming child is right out front for everyone to see. People really will try to help you get what you need or want now. Enjoy this period, for it is very difficult to get a lot accomplished during the sextile between natal and progressed Venus. If you have particularly difficult aspects from outer planet transits or progressions while the sextile is present, you will have the support of loved ones to help carry you through the other stresses.

You'll be able to pull together different areas of your life during the sextile. Children, partners, friends and relatives can come together in a way that is most gratifying. Yes, you'll probably have to do some manipulating to make them all get along, but right now that is something you can do very well.

VENUS-MARS ASPECTS

Love is going to get you someday—and frequently the someday is while you have these two planets aspecting each other. It doesn't seem to matter much what the aspect is—any connection between these two by progression brings opportunities to begin a new relationship or review a current relationship. A single transit of Venus to natal Mars or Mars to natal Venus indicates that a good time was had by all. These transits usually occur too fast to indicate that the love of your life shows up in splendor at the local pub. Transits of Mars to natal or progressed Venus act as triggers for an outer planet or progressed pattern, while transits of Venus are much milder triggers. Don't abandon the simple transits, though. Plan a party, go to the beach, kick back and have a good time.

Sometimes we go out of your way to avoid being in situations that might allow us to meet an appropriate member of the appropriate sex during your Venus-Mars connections. If you are already in a primary long-term relationship, this makes a lot of sense. Why ruin a good thing? If, however, you are theoretically playing the dating game, or at least looking, and you go visit your mother during your Venus-Mars connections, you should take another look at your natal chart. Maybe you really don't want an intimate relationship after all.

Variable: Conjunction (0°)

This conjunction symbolizes energy unlimited. A line in an old R&B song says, "It ain't the meat; it's the motion, baby," and that's what this conjunction is all about. It doesn't matter whether you are fat, skinny, lumpy, tall or short, when you've got the moves, others are attracted to you. During the conjunction, you've got the capacity to completely enjoy everything you throw yourself into. Of course, you can throw yourself into lots of projects that have nothing whatsoever to do with relating to other people. If you are not looking for a new relationship, these other options are naturally the ones you'll be manifesting. However, even if you've been married to your prince or princess for a hundred years, a little spice enlivens any relationship. Hit the town with your one and only; both of you will have a great time.

I am obviously prejudiced in favor of relating as the nicest way to manifest this conjunction. There are other equally valid possibilities, however. You can have a baby. If you don't want a baby, be scrupulously careful during this time. Your insides want a baby, whether or not your brain does. Your inner charming child can get nearly anything it wants now. Maybe you'll turn into a "honeydew." You know, "Honey, do this. Honey, do that." It will work until the conjunction separates. Then honey will get tired of being a personal slave.

Tension: Semisextile (30°) and Inconjunct (150°)

If you have any lingering guilt about your sexuality, your body, your relationships, or your materialistic side, you'll turn this up to full volume during the tension aspects between Venus and Mars by progression. It is possible to use this to beat your body into physical shape. Unfortunately, if you are manifesting a deep dislike for your physical self, you may go overboard and starve yourself, or pull all your muscles or do some other kind of major physical damage. You can become involved in a really rotten relationship and let someone else show you just how unworthy you are. If you convince yourself to try some sort of therapy, you may be able to discover where your fears about relating or about sex originate. At least you'll have someone to talk to while you are busy wallowing in guilt.

If you are involved in an abusive relationship, join one of the support groups (al-anon, adult children of alchoholics, love addiction, etc.). Then PAY ATTENTION to the things the other people say. Never mind whether you were a perverted monk in another life. You are living in this life now. It's up to you to make it as happy as possible.

Stress/Action: Semisquare (45°), Square (90°), Sesquiquadrate (135°) and Opposition (180°)

With the current threat of sexually transmitted disease, it's unwise to allow yourself the sixties manifestation of this combination. Jumping from bed to bed used to be simply stupid. Now it could be deadly. (I sincerely hope that sentence will have to be deleted from future editions of this book.) There always was another way to express the stress/action aspects between Venus and Mars. No matter how lusty you feel, you can use the energy to start a relationship that could be longer lasting.

Lust can cloud your mind. If you don't have anything in common with a partner except an incredible desire to get into bed, you probably don't have the potential for a long-term committed relationship. If you have all kinds of things to talk about and do together, but you don't have the Venus-Mars energy going, you probably won't stick it out either. During this aspect, exercise your other planetary energies. Let Venus-Mars take care of itself. You'll find people who attract you physically. Don't settle for the first one who comes along, particularly if he or she has trouble completing a sentence.

Ease: Sextile (60°) and Trine (120°)

This combination is the easiest to transfer to situations other than relating. Your current relationships will flow along without any hiccups during the sextile or trine between Venus and Mars. If you have your reasons for avoiding relationships, you'll be able to substitute any kind of group involvement here. These connections are as comfy as an old flannel shirt, but all the comfy old flannel shirts I own are not fit to wear in public. If you retreat into your comfortable places and people, you'll effectively prevent any new connections, while enjoying the other sides of the ease aspects.

Before this aspect becomes exact, sit down with yourself and think about what you want at this time in your life. You can expand your circle of friends with ease. Are you looking for a congenial group of people? Decide what your interests are; then look for a group of similarly inclined people. Are you looking for a long-term commitment? Make sure any group activities you pursue allow you to meet single other people of the appropriate sex. For instance, you'll probably find more single men at a motorcycle rally, while a ceramics class would probably have more single women.

VENUS-JUPITER ASPECTS

When moving as fast as possible, Jupiter progresses about 14 minutes per year. The maximum distance Jupiter can travel in sixty-five years is about 15 degrees. Pay attention to the year in which a Jupiter-Venus aspect is exact, for it can be triggered easily by transiting Mars. Venus progresses up to a degree and a half per year. Watch the month surrounding the exact aspect for events connected with the aspect. Transiting Jupiter can zoom by the aspect to natal or progressed Venus, or it can dally a while, going retrograde over the aspect position. When the transit only makes one contact, it won't prompt a major change. The longer the aspect is there, the more power it presents.

Sometimes Venus-Jupiter connections signify too much of a good thing. When the greater benefic and the lesser benefic get together, you can expand a mess into unbelievable proportions. Some folks win money with these connections. I've seen more people manage to lose a lot of money gambling with Venus-Jupiter connections. They had a good time while the aspect was there. The winning streaks I've seen seemed to occur when Saturn followed the Jupiter-Venus connection.

Variable: Conjunction (0°)

No limb is too tiny for you to crawl out on during the conjunction of Venus and Jupiter. Nothing seems impossible, nothing seems too difficult, failure appears to be the only possibility you won't consider. Marriage is only one of the major leaps into the unknown that will satisfy this conjunction. You can charge to the limit on a nearly unlimited assortment of plastic. Watch out for this one. Sooner or later Saturn comes around, then you've got to pay or give back the goodies. You can get yourself into a nasty compulsive gambling habit with this conjunction. If you limit your wagering, however, you can win money. If you catch the gambling bug, you'll rue the day you started.

You can harness the wonderful sides of this conjunction if you exercise some self-control. Do your homework before you take a chance on anything. If you are a stock market investor, pay some attention to fundamentals as well as your "feel" for the companies. Don't get greedy. Determine in advance what you want out of a project and quit when you have received that return. If you moderate the wild enthusiasm of this connection, you can accomplish more than at any other time in your life.

Tension: Semisextile (30°) and Inconjunct (150°)

Watch out for the "sugar blues" during the tension aspects between Venus and Jupiter. If you already have a problem with your sugar metabolism, the inconjunct can be troublesome. Expanding waistlines are a perennial hazard when there is tension between Venus and Jupiter. The two benefics can combine to let you shoot yourself in the foot. You are afraid to take too many risks, yet at the same time, you are not content to leave things the way they are. This results in a series of fits and starts during which you over-expand then pull back too far. You just about get the rock over the top of the hill, then you let go. Sisyphus must have had this aspect natally.

Most people question their basis for love and deserving during the tension aspects. If you lock into a concept of worthlessness, you can spiral into quite a few self-destructive behavior patterns now. Talk about what's going on. Bounce back into Mercury and analyze the situation. Pull out the rest of your chart, for you can learn a lot about your fears now.

Stress/Action: Semisquare (45°), Square (90°), Sesquiquadrate (135°) and Opposition (180°)

These aspects are more often positive than negative, although when they backfire, they do it in a most amazing manner. Most of the folks I know have found business opportunities, partners, serious relationships, promotions, long trips, engagement rings or wedding rings during the stress/action aspects between Venus and Jupiter. The kick of the stress/

action connection prompts you to do something with the two energies. It is up to you to do something that is not only fun but provides a long-term result.

You can become a wanton spendthrift, putting nothing aside for tomorrow. Then you may vacillate between go-go optimism and depression about what happens next. You'll swing back and forth in a grand manner while the aspect is close. You can stop paying your bills and let the bank repossess your house, car and teeth after the aspect passes. When you are up, you are very very up; when you are down you are devastated. Exercise a little forethought. A minimum dose of Saturn will insure that you experience the fun, optimism and long-range benefits possible now.

Ease: Sextile (60°) and Trine (120°)

Plan a party, have a ball, get together with your best friends—it's time to let the good times roll. Ask for the raise (you'll probably get it), and forget the word "diet." Self-control is a difficult thing to maintain, but if you can hang on to some pretty basic shoulds and oughts (keep paying your bills) you can have a pretty good time with either of these aspects.

Trines and sextiles are not action aspects, so you'll have to look for a stress/action aspect from another planet (progressed or transit from Mars to Pluto) to get yourself in action during the ease aspect. If you've spent a lot of years toting that barge and lifting that bale under Saturn, take a break during the Jupiter-Venus sextile. If you have not done a lick of work in more years than you can remember, you aren't going to change your habits now.

You can handle whatever tough aspects come up during this combination with grace and wit. Furthermore, you can spend a few months as Gladstone Gander. Your projects now stand an excellent chance of succeeding. Most of us don't start anything, though, because it feels so nice to spin pipe dreams and think about what we'll do after the aspect passes.

VENUS-SATURN ASPECTS

Red Riding Hood meets the Big Bad Wolf . . . or perhaps more accurately, the sensualist meets the ascetic. Saturn gets a lot of bad press, most of which it deserves. Venus gets a lot of good press, most of which it deserves. Neither one deserves the extremes of fear or adulation sometimes assigned to it. You could match up lists of good results and rotten results for either symbol and probably come up with about the same number of things in the positive and negative columns of each. We enjoy the sins of Venus, but the sins of Saturn are no fun at all.

Transiting Venus moves much too fast to make more than a mild ripple in your life. When Venus makes a station within a degree of a major aspect in your chart you can sometimes see its influence. Progressed Venus makes much more of an impact on your consciousness, for it usually takes about a month to come into and leave an orb of 10 minutes or so. Transiting Saturn can spend a year in aspect if it goes retrograde over an aspect position. Progressed Saturn only moves 8 degrees in sixty-five years (when in direct, fast motion) or 7 minutes per year. The aspects formed by progressed Saturn indicate the culmination of a very long-term influence. The following section describes the influence of progressed Venus and transiting Saturn aspects.

Variable: Conjunction (0°)

Eros has been frozen in place by the breath of winter. When progressed Venus comes to conjunct natal and progressed Saturn, all your need for structure and control focus on the Venus symbols in your present life. Sometimes this does not have anything to do with people, because it means you have to get your "stuff" together. Companies call this a consolidation of assets. For some reason you have to sort through piles of things, evaluating, discarding, eventually ordering the mess. When this deals with people, you have to straighten out your individual responsibility for the other people around you.

When transiting Saturn conjuncts natal or progressed Venus, you may feel very lonely. You may be so afraid of rejection that you refuse to become involved with others. If you already are in a relationship, the ardor cools while you assess the reality of your situation. This is a wonderful aspect to have occur during an engagement, before the marriage date, because if you still love your "significant other" after the conjunction, you can probably stick together "in sickness and health." If you do start a romance during the conjunction, the relationship will last at least through this lifetime.

Tension: Semisextile (30°) and Inconjunct (150°)

Every human being I've ever counseled has some sort of fear of abandonment. Some have a huge fear, others have a tiny fear, but it lurks there as part of the package called life. During the semisextile, this fear is whispering in the background, telling you that you had better be good or Santa won't show up. Manage your money well, keep your indulgences in line, don't get too lazy. If you do not have a serious problem with lack of nurturance, the semisextile just aggravates you about paying bills and working.

In contrast, the inconjunct aggravates even the nearly perfectly adjusted among us. If you are in a relationship, the inconjunct usually surfaces as some sort of fear of being left by your loved one(s). If you are just starting a relationship, you worry that someone smarter, sexier, better-looking or richer will win away your beloved. It looks a lot like jealousy, but it is really fear. People with long-term stable relationships tend to manifest this inconjunct much more directly, as a fear of death of their partners. If this is coming up in your chart, ask your partner to get a physical exam. Clear up things like wills before the darned thing becomes exact. Then you will be able to ride it out without driving yourself and all your friends nuts with groundless worry.

Stress/Action: Semisquare (45°), Square (90°), Sesquiquadrate (135°) and Opposition (180°)

When someone comes to ask me for an election chart for a marriage, I want to know how long the people involved have been going out with each other. What I'm looking for is one of these aspects (or the conjunction) between Venus and Saturn in each of their charts during the courtship time. If neither one has had any tough Venus-Saturn connections during the time they've been involved with each other, they have only seen the fun parts of being together. I then suggest waiting until they have weathered at least one Venus-Saturn connection. In my opinion, the best chance of success for a marriage occurs when the election is set as the Venus-Saturn aspect separates for the last time. These are not once-in-a-lifetime aspects, for when you add up progressed Venus, natal Venus, natal and transiting Saturn, you find the probability of a stress/action aspect or a conjunction during a six-month period is pretty high.

It's hard to start a relationship during stress/action aspects between Venus and Saturn. Most of us retreat into our own spaces, mumbling self-reliance and other great stuff about doing it alone. Responsibilities intrude on existing relationships, making the open expression of affection more difficult. For the single person, celibacy is a common state during these aspects. Instead of spiraling into depression over the bleak relationship outlook, refocus your energy into career or financial issues. Your chart will tell you when the period ends, and meanwhile you can get your financial matters in order. Take a course in finance, money management, or study for a new career. It is possible to find interesting other people (maybe that Saturn "forever" person) while you are busy doing something else. In fact, during Saturn-Venus stress/action aspects, you will only find a partner after you quit looking for one.

Ease: Sextile (60°) and Trine (120°)

These connections between Venus and Saturn cool down the ardor and stabilize the relationships in your life. In new relationships, the ease aspects usually don't put out the fire, but they do put some larger logs on the blaze. If the fire catches, you have something that can warm you for a long, long time. You're taking the time to evaluate just how you feel, and what you are responsible for within a relationship. None of this feels negative. If the bigger logs don't catch fire, the separation is usually amicable. If, on the other hand, you are in a stable relationship, sextiles and trines between Venus and Saturn enrich and deepen your feelings about your loved ones.

The ease aspects don't indicate any action, but if you can motivate yourself to look into your finances, you will be able to establish long-term security now. Clear thinking about material goods or money helps you make appropriate choices. You can combine luxury and pragmatism to get the car, condo, painting or pension plan that offers the largest real return for the money invested.

VENUS-URANUS ASPECTS

"Happily ever after" confronts "I've gotta be me" whenever these two get together. Above all else, Venus loves comfort, while Uranus revels in the new and unusual. Can the champion of the white water rafting crew come to an agreement with the devotée of satin sheets? Can you take a waterbed on an expedition to the upper Amazon? Since both Venus and Uranus, the explorer and the Sybarite, are parts of your own personality, some sort of compromise has to be worked out, even if it seems that the two sides can't inhabit the same planet.

Transiting Venus travels too fast to have much of an effect, while progressed Uranus crawls along too slowly to do more than intensify an already present natal aspect. The following analysis involves progressed Venus aspecting natal and progressed Uranus, and transiting Uranus aspecting natal or progressed Venus.

Variable: Conjunction (0°)

There is a clear difference between progressed Venus conjuncting natal and progressed Uranus, and transiting Uranus conjuncting natal or progressed Venus. If transiting Venus makes a station conjunct your natal and progressed Uranus, you'll get a little taste of the meaning of the progressed conjunction.

When progressed Venus conjuncts natal and progressed Uranus, you investigate your own needs for creativity or freedom in your life. You may find unusual people attractive, but this attraction is based in the present and won't necessarily disrupt prior commitments or relationships. For many people, the conjunction brings a determination to get that motorcycle or big brass giraffe they have wanted for a long time regardless of what other people might say about it. What you have now is a desire to indulge your internal child. All of us have that kid inside, and when progressed Venus conjuncts Uranus, we tend to pay more attention to the kid. This may rattle the status quo a bit, but does not usually result in huge upsets.

In contrast, when transiting Uranus conjuncts natal or progressed Venus, you look for excitement and change in love situations. If your loved one suddenly does something quite bizarre, you won't be able to do anything but hang on for the ride. Uranus isn't something you can control. If your loved ones are completely predictable, you'll be the one chafing at the bit, looking for adventure. Uranus can devastate even the most upright person with an unexpected attraction. You don't have to *do* anything, but your view of how and who you love won't be the same after the conjunction. The only nearly universal prediction possible about

Uranus conjunct Venus is that you'll understand a lot more about the inherent instability of human relationships after the conjunction has passed.

Tension: Semisextile (30°) and Inconjunct (150°)

These connections bring out the problem of adjusting to simultaneous desires for comfort and freedom. Nobody wants to let go of either Venus or Uranus, but it seems harder to have both during the tension aspects. The semisextile frequently pits materialistic desires (your own home, bank account, car) against your desire to be a beach bum. Do you go home and run the family farm, giving up your job as a computer programmer (which you like)? This is the ordinary kind of mess the inconjunct indicates. The inconjunct can work through issues of lost freedom, martyred hopes, service to others. These things come up if you decide to give up your dreams (Uranus) for the people you love (Venus). The problem with this analysis is that it is only part of the truth. You are also afraid of giving up comfort, stability, or things like the house you grew up in, the land, the farm and the rest of the package. The tension here can get so great that you become physically ill. Any chronic problem such as high blood pressure can become much worse while you grapple with the adjustments necessary during the inconjunct. Take care of yourself, watch the physical side, and use the time to sort out what is really most important to you.

Stress/Action: Semisquare (45°), Square (90°), Sesquiquadrate (135°) and Opposition (180°)

Something's gotta give when Venus and Uranus are in a stress/action aspect. You have to provide some way for your unique, creative kid to come out. All your love relationships are subject to sudden, bizarre changes. Don't count on stability; it isn't one of the principal ingredients in your life right now. You don't have to subvert your own relationships, but you really have to find a way to channel your restlessness. Those of us who are supremely confident of our ability to stay in control of ourselves at all times (like Capricorns before Neptune invaded Capricorn) have the most trouble with the hard aspects between Venus and Uranus. We who are loyal, steadfast and true hate it when we are offered a delicious affair at the office. We don't do things like that. If we give in we are guilt-ridden, if we don't we are crabby and miserable. Time to sublimate. Even if you aren't dominated by Saturn, even if you are single and actively looking, it helps to deflect some of this energy into a creative new project. You don't need to have your love relationships do back flips for extended periods of time. Some of the more successful ways to combat this itchiness include classes in computers, modern dance, electronics, astrology or other occult areas. Any kind of weird science helps. Groups devoted to saving whales or stopping nuclear proliferation come in handy, for they are actively engaged in changing the status quo. The trick is to get involved and use up your spare time, rather than allowing yourself to be crazy with your loved ones.

Ease: Sextile (60°) and Trine (120°)

Your independence attracts and intrigues others. You can combine your self-expression with your need for security and comfort while you have the ease aspect between Venus and Uranus. You've got a definite flair for the outrageous, the unusual in all areas of your life. Most of us don't do too much with the ease aspects, but they are certainly fun to have around. You can flirt and not be expected to follow up on it; you can be silly and not feel stupid afterwards.

The sextile or trine between Venus and Uranus can moderate nearly any nasty combination by transit or progression. Whenever you see this aspect, change your opinion about what the rest of the progressions and transits mean. The easy creative flow can find the best way to make lemonade out of the bushels of lemons life pitches your way. It also means you'll find a way to market a million gallons of lemonade.

VENUS-NEPTUNE ASPECTS

Transiting Venus moves much too fast to have a major effect on your life, while Neptune progresses so slowly that it won't make any aspects that were not there in your natal chart. Therefore, this section is addressed to transits of Neptune and progressions of Venus.

When you combine these two symbols, you get romance, fantasy, art, music, drugs, pleasure and confusion. What you don't get is a lot of sober-sided reality. Any connection between these two can provide marvelous dreams, but you have to look elsewhere for the ability to bring the dreams to a reality on the Earth plane. Neptune has a marvelously uplifting spiritual side, but it also has a sneaky, deceptive, escapist side. Venus has all the goodies connected to relating and comfort, but it also has the (shudder) materialistic, selfish, self-indulgent side that nobody likes to acknowledge.

Any aspect between Venus and Neptune gives you an opportunity to explore both positive and negative sides of each symbol. Neptune is so elusive that we often don't realize just what we're getting into. It's important to hang on to other reality indicators in your chart when you've got these two combined, because you can rationalize and excuse and drift farther and farther out to sea in the fog.

Variable: Conjunction (0°)

In his poem *Kubla Khan*, Samuel Taylor Coleridge demonstrated his understanding of his natal Venus-Neptune conjunction. (He had Saturn conjunct Venus natally, too.)

> In Xanadu did Kubla Khan
> A stately pleasure dome decree:
> Where Alph, the sacred river, ran
> Through caverns measureless to man
> Down to a sunless sea.

When you are seeing love and pleasure through Neptune's filter, you gaze upon castles in the air, fabulous fantasy lovers, subtle pleasures seductive with promise. Your view of a loved one may have no connection to the person present in your life. Sometimes active deception is part of the package, but more frequently you are deceiving yourself.

In the worst-case possibility, you can sink into an alcohol- or drug-induced stupor with this conjunction. On the other hand, if you are an artist or musician, this can be an extremely positive time, for it can raise you to a creative high. Just stay away from those chemicals! You may even find your soul-mate now. Please don't marry him or her until the conjunction passes, or at least until you get a nasty Saturn aspect to your chart. Saturn is about the only planet that can counteract the overly romantic Neptune.

I realize that I have not given a lot of positive possibilities here. That is because the pitfalls of this conjunction are potentially devastating. You won't need rosy predictions to tell you you are feeling fantastic. You do need to know that there could be quicksand in the meadow.

Tension: Semisextile (30°) and Inconjunct (150°)

My dog is afraid of raccoons. When one comes up on the porch outside my office, he won't look at the porch. He doesn't want to leave the office if I'm working there, but he certainly would rather be in the front room. He will run in front of me and bark fiercely (while shaking terribly) if I go to shoo the raccoon away. He would rather I pretended the thing was not there, too.

During the tension aspects between Venus and Neptune, you may know perfectly well what you are not looking at, but you are afraid of what you'll see if you look closely. The longer you avoid it, the more stress you will experience.

Sometimes the dilemma manifesting during the semisextile or inconjunct concerns the behavior of a loved one. What do you do when someone you love does something immoral, illegal or just downright bad? You probably still love the person, but you can't live with what he or she is doing. There are no pat solutions to these tensions. The adjustments you have to make concern how you will view what is going on in areas of love, relating and material goods. You don't have to be the victim; you don't have to get sick over it. Try to determine what the worst results of taking a close look at the situation could be. Then decide whether you want to keep pretending that there is no raccoon on the porch.

Stress/Action: Semisquare (45°), Square (90°), Sesquiquadrate (135°) and Opposition (180°)

An awful lot of people get married during one of these combinations of Venus and Neptune. They think I'm impossibly negative when I express reservations about the reality of the love situation. They usually won't consider waiting, especially if the aspect is from transiting Neptune to natal Venus, because the wait could be a year or so. Some of the marriages work out just fine. Other people discover that the things they didn't notice while courting were pretty important, after all. It is very difficult to tell where you or your lover stands during a stress/action aspect between Venus and Neptune.

Sober musicians, artists and sailors fare the best during these combinations, for they can manifest strong, positive Neptune. I've never counseled a spiritual guru, so I don't know if they do well or not. People who take up painting, music, swimming, sailing or some other form of Neptune-connected hobby provide themselves an area for Neptune to function. After Neptune leaves, you might discover that you are not the next Picasso, but these coping strategies do let you escape reality without long-range rotten results.

Ease: Sextile (60°) and Trine (120°)

Soft, gentle, romantic and warm feelings fill you now. No matter what else is going on in your life, you can see the sunset, smell the roses. The hard edges of life seem cushioned during the ease aspects between Venus and Neptune. Enjoy the stillness within which allows you to appreciate the beauty around you.

By itself, this combination does not indicate any action. Yet it often changes the meaning of other aspects by adding the component of romantic love. Thus, if transiting Pluto conjuncts or opposes Venus while Neptune is making a sextile or trine, you may become involved in a compulsive love affair. If you have some sort of Sun-Uranus connection while either progressed Venus sextiles or trines natal Neptune, or transiting Neptune makes an ease aspect to natal Venus, your love life may go through sudden upheavals, or you may be separated from a loved one due to business or other conditions. This connection adds the probability of "romantic love" or "internal harmony" to the other transits and progressions taking place.

VENUS-PLUTO ASPECTS

The king and queen of manipulation are joining forces when Venus is connected to Pluto by progression of Venus or transit of Pluto. Of the two, the transit lasts longer and probably will indicate situations or events etched deeper in your memory. Of course, you might not get a "simple" Pluto transit. Instead you might get a combination of Pluto and Neptune, because these outer planets are sextile each other now.

Pluto brings change—permanent change. Pluto also symbolizes your personal power. Venus symbolizes what and who you love, but more importantly, it stands for your belief about whether or not you can love or be loved. Astrologers often talk about the transformation brought by Pluto. Well, nature and people abhor a vacuum, and when you have to let go of something (or someone), something else takes its place. Sometimes what you get after the Pluto-Venus aspects are done is better. You can't really tell, because you can't put things back the way they were before the contact was made. Regardless of what the aspect is, you will know a lot more about amor, eros and agapé—the three faces of love—as well as a lot more about your own ruthless power side after you have experienced a Venus-Pluto tie.

Variable: Conjunction (0°)

When this conjunction manifests through a relationship, the passion, compulsion, ecstasy and despair of that romance equal or surpass all the poetry ever written about the insanity called love. During the conjunction, little inner planet transits to the conjunction often mark daily mood swings as you go through the "loves me, loves me not" syndrome. Jealousy slips in, no matter how enlightened and non-possessive you think you are. If you move to the Moon, you might be far enough away to restrain yourself from hourly telephone calls.

You can experience Pluto-Venus conjunctions through things rather than relationships. A long time ago, when Pluto was in Virgo, someone I knew bought himself a brand new Corvette while transiting Pluto conjuncted his natal Venus. He lived in a city and had no garage. He spent every night in agony, getting up every few hours to make sure his Corvette was still parked outside his apartment. He put tape all over the seats so that the local hoods would think that someone else had already slashed up the seats and leave them alone. Within six months he sold the Corvette and bought a nondescript used car.

Tension: Semisextile (30°) and Inconjunct (150°)

Your fear of being dominated may get you into manipulation games in relationships. You need to take a close look at what is behind the tension now, or you can slip into potentially destructive battles with everyone you know. Money is one of the clearest symbols of power in our society. When partners start arguing about finances, power is often the real subject. These tensions eventually affect what goes on in the bedroom. With a semisextile or inconjunct between transiting Pluto and natal or progressed Venus, or between progressed Venus and natal and progressed Pluto, the manipulation is not necessarily conscious. The headache or lack of sexual response is real. You can develop a real physical ailment, which can lead to all sorts of problems with anything ruled by Pluto or Venus. Pluto rules, among other things, the reproductive and excretory systems. Venus rules the kidneys, ovaries, uterus and, some people say, breasts. Together, Venus and Pluto cover everything that has anything to do with sex or reproduction. You don't have to get sick. Take some time before the aspect becomes exact to examine how you use and express power, particularly in sexual relationships. If you work for a sexist boss (these come in both male and female bodies, and they discriminate against men as well as women) the stress may come from the work situation, not your home life.

Stress/Action: Semisquare (45°), Square (90°), Sesquiquadrate (135°) and Opposition (180°)

When progressed Venus is in hard aspect to natal and progressed Pluto, or transiting Pluto is in hard aspect to natal or progressed Venus, we get into "all or nothing" situations with loved ones. Even folks with natal Venus in Aquarius, who are usually detached and intellectual in love relationships, discover the green-eyed monster jealousy raging within when transiting Pluto squares their natal positions. All of us get a chance to understand compulsion in relationships when we have to deal with these stress/action aspects. Changes you make now are likely to be permanent changes, so use your head as well as your heart when dealing with love issues.

Some of us don't manifest these stress/action connections in relationships at all. We get intense and compulsive about our houses or cars or clothes instead. This crazy single tracking eventually will affect all the other parts of our lives, because friends and relatives will get sick and tired of listening to our obsessions after a while. The underlying conflict involves personal power and personal worth. During the stress/

action aspects we have to determine how to use power and how to judge worth.

Ease: Sextile (60°) and Trine (120°)

Do whatever you want to do—it will work now. You have the ability to entice with the sweetness of Venus and push with the power of Pluto. While the two symbols are sextile or trine each other, you gravitate towards the perfect balance of persuasion and coercion. Relationship ties usually deepen during the ease aspects. If you are not in love, you could be! If you have a strong fear of relating, or some other reason to avoid forming a romantic tie, the ease aspect won't push you into one. In fact, you can be quite contented with a dating period during which you reject every possible suitor, for you feel that your demands are quite reasonable.

The ease connections between progressed Venus and natal and progressed Pluto or between transiting Pluto and natal or progressed Venus provide an escape hatch for any difficult aspects by transit or progression. You have the ability to maneuver, finagle, contrive, circumvent, scheme, persuade, convince, convert, win over or bring around any person or situation to your advantage. If you have spent your life ignoring or trying to disown Pluto, you may choose to beat your head against other difficult aspects rather than use the sextile or trine. This background aspect gives you the chance to take hold of the wheel and drive the other aspects. It's up to you to seize the opportunity.

CHAPTER 9

Pushing
Your Buttons:
MARS ASPECTS

Mars symbolizes energy, initiative, aggression, action, anger and irritation. Some cultures believe that men should own a well-disciplined Mars, while women should have that planet surgically removed at birth. Other cultures believe that having Mars in your chart is a breach of etiquette. The tales about the Vandals, Visigoths and Huns indicate that at least the Romans thought these folks all had Mars conjunct all their angles and both lights. The United States has a peculiar attitude towards Mars, for we pay lip service to the ideal of eliminating any negative expression of Mars while refusing to pass any comprehensive laws to limit the sale of weapons. We want our sons to be competitive and compassionate, gentle and strong. Yet when our six-year-old sons come home in tears, with bloody noses, many of us proceed to teach them how to box. When our daughters come home in the same state, we get on the telephone to berate the parents of the kids who punched them. We give mixed messages to ourselves and our kids. On the whole, we don't handle anger well.

Transits of Mars are the single most effective trigger for outer planet transits or progressions. While other planets can move a backround aspect into action, no other planet does it with the speed of Mars. Use transiting Mars to time the events indicated by the slower-moving aspects. Mars adds energy, aggression or anger to the meaning of the other slower aspects.

Progressed Mars energizes any other planet it aspects. During the few months that the aspect is within a few minutes of orb, you get a good look at whatever the other planet symbolizes, for the two energies will be prominent in your life. Of course, you have a chance to review your own irritation quotient any time progressed or natal Mars is activated. The best thing about Mars aspects is you usually get to do something about whatever is bothering you. Sometimes the events are "great learning experiences" (humanistic language for really lousy). If you have your wits about you and get ready for these aspects, you can avoid experiencing the learning experience through a serious accident. It is sometimes healthy and sometimes helpful to have a full-bore temper tantrum around the time of tough Mars aspects. The universe is used to human temper fits. It won't collapse if you shriek like a crazy person once in a while. However, you may decide that you'd rather have the temper fit by yourself rather than at your boss or spouse or mother, for you might like to be able to speak civilly to these people after Mars leaves.

MARS-MARS ASPECTS

Transiting Mars makes an aspect to your natal Mars nearly every month. Sometimes the contacts are difficult, but they are most often the little, annoying things that make up the fabric of life. Unless there are other major aspects to natal Mars, most of us shrug off the fast transit. If someone cuts us off in traffic, or a clerk in a store is rude, or dinner burns, most of us don't decide to run the stinker off the road or shoot the clerk or blow up the house. We may mumble and grumble, or exchange heated words with the clerk or throw out the dinner, but a simple transit doesn't indicate a need to escalate the event into a minor war.

If you are following the transits to your natal chart, experiment with scheduling your heavy activities to coincide with various transiting Mars positions. For example, some of us find that our productivity increases during the sextiles and trines, while some of us get lethargic during the soft aspects. Some of us really get moving under the stress/

action aspects. We respond to the initial kick of the hard aspect by increasing our efforts. For us, a semisquare isn't a time to dread, but a time to plan a party or a trip. We'll probably be impatient or irritable during part of the activity, but if that's our method of projecting natal Mars energy, we are not upset about slight irritation.

In general, if your natal Mars is well aspected (mostly trines and sextiles), you respond well to transiting (or progressed) soft aspects. If you don't have a nice natal Mars (people gasp when they look at your natal chart), you actually may feel more energetic, more alive and happier during the stress/action aspects from transiting or progressed Mars to your natal position. You see, if you have a difficult natal Mars, you function best when there really is something to be done. The only aspects from transiting Mars to its natal position that nobody likes very much are the tension aspects. Since I have not personally met every person in the world, there may be some exalted folks who have completely integrated their expression of energy, aggressive behavior, initiative and drive. They would not be bothered by the mild guilt and doubt that my clients experience during the semisextile or the inconjunct.

Variable: Conjunction (0°)

Everybody gets transiting Mars conjunct natal and progressed Mars every two years. If your natal Mars is retrograde or if Mars goes retrograde shortly after your birth, your progressed Mars may conjunct your natal Mars at some time during your life. You have an unusual opportunity to actually change your expression of energy, because the conjunction amplifies the natal condition of Mars. You can't deny, repress or shift the blame, no matter how hard you try. During the conjunction it is obviously *your* Mars functioning.

Transiting Mars gives you a kind of biannual check-up on all the Mars functions in your life. If your natal Mars is heavily afflicted, the transit reminds you that you have not yet transcended the Earth plane. At least it does this to me. I keep trying to rise above it, to learn to integrate it, to arrange around it, but every other year something happens to remind me that I'm still here and Mars is still functioning. If your natal Mars is well aspected, you can expect a positive infusion of energy with each conjunction.

Tension: Semisextile (30°) and Inconjunct (150°)

Mars can progress to semisextile its natal positon. The inconjuncts I will discuss in this section are from transiting Mars. The semisextile symbolizes a period of questioning your own expression of energy.[21] Every time you have to *do* something (in other words, use your Mars) you pick away at yourself about how you could do it better, faster, easier. The stronger your progressed Mars is, the tougher the transition indicated by the semisextile will be. If your natal Mars is in Pisces, and it has progressed to Aries, you struggle with the current clear expression of energy conflicting with the "what ifs" that plague the natal Pisces position. When the natal position is the stronger (natal Mars in Capricorn progressed to Aquarius, Scorpio progressed to Sagittarius or Aries progressed to Taurus) you question your automatic strength, you hesitate to apply your conviction.

The semisextile from transiting Mars does the same thing, but in a much faster and (usually) milder form. The inconjunct from transiting Mars brings a different set of symbolism. When this occurs by itself (no other outer planet transits or progressions to the natal Mars position), the tension often surfaces through a set of outer circumstances which point out an inappropriate use of Mars energy. This can be reading a front-page headline about an assault, seeing a documentary about an atrocity, or witnessing an unnecessary aggressive action. When transiting Mars is triggering another set of aspects to your natal Mars, the situation involves you much more personally. You don't have to get sick or be the victim of an attack, but if transiting Mars is acting as a trigger from an inconjunct position, don't place yourself in circumstances where you could be the victim. In other words, this isn't a good day to visit the really seamy parts of a city. Mars moves fast enough to indicate which day you are most likely to have an incident occur. You are responsible for taking appropriate action so that you are not in a situation that could provide lots of hindsight ("of course, look at what's going on in the chart") discussions in astrological circles.

The day that the inconjunct is exact is a tough day to get anything done. Use the tension to uncover the underlying conflict, which has to do with the appropriate expression of aggression in your life.

---

[21]See figure 2 on page 18 for combinations possible with the semisextile.

Stress/Action: Semisquare (45°), Square (90°), Sesquiquadrate (135°) and Opposition (180°)

The open aspects (square and opposition) from transiting Mars are usually the finest triggers possible for a background aspect from an outer planet transit or progression to natal Mars. When transiting Mars forms a square or opposition, you almost always see who just kicked you in the shins. You have to figure out what to do about getting kicked, but you know what is going on. When the trigger comes through the semisquare or sesquiquadrate, you can't see the perpetrator as clearly. In this case, you have to figure out what to do next even though you aren't sure of who or why.

There was a song on *Sesame Street* in the early seventies that pretty well summed up a stress/action aspect from transiting Mars to natal Mars. "Makes you angry, very, very angry. Makes you mad." The rest of the song went on to outline positive responses to irritating events. And there are lots of ways to turn the energy here into positive results. It is, after all, only energy, which can be used any way you want to use it. Don't hide under the bed when these aspects are coming up. You'll have the initiative and the drive to accomplish quite a bit. It's up to you to use it to get yourself moving in a positive direction.

Ease: Sextile (60°) and Trine (120°)

These aspects flow so smoothly that most of us never even notice them. If you watch the transits to your chart, you can take advantage of the free flow of activity by scheduling potentially difficult appointments while you have a sextile or trine from transiting Mars to natal Mars. You will be able to channel your energy productively during these times. The ease aspect doesn't guarantee that you will get everything you want, but it does indicate that you will like (or at least be able to live with) whatever compromises are needed.

Sextiles and trines usually don't trigger activity, regardless of the background aspects. However, they provide a time during which you can explore positive ways to circumvent difficult background aspects. Suppose you have transiting Pluto opposing natal Mars, and you are getting a little obsessive about your ability to do anything at all. The sextile or trine from transiting Mars softens the background opposition.

If you take advantage of this combination, you can set up positive channels through which you can express the incredible energy of that opposition without destroying everything in sight.

MARS-JUPITER ASPECTS

The fastest Jupiter progresses is about 14 minutes per year, or 15 degrees in sixty-five years, so a Jupiter progression frequently represents the perfection of a natal aspect. Progressed Jupiter will be within a minute or two of exact for a couple of months, so you have to look at the other transits or faster progressions (progressed Moon is a good one) to trigger this aspect. Unless Mars is close to a station in your progressed chart, it moves fast enough so that the aspects it forms will be exact for a week or two at most. Both transiting Mars and transiting Jupiter can trigger slower aspects. Both of them are pretty easy to time, using any standard ephemeris.

When the greater benefic teams up with the lesser malefic, you can be pretty sure there will be some action. Whether the events are great learning experiences (which we all usually hate) or wonderful experiences (never referred to as learning experiences—I wonder why) has more to do with how you deal with your own natal Jupiter and Mars than with whether Mars or Jupiter is stronger in the aspect. When the two are working well, there isn't anything you can't get done. When the two are not quite so terrific, any pre-existing mess can expand outward at an exponential rate during the connection between Mars and Jupiter.

Variable: Conjunction (0°)

This conjunction usually gets your attention, one way or another. When your natal Mars is joined by progressed Jupiter, you've felt it coming for a while. Leaping off tall buildings is no problem. Make sure you've got some sort of plan for landing, though. Transiting Jupiter isn't quite so dramatic. After all, even if it makes a station on top of your natal Mars, it gets past the exact position in a few days. Nonetheless, most of us notice transiting Jupiter conjunct natal or progressed Mars, because we get an energy boost. If you have a lot of difficulty expressing aggression, anger or irritation, you may find this conjunction quite irritating. The better integrated your energy levels are before the conjunction, the more fun you will have during the conjunction. Before Jupiter gets to your Mars, practice asking yourself "How important is it?" before you deal with any situation. Meditation and centering exercises also help to integrate your energy levels. With these advance preparations, you, too can have fun during the conjunction.

Transiting Mars conjuncts your natal Jupiter every two years. It often provides a shot of enthusiasm that can help you jump into a new venture. When the conjunction is from progressed Mars, it lasts a month or two. You have time to explore the ways you actually grow, the ways you express faith, the risks you really are willing to take in your life. If you won't take any risks at all, you won't get much from the conjunction. If you are always walking right on the edge, you might find this conjunction too much of a good thing, for you could leap into a new venture without spending any time thinking about what the other possible outcomes of your idea might be.

When the transit of Mars triggers an outer planet or progressed aspect to your Jupiter, you take action with the transit. Try to decide what the long-range benefits and difficulties will include before transiting Mars gets to your Jupiter. Then you can turn a potential crisis into a golden opportunity.

Tension: Semisextile (30°) and Inconjunct (150°)

The twin pitfalls of the tension aspects between Mars and Jupiter are pride and righteousness. Sometimes you find yourself completely frustrated by someone who is always right and won't discuss anything. If you find that friends or business associates seem to be cooling off or avoiding you, you may be the one who won't listen to anything but your own ideas. The semisextile nags away at you, often bringing up unconscious attitudes toward risk-taking or success. If you have incorporated a fear of success into your life pattern, this semisextile may practically paralyze you. If you don't do anything you won't fail, but you won't be able to succeed, either.

The inconjunct poses similar, but more intense situations. You may have to completely let go of a plan or scheme before a new one can develop. The more effort you have put into the plan that needs revision, the more it feels like you are killing the idea completely. Yet the harder you try to hang on to the concept, the less of the original plan you will be able to rescue. The major difficulty here is an inability to compromise. An example of transiting Mars inconjunct natal Jupiter (fast, not stationary, no big deal) comes from one of my daughters. She needed a semi-formal dress for a college function. Instead of going to see what was available, she decided what she wanted. After six stores, I quit. I gave her my credit cards and went to see a movie. She stayed up all night the night before the function, sewing like a madwoman. She had a lousy time because she was exhausted. The dress was very nice, but (in my parental opinion) not worth the grief that refusing to compromise engendered.

When the inconjunct comes from progressed Mars or transiting Jupiter, the situations involve more important issues than a dress for a college semi-formal, but the rigid bahavior patterns are identical. When you are in the midst of one of these aspects, stop and ask yourself whether or not you are creating a major mess by refusing to bend a little. Adjusting to the current situation involves flexibility. The more you try to preserve the status quo, the more likely you are to drive yourself into a physical problem. You don't have to be hospitalized before you decide to let go of whatever is creating the tension in your life.

Stress/Action: Semisquare (45°), Square (90°), Sesquiquadrate (135°) and Opposition (180°)

The stress/action aspects between Mars and Jupiter can bring boundless enthusiasm and the energy to launch into new ventures. When transiting Mars is triggering an outer planet transit or progression to Jupiter it gives the initiative to do something about the other background aspect. The symbolism of the outer planet transit or progression tells you what the action involves. Transiting Mars just tells you when you will do something about the situation.

When the stress/action aspect is from progressed Mars to natal or progressed Jupiter, or from transiting Jupiter to natal or progressed Mars, you are deciding how to direct your energy for your growth or expansion. This means that you're dealing with taking chances in personal or professional situations. You may be asked to do something you are not certain you can do. You may have done similar things before, but this one is much bigger. The safe response is to decline, but the exciting response is to give it a try. Suppose you run your own decorating business, usually doing individual apartments or homes. A major hotel chain asks you to design and implement their new look. Examine the other aspects surrounding this one in time. Maybe you have several other tough aspects coming up after the Mars-Jupiter connection. I'd urge you to leap at the offer, because you now have the perfect manifestation for those other aspects. It's nicer to be stressed out because of a major expansion of your horizons than to be sitting around in your little puddle waiting for the universe to throw some garbage at you.

Ease: Sextile (60°) and Trine (120°)

Although these connections don't indicate any action, you can schedule things to take advantage of them. Most of us float through the ease aspects feeling good and doing nothing. If you have any negotiating to do, do it when the sextile or trine is exact. You will have a much better shot at getting what you want. Do your homework, for if you are not sure of your goals, you can get a good short-term result, but be disappointed in the eventual outcome.

Your gains are limited only by your vision (or lack of it) during the ease aspects. This connection usually does not mean that the universe simply showers you with goodies. You do have to be willing to put some effort into achieving the ideas you have now. If you can avoid the inherent laziness of the sextile or trine, you can do better than spin out possibilities. This combination can provide the background energy to turn any other problem aspects into opportunities for positive gain.

MARS-SATURN ASPECTS

Traditionally, Saturn is known as the greater malefic and Mars is the lesser malefic. There are good reasons for these designations, in spite of the fact that those terms are labeled "negative astrology" by many people. It is difficult to integrate either symbol into your life.

Saturn symbolizes reality, responsibility, duty, the "shoulds and oughts" of life. Saturn is like Jimminy Cricket, a constant nagging conscience that harasses you whenever you are not living up to your best potential. Sometimes Saturn acts like a giant critical parent, asking why the B wasn't an A, why the one million dollars wasn't two million dollars, why the garden has weeds.

Mars is your energy in action. Whatever you do, you can always think about another way to do it after the fact. You can be wrong no matter what you do with Mars. If you get angry, someone may tell you you could have mastered your temper better. If you stay calm, someone may tell you that your lack of aggression allows others to take advantage of you.

When the two malefics are combined, the two hardest areas of life are connected. Nobody who is in a physical body has completely integrated Mars and Saturn. So we act, then doubt, then react, then get clobbered with the results of our actions. Saturn always brings us what we deserve. Mars ensures that we get it pretty quickly. Transits of Saturn to Mars and progressions of Mars to Saturn indicate times during which we undergo some of life's bigger learning experiences.

Variable: Conjunction (0°)

During this conjunction it often seems that the harder you try, the further behind you get. The frustration of this connection tests your ability to keep going in the face of delays. You have to keep coming at the problem from different directions. The longer the conjunction is present, the more important it is to keep plugging away at the situation. A station of transiting Saturn within a degree of conjunct your natal Mars presents a situation with no apparent solution. If you persist, however, you will get past the block. You are responsible for whatever you do during the conjunction. If you try to do nothing, chances are you will be nailed for your inaction. When progressed Mars conjuncts your natal and progressed Saturn, the issues involve personal responsibility. Whatever areas you have shirked will come back to demand your attention.

For most of us, the conjunction indicates a time of hard work and delays. If you choose to lead your life at the lowest level of awareness, the worst of the negative symbolism can occur. You may be arrested or convicted for prior illegal actions. You will reap exactly what you have sown when progressed Mars conjuncts natal and progressed Saturn, or when transiting Saturn conjuncts natal or progressed Mars.

Tension: Semisextile (30°) and Inconjunct (150°)

You have to make some compromises between your expression of energy and your response to authority during the semisextile or inconjunct between Mars and Saturn. On an everyday level, this means that you may have some trouble getting along with your boss. If you are your own boss, the symbolism still holds, for you would quit if anyone else tried to do what you are doing to yourself during the semisextile or inconjunct. Try to back off and rethink your attitudes towards control and action. You have to adjust between doing and being responsible or you'll get lost in incredibly bad timing.

Sometimes the issue is delegation of responsibility. If you try to do everything yourself, you can burn out quickly during the semisextile or inconjunct. Or, you may need to learn when to refuse to accept any more responsibility. If you don't allow yourself to adjust between the two symbols, you can become more and more stressed. If this aspect indicates major control problems in a work situation, you'll have to find a way to defuse the situation. Your body will quit if you won't let yourself stop. No job is worth your health.

Stress/Action: Semisquare (45°), Square (90°), Sesquiquadrate (135°) and Opposition (180°)

The worst possible time to ask for a raise is while transiting Mars is in a stress/action aspect to your natal Saturn. Wait until transiting Mars gets over to the sextile or trine. The stress/action aspects indicate difficulty with authorities, difficulty in personal advancement. The magnitude of the difficulty depends on what you've done up to now in your personal and professional life. You can be sure the boss will catch up with you if you've been spending half an hour a day on company business and seven-and-a-half hours a day goofing off. At best you'll get a poor review and no raise.

Suppose you've been putting in ninety hours a week for the past year. Then along comes the stress/action aspect and you put in a hundred hours a week (your kids forget what you look like). The projects take longer to complete, the results are less certain. Then the aspect finally goes away. The job is done, you can go back to sixty hours a week. You may find a follow-up transit of Venus, Mercury, or even the Sun brings a raise, a promotion, some sort of recognition.

You have to figure out a way to organize your effort during the stress/action aspects. If you beat your head against a wall instead of taking charge of your own responses, it will be hard to glean any positive results from the events occurring now. If you can develop patience and self-control, you eventually will discover how to use the experience you are gaining during the stress/action combination of Mars and Saturn.

Ease: Sextile (60°) and Trine (120°)

Even though this is not an easy combination, it is a strong success indicator. In order to achieve the success symbolized, you must be willing to plan ahead and work hard. The sextile or trine shows that you have the ability to concentrate on a goal. Most people can evaluate their efforts fairly during these periods. This means that if you ask for a raise, you have a better than average chance of getting it, because you are asking for something you have earned.

Occasionally someone will use this combination to circumvent authority or get away with illegal activities. However, the outlook for long-term evasion of responsibility isn't spectacular with this combination. Transiting Saturn will bring the situation out into the open with its next stress/action aspect to your natal Saturn. Saturn makes a stress/action aspect to its own natal position every three-and-a-half years. If the next hard aspect is the semisquare or sesquiquadrate, you may worry yourself half to death. If the next hard aspect is a conjunction, square or opposition, you may have to face the judge.

MARS-URANUS ASPECTS

Hang on to your hat; you're in for a wild ride whenever these two planets get together. Uranus plays the cosmic jester, turning a humdrum trip through life into a psychedelic roller-coaster. Mars can be like the carnival man who starts the ride once the people are all aboard. Sometimes this carnival man does not look to be sure everyone is seated before he throws the switch. Then it is up to you to hang on and find your seat as best you can.

Neither Mars nor Uranus represents areas of expression that are universally accepted in today's culture. We don't handle aggression any better than we handle abrupt change. Progressed Mars connections to natal and progressed Uranus[22] are a little bit easier to handle than transiting Uranus connections to natal or progressed Mars. You simply have to figure out what to do with your inner rebellious child during the aspect from progressed Mars. In contrast, transiting Uranus aspects to natal Mars demand action. Whether or not you like your aggressive side, it will be activated. If you won't claim it, someone else will do it to you.

Any aspect other than the sextile or trine between these two can set a background for an accident. You don't tend to pay a lot of attention to your surroundings during Mars-Uranus connections. Carelessness or inattention invites accidents.

Variable: Conjunction (0°)

It won't take much to set you off during the conjunction. The trick is to harness the power generated during this potentially creative period. Notice I said *potentially* creative. Most of us explode all over the place rather than channeling this energy. You don't have to respond negatively to this conjunction. Some of my clients have launched into wonderful new areas during the conjunction of Uranus and Mars.

Even the clients who used this conjunction in highly creative, energetic new ventures admitted to being extremely touchy when transiting Uranus was closest to their natal Mars. It's like being supercharged. You've got so much energy that you have to find more than one outlet for it. As much as I hate to admit it, the people who fared best with the conjunction were the ones who did something physically strenuous every day. The folks who sat around waiting for something to happen were often the ones who got hit with disagreeable events. Couch potatoes had a tendency to perceive similar events as far more difficult than the people who were physically active did.

When transiting Mars triggers other outer planet transits or progressions to Uranus by conjuncting Uranus, you are more accident prone. You don't pay enough attention, or you drive too fast. Be a little more cautious the day of the conjunction.

---

[22]Uranus progresses 3 degrees at most in 65 years. Aspects from progressed Uranus are almost always the perfection of a natal aspect. The aspect will be exact to the minute for at least a year, possibly two or three years. During this time you may be more volatile.

Tension: Semisextile (30°) and Inconjunct (150°)

During the semisextile or inconjunct between Mars and Uranus you need to keep your wits about you. The semisextile does not produce quite so much tension as the inconjunct, but both of these aspects indicate a tendency to be careless in the face of obvious danger. It helps to take a look at the cause of the tension (usually anger). The anger surfaces as incredible impatience. Then you do dumb things, like reach into a running machine or saw up a piece of metal without safety goggles.

The toughest of these aspects come from transiting Uranus or progressed Mars, because they last the longest. If you won't acknowledge the tension you can be an accident looking for a place to happen. If you insist on taking the shortcut through the alley behind the roughest bar in town at two in the morning, you're asking the aspect to manifest in a really rotten fashion. Choices that would be unwise under ordinary circumstances can be catastrophic during an inconjunct from progressed Mars to Uranus or from transiting Uranus to Mars. You don't have to be the victim. Slow down, take your time, THINK! Then the events symbolized don't have to include a trip to the hospital emergency room.

Stress/Action: Semisquare (45°), Square (90°), Sesquiquadrate (135°) and Opposition (180°)

Like the conjunction, the stress/action aspects between Mars and Uranus galvanize your life. You have to slow down a little to avoid a short circuit. Transiting Mars makes eight of these connections every two years. Unless Mars is triggering another aspect from an outer planet transit or a progression, most of us don't notice the hard aspects as more than passing irritation. However, if you have transiting Uranus opposing natal Mars and transiting Mars comes along to square or oppose either natal Mars or natal Uranus, you have so many things happening at once that it is difficult to pay attention to all of them. In a situation like this, don't go out of your way to schedule events. Try to get your work done before transiting Mars hits. Then assume that other drivers will behave like lunatics, and be appropriately cautious.

Somehow or other you're going to experience a sudden, complete change in the way you express either energy or creativity. Most of my clients prefer changes that were their own ideas. Take time to assess your effectiveness in different areas of your life. If you feel that your efforts don't produce much change, now is the time to try a different approach. Assertiveness training may be in order, or, conversely, a workshop on developing negotiating techniques.

Ease: Sextile (60°) and Trine (120°)

In spite of the fact that sextiles and trines don't indicate action or events, these connections between Mars and Uranus are terrific. Transiting Mars does not stick around long enough to bring you more than a mildly pleasant day on which just about everything works the way you thought it would. When the aspect involves transiting Uranus or progressed Mars, however, you have a background aspect that can turn any other aspect into a glorious opportunity. When you add creativity to energy in a positive fashion, you get sudden inspirations that show you how to capitalize on whatever situations occur in your life.

Physical coordination usually improves during these aspects. If you can't smoke up the court in raquetball or tennis, you'll at least improve your game. Part of the improvement in sports as well as other areas of life stems from your willingness to change the way you always do things. Why not consider keeping this flexible attitude after the aspect passes? You can turn it into a part of your everyday pattern of life, if you want to.

MARS-NEPTUNE ASPECTS

Neptune, like a moving fog, tends to obscure anything it touches. Whether or not you benefit from blurring the edges of Mars depends on how you express your own initiative, drive and aggressive tendencies. If you are overly intense, driving yourself and others mercilessly, you may discover a more conciliatory approach during a Neptune transit. It's usually pretty hard to be definite about anything when Mars and Neptune are connected. The ability to compromise arises from an inability to make snap decisions. Balancing this extreme are you folks who usually don't jump into things. You may already have a bit of difficulty balancing all the possibilities in any given situation. When you add transiting Neptune to your natal or progressed Mars, your confusion can multiply. If you are adding progressed Mars to natal and progressed Neptune, you are softening your current approach to aggressive action. Transiting Mars can precipitate action when something else is in a long-lasting aspect to Neptune.

Add some sort of Neptune symbolism to your life during these connections. If you are already involved in art, music, dance or anything to do with the ocean, you don't need to add anything. If you don't fit into one of those categories, you can buy a radio or tape player, go to a dance or two, take swimming at the local Y.

Variable: Conjunction (0°)

One of my friends had transiting Neptune conjunct her natal Mars in the third house the day she picked me up from the airport to drive me home. She has made that trip many times because her husband travels constantly on business. At every intersection where she could take a wrong turn she started to go the wrong direction. Unfortunately for my friend, transiting Neptune stationed within a few minutes of her natal Mars. She got lost over and over again even though she never went farther than forty miles from home.

Not everyone will manifest this conjunction by getting lost. But confusion with daily action is typical of this conjunction. You may have made hundreds of apple pies in your lifetime, and suddenly can't remember whether to use cinnamon, cloves, nutmeg or all three. You probably are not going crazy. When you combine transiting Neptune with natal Mars, or progressed Mars with natal and progressed Neptune, it becomes hard to tell what is bothering you. It's as though your unconscious mind is very busy processing information, but hasn't come up with an answer yet. Meanwhile, actions that are usually automatic get confused. So you put the ice cream in the pantry, the shoes in the freezer, and the canned soup in the shoe bag. Turn up the stereo or plug in the earphones and take a break with some Neptune music. Life will get back to normal eventually.

Tension: Semisextile (30°) and Inconjunct (150°)

The semisextile or inconjunct between Mars and Neptune often indicates that you don't have all the facts. Thus, action really is not appropriate.

Sometimes deception (of you or by you) is part of the reason for confusion. Perhaps you weren't actually told a lie; you only were told part of the truth.

If you are a musician, artist, dancer or sailor you may find the tension due to some difficulty with your chosen profession. Ingrown toenails do for a dancer what laryngitis does for a singer, while seamen can be plagued by anything from capricious winds to longshoremen's strikes. Most of us don't work in those glamorous Neptune areas. We get tense about how we do what we do. This is the great second-guessing aspect. If you get upset and display your Mars, you brood about it (or someone else tells you you are projecting your inner anger). If you avoid dealing with what is bothering you, you brood about it (or someone else tells you you are out of touch with your inner anger). You are tempted to go out and get roaring drunk. Serious problems with addiction can surface during the semisextile or inconjunct. Drug reactions (even to things like aspirin) can occur, and infections are more likely. This is not a wonderful time to schedule any type of elective surgery.

Stress/Action: Semisquare (45°), Square (90°), Sesquiquadrate (135°) and Opposition (180°)

When transiting Neptune makes a stress/action aspect to your natal or progressed Mars, both lethargy and confusion creep in. Snow White bites the apple offered by the wicked Queen, Dorothy is swept up in the tornado, the Prince turns into a toad. Whatever action you try to take gets turned around somehow, producing results that confound you. It is quite difficult to tell who or what is behind the events occurring. The effect of Mars making a hard aspect to natal and progressed Neptune can be a little different. First of all, progressed Mars is unlikely to be around for more than a month or so, while transiting Mars only stays in aspect for a day or two. Transiting Neptune hangs around for a year or more. Second, you are prodding your Neptune into action when Mars makes the aspect, rather than having your action dissolved through Neptune. It is somewhat easier to manifest Neptune activities (painting, music, swimming, etc.) when Mars makes the aspect. If you are working towards the lowest manifestation of life, it won't matter whether Mars makes the aspect or Neptune does. The deception, confusion, escapist behavior will be identical. Problems with addiction or infection are the same. If you choose to manifest on a higher level, Mars won't make you Fred Astaire, but you will be able to develop some grace, some ability, or just have some fun in the areas of life connected to Neptune.

Ease: Sextile (60°) and Trine (120°)

If you can trust your intuition, you can use the ease aspects between Mars and Neptune. You will have an instinct for the right choice, the productive area, the easiest path. You can defeat the sextile or trine by picking apart your own reasoning. These aspects don't imply logic. They suggest ease of action. On an everyday level, you discover yourself taking the longer way home from work. If you get locked into your own Saturn and turn around to take the logical way home, you may discover a gigantic traffic jam on your usual path. How did you know? Did you know? Does it matter?

You can drive yourself nuts trying to answer the above questions. Maybe you are more psychic; maybe you heard the traffic report on the radio of the car next to you at the first traffic light but because you were busy thinking about something else it only registered in the back part of your brain. You can accept whichever explanation makes you feel more in control of your life. The point is, if you will let yourself flow with the sextile or trine, you can sidestep many of life's little irritations. Your own automatic pilot is working well now. Trust it.

MARS-PLUTO ASPECTS

Here we mix the symbols of power and energy. This combination can concentrate energy like a laser beam, able to cut through the dross of daily life quickly and efficiently. Just as you wouldn't hand a laser to a five-year-old, you need to take care where you aim this combination. Otherwise you could find that you vaporized your job by taking aim at your boss.

You will never have more ability to concentrate on a project or desire than you have while an aspect between Mars and Pluto is in effect. Sometimes this concentration increases until it becomes an obsession. Then it can take Herculean effort to get you off whatever thing, project, person you have fixated upon. We all hope our friends care enough about us to try to deflect us when we get these blinders in place. We further hope we still have these friends after we tell them where to take their advice.

The worst thing you can do during any of these aspects is to underestimate your own power to make things happen. You have a complete arsenal of persistence, persuasive ability, explosive potential—in short, every possible means available to humans to achieve your ends. Make sure you really want whatever you are going after.

Variable: Conjunction (0°)

If you persist in lighting your hibachi with a flame thrower, the only folks who will come to your barbecues are the local firefighters. This conjunction can fry anyone who gets in your way. When transiting Mars hits natal and progressed Pluto, you deal with some kind of power play. This one is usually fast and, in the greater scheme of things, pretty trivial. If the transit is triggering an outer planet aspect to your Pluto (like transiting Pluto square natal Pluto) or a progression to your Pluto, it may be the final straw, indicating action along the line of the other aspect. When the combination is transiting Pluto conjunct natal Mars (which lasts almost a year), or progressed Mars conjunct natal Pluto (which lasts a month), it isn't a little flare-up. The underlying issue is power. How much do you have, how much do they have, and how are you going to respond to pressure?

There will be pressure with this conjunction. You will learn what happens when you lose your temper and what happens when you endure without a flare-up. Your idea of your own power base and your own energy level will not be the same after this conjunction. It's very easy to get locked into an obsession now. Whether you are focused on a job, a project, a person, your passion may completely distort your judgment. If ever there was a time to back away, center, meditate, take a mental vacation, it is right now.

Tension: Semisextile (30°) and Inconjunct (150°)

If you have progressed Mars approaching the semisextile or inconjunct to natal and progressed Pluto, or transiting Pluto about to semisextile or inconjunct natal or progressed Mars, take a little time to track transiting Mars. What kinds of little things have happened in the past two years when transiting Mars made these aspects to your natal Pluto? This isn't a silly pursuit, because individual reactions to the tension aspects depend on the entire gestalt of your natal chart. There isn't enough paper in the world to write about all the possible variations inherent in this combination.

Of the two aspects, the inconjunct seems stronger. Often the semi-sextile is mildly uncomfortable, symbolizing questions of finance or subconscious motivations rumbling in the background. In contrast, the pressure of the inconjunct often seems to mount with no means of release. You have to reach some sort of compromise between power and initiatory energy. Although this is an area most reasonable people avoid confronting, if you try to slide by this without making any changes, you may be opening yourself up to be the victim. You can drive yourself into severe medical problems or walk right into a mugging unless you are willing to examine your own response to pressure, anger, force, manipulation. Never mind the way things should be. Even Rambo can get beaten up if he isn't careful.

Stress/Action: Semisquare (45°), Square (90°), Sesquiquadrate (135°) and Opposition (180°)

During the year that progressed Mars makes a stress/action aspect to natal and progressed Pluto or transiting Pluto makes a similar aspect to natal or progressed Mars, you will change both how and why you use your energy and your power. Backtrack through the transits of Mars to your natal Pluto for the last few years. How have you responded in the past to the combination of these symbols? Unless the transit of Mars is triggering an outer planet transit or a progression, it usually happens too fast to signify a major event. However, it will graphically illustrate your personal reaction to the use of overt or covert force. If firecrackers go off every time transiting Mars makes a hard aspect to your natal and progressed Pluto, you may be in for a big explosion during the longer-lasting aspects. Before the aspect becomes exact, take the time to review your inner script concerning how nice folks deal with life's garbage. Since therapy provides a place to dump garbage, you may want to consider starting before the heat becomes intense.

If you hardly notice transiting Mars, you'll probably shrug off the longer-lasting aspects as well. You may become completely wrapped up in a new passion, which could involve anything from a new hobby to a new job or even a new relationship.

Ease: Sextile (60°) and Trine (120°)

When transiting Mars makes this aspect to your natal and progressed Pluto, you have a day to schedule the toughest meetings, because you'll probably get whatever you're after. The longer the aspect stays there (transiting Pluto remains for a year or so) the more it modifies all the other transits and progressions occurring simultaneously. You can use it to steamroll over everyone else in your life, getting exactly what you want all of the time, or you can use it to grease the gears. You are the one who chooses whether to use the persistence and energy to nag someone else to death or to get your own ideas in motion.

Although the ease aspects can give you the power to demolish the opposition, they also can provide the ability to go around obstacles. If you don't have long-term tough transits or progressions during the ease aspect between Mars and Pluto, you may not do much of anything during this time. It's hard to get intensely motivated when everything flows along exactly as planned. If you have a number of tough transits (say, transiting Saturn and/or Uranus making stress/action aspects to everything else in your chart), things may not go according to plan, but everything will get done, one way or another.

CHAPTER 10

Over the
Next Mountain:
JUPITER ASPECTS

Jupiter progresses 14 minutes per year or about 15 degrees in sixty-five years when in fast direct motion. During the first half of your life, most aspects from progressed Jupiter are the perfection of a natal aspect. During the year in which the aspect is exact, that aspect probably will be the most important natal aspect in your chart. It won't be unfamiliar, just much stronger.

As the greater benefic, Jupiter has a wonderful reputation. Jupiter's action depends on your current state of mind much more than on the positive or negative tone of the angular separation. If you are locked into negativity, Jupiter can be awful.

Whatever Jupiter brings, it's big. Jupiter travels around the zodiac once every twelve years. The Jupiter cycles mark off times in your life when your growth and development shift. If you are more than twelve years old, you can check your own response to Jupiter by backing through the ephemeris and marking down every time transiting Jupiter made major aspects to your natal planets. For many of us, the aspects between transiting Jupiter and natal Jupiter are not as striking as the aspects from transiting Jupiter to patterns such as T-squares, grand squares or oppositions in our natal charts.

JUPITER-JUPITER ASPECTS

The planets from Jupiter out have long term cycle effects.[23] When you are looking at an aspect from transiting Jupiter to its own natal position, you are looking at part of that cycle. The solar arc of any planet to its own place is included in the Sun's solar arc aspects to itself, for all the planets aspect themselves at the same time by solar arc.

Jupiter symbolizes faith and growth, optimism and expansion. It's a symbol we look at to see what "they" think, and how our own faith or belief systems match up with what "they" think. Whenever you decide that "they" agree with us, you become optimistic. All of us look for people with compatible belief systems. We may not be aware of the importance of basic beliefs in relationships, but this determines whether we get past "Hello."

When transiting Jupiter sextiles or trines its natal position, it's easier to find friends who are philosophically compatible with you. You feel bouyant, successful. Hard aspects from transiting Jupiter to natal Jupiter challenge your inner philosophy. For some of us this is fun. If you aren't too sure of yourself or your beliefs, however, examining foundations of sand can be painful.

Variable: Conjunction (0°)

New people appear in your life around the time of the conjunction between transiting Jupiter and natal Jupiter. If transiting Jupiter is going to retrograde over your natal position you may get pretty righteous about your beliefs during the first pass. After all, you've had them for a while and they are pretty comfortable. The righteous stance is a clear clue that you are about to change your mind. If you are not going to change, you don't get defensive about your philosophy.

This is an excellent time to get involved in a "good cause" that you really support. If you try to keep everything to yourself during the Jupiter-Jupiter conjunction, you may pack on the pounds. It's as if your

---

[23]See Betty Lundsted, *Planetary Cycles* (York Beach, Maine: Samuel Weiser, Inc., 1984) for a discussion of the planetary cycles. Her book has a more complete description of the aspects between the outer planets and their own natal positions than there is room to include in this book.

body hears your command "Keep everything." So it does. Every drop of water, every calorie, every speck of fat travels to your belly or hips or thighs and STICKS. The defense isn't diets or aerobics or running, it is becoming involved in something besides yourself. This transit has the promise of new people, travel, new ideas, new ventures. If your head is stuck in your refrigerator, you won't see any of the possibilities.

Tension: Semisextile (30°) and Inconjunct (150°)

The semisextile between transiting Jupiter and natal Jupiter creates a nagging undercurrent of dissatisfaction with your goals, your material desires, your unconscious motivations behind beliefs or faith. It may surface as criticism. You'll end up getting as much criticism as you dish out. The nagging undercurrent makes swirls on the surface of the waters during the inconjunct. You have to adjust your philosophical outlook, for you can hear the waterfall ahead.

The challenges presented by the inconjunct make your sacred cows sick. How well you cope with this period depends on the size of your herd of sacred cows and on how quickly you examine them to determine the best way to cure the illness. You may lose one or two of them if transiting Jupiter retrogrades over the inconjunct position. If you try to keep them all, you may end up infecting the whole herd. Then you won't have any sacred cows left to depend upon. That's an interesting situation if you think about it. I don't know anyone who doesn't have at least a couple of sacred cows. Some of these beliefs are like Elsie, the Borden cow, with big brown eyes and a gentle outlook, while others are like wild Brahma bulls, magnificent to watch from a safe distance. No matter which kind you own, you'll have to take care of them during the inconjunct.

Stress/Action: Semisquare (45°), Square (90°), Sesquiquadrate (135°) and Opposition (180°)

The stress/action aspects from transiting Jupiter to natal Jupiter often bring opportunities for promotions, marriage (or engagement), travel, money or material goods. Most of us don't find these events terribly stressful. Every single one of them requires that you take a risk. What if you can't handle the responsibilities the promotion entails? What if the marriage doesn't work? What if the people far away are not nice? Is it spiritual to have lots of money and stuff, or should you give it away before it corrupts you?

If you play the "what if" game thoroughly, you can turn the stress/action aspects into a total disaster. You won't find a wonderful love, because your inner script won't allow a relationship that might fail. You'll argue and nit-pick with anyone who comes close. You won't get the promotion because you'll mess up your current position before anyone can consider you for the one higher up. You'll get yourself stuck in huge traffic jams every time you decide to leave town, and you'll suspect the motives of anyone who offers you money or material things. If this is what's going on, slow down. Your beliefs are denying the better side of Jupiter. You are the only one who can change your inner script.

Ease: Sextile (60°) and Trine (120°)

Everybody loves a lover, and during the ease aspects between transiting Jupiter and natal Jupiter, you're a lover. You'll find people just like you everywhere you go. These aspects smooth the path to most other things going on, because you've got some kind of support group behind you. You may not think of the folks you know as a support group, but if you've got other difficult aspects during the sextile or trine between transiting Jupiter and natal Jupiter your friends will rally 'round and help you out.

Laziness is the major block to achievement during these aspects. If you really have to get a lot done, schedule things for the days the aspect is the closest. You will be able to get what you want while the aspect is within a degree of exact. On the other hand, there is quite a bit to be said for enjoying these aspects without laying a Saturn trip on yourself. If you are a driven, type A personality (industrial strength Saturn), Jupiter trines or sextiles to natal Jupiter can provide times of rest and relaxation, which prevent you from burning yourself out. You actually may be able to take a few days off without bringing home paperwork or guilt. Try it! A couple of days probably won't turn you into a permanent beach bum.

JUPITER-SATURN ASPECTS

Success on the material plane often is connected to times when these two symbols are contacting each other. Aspects between these two by secondary progression can last for years. Unless the aspect has a 0 degree orb, it is only background. It may be triggered by the progressed Moon or a transit, but won't indicate events by itself. Solar arc aspects between the two last two months, with a 5 minute approaching and separating orb. The transit of either Jupiter to natal Saturn or Saturn to natal Jupiter can last longer if the transiting planet retrogrades over the aspect position.

Saturn seems to ground Jupiter, bringing Jupiter's grand schemes closer to reality. Jupiter seems to enliven Saturn, loosening up some of the grim duty often associated with Saturn. Each of you tends to develop a response pattern to each of these planets. Those of you who do very well with Jupiter transits don't usually find Saturn transits as easy. Yet some of you do very well with transiting Saturn, finding transiting Jupiter a major trial. Your natal chart can indicate which pattern you will establish, but you can discover the pattern for yourself by simply backing up through the cycles of transiting Jupiter aspecting natal Saturn and transiting Saturn aspecting natal Jupiter. What kinds of things happened?

Variable: Conjunction (0°)

If transiting Jupiter races by your natal and progressed Saturn without retrograding back past the positions, any events will occur during the week that Jupiter is between the exact conjunction to the natal and the progressed positions of Saturn. This kind of conjunction doesn't indicate major life events unless Saturn has other outer planet or progressed aspects going on simultaneously. In that case, transiting Jupiter works like a trigger, activating the other aspects. Just ask someone with natal Saturn between 9 and 12 degrees of fixed signs what happened in 1988 when transiting Jupiter ignited the Pluto aspect.

To get ready for Jupiter's amplification, whether by a transit that retrogrades over your Saturn positions or by solar arc, you have to imagine a sudden quadrupling of Murphy's Law. Simplify your life, for the outside world will provide plenty of complications. Delegate extraneous duties. If you pare down the responsibilities you carry, you may be able to take advantage of the conjunction to get into a new area for your own growth. If you don't think ahead, you may become burdened with so many extra responsibilities that you simply can't take care of everything.

The conjunction from transiting or solar arc Saturn to your natal and progressed Jupiter will push action when it is exactly conjunct natal

Jupiter, exactly conjunct progressed Jupiter, and exactly between natal and progressed Jupiter. The kind of action stimulated depends on what you've dared to dream with your Jupiter. If you have detailed your aims, transiting Saturn often provides the mechanism (you have to furnish the work) to bring these schemes into reality. You want to write? Saturn appears as a publisher who wants the book. You want to quit your 9-to-5 and make ceramic eggs? Saturn provides a buyer who wants a million eggs. You want to sail a boat to Madagascar? Saturn provides a sponsor. Saturn won't write the book, make the eggs, sail the boat. You have to do the work. But Saturn makes you decide if you ever really meant what you've been saying with Jupiter. This is the time to put up or shut up. Saturn won't guarantee that you'll succeed, only that you'll be able to try. Jupiter demands risk. This can be one of the scariest conjunctions you'll ever face. It happens once every twenty-eight years. That's how long you'll have to wait if you decide to defer your dream.

Tension: Semisextile (30°) and Inconjunct (150°)

When transiting or solar arc Jupiter makes one of these tension aspects to natal and progressed Saturn, you have to make some decisions about how much responsibility you can (or should) carry. If you've been dragging around a cross, someone will show up with some nails. If you really want martyrdom, you'll find it during the tension aspects. If that's not what you had in mind for this lifetime, you had better take a look at how you handle responsibility before the semisextile or inconjunct becomes exact. If transiting Jupiter is running right past the semisextile or inconjunct position, you'll just get a little burst of unreasonable demands. If, on the other hand, transiting Jupiter is going to stick around a while, retrograding over the semisextile or inconjunct, or if the aspect is from solar arc Jupiter, it is a very good idea to re-evaluate the whole concept of responsibility before the aspect gets tight. You don't have to drive yourself into serious medical claims by working from 11:00 P.M. to 7:00 A.M., then coming home to take care of a two-year-old while your significant other goes to work. This is when the word "burnout" takes on special meaning. Take into account your own needs as well as the needs of the folks around you.

When transiting or solar arc Saturn makes the semisextile or inconjunct aspect to natal and progressed Jupiter, you are likely to become very discouraged about your ability to achieve your goals. You have to adjust your efforts, somehow make changes between what you can accomplish and what you wish you could accomplish. The more rigid you are about what you want to do, the harder the semisextile or inconjunct will be to assimilate. Your sense of humor suffers a severe setback, as the whole process of life looks like work, work, work.

Sometimes the events surrounding the semisextile or inconjunct are the consequences of irresponsible behavior. If you've been indulging yourself with Jupiter excesses, Saturn can rain all over your parade. Daddy repossesses the keys to the wonderful Jupiter car. When you are on your own, your Saturn Daddy may be the bill collector. The moral of the Saturn story is to practice responsibility before the semisextile or inconjunct becomes exact. Saturn brings exactly what we deserve, which is why most of us find Saturn transits so miserable.

Over-indulgence (another negative Jupiter possibility) can make you very sick during the semisextile or inconjunct from Saturn. This is not the time for twenty-course meals of cream and marbled fat. The time to get a physical, quit smoking, change your diet, (in other words, use your natal Saturn) is BEFORE the semisextile or inconjunct from transiting Saturn to natal and progressed Jupiter. Then you can play out the tension aspect with the irritability that usually accompanies changing over-indulgent lifestyles.

Stress/Action: Semisquare (45°), Square (90°), Sesquiquadrate (135°) and Opposition (180°)

There is almost always a silver lining when transiting or solar arc Jupiter makes one of these aspects to your natal and progressed Saturn. Take the time to examine the obstacle when you first stumble. There really is an easier way to accomplish your aims. Think about how to simplify the responsibilities between the first stress/action contact and the last. (Even with one pass by transit or solar arc, it will aspect both natal and progressed Saturn.) Let yourself use this contact. Instead of trying to figure out how to be three people at once, figure out how to reduce your work load to manageable size. Often this connection signals a time to delegate your Saturn. The stress involves a very human desire to do everything yourself. The action involves deciding what is necessary, and letting go of the rest.

Transiting or solar arc Saturn aspects to natal and progressed Jupiter signal changes of a different type. You have to put some time and effort into bringing your Jupiter hopes into manifestation now. If you can bite the bullet and get going, the results of the stress/action aspect between Saturn and Jupiter will amaze and astound everyone. If you never wanted to do any work to get the Jupiter you wanted, your little pretentious dream may be exploded now. Saturn asks you how much you are willing to drudge to get the Jupiter reward. Saturn gives no free lunch. This is the archetype for the critical parent, and you do it to yourself. It's not all bad news with this aspect, though—not even close. If you are willing to buckle down during the aspect, you will get the win at the end. If you just talk about doing the work, you may get an offer but you won't get the big pay-off because you wouldn't do the required work between the offer and the deadline.

One way or another, this aspect makes you aware of how much you will risk as well as how much work you are willing to do to achieve the Jupiter dreams you have. Sometimes this contact seems very lucky. On the chance that this is the way it will surface in your life, risk a dollar or two on a lottery ticket. Don't bet your house, though, unless you can walk away, having lost, and start again.

Ease: Sextile (60°) and Trine (120°)

These connections between Jupiter and Saturn provide background protection. No matter what the other planets are doing by transit or progression, you can get around obstacles now. You can tell what requires attention and what is really a guilt trip imposed by someone else. If transiting or solar arc Jupiter is aspecting your natal and progressed Saturn, you can understand the real "shoulds and oughts" in your life. You can tell the difference between an actual need and a frivolous request. No, a Porsche is not necessary for your teenage son. Yes, maybe a fourteen-year-old Chevy would be appropriate. You can decide how much responsibility you want to accept. Do you want a baby or would a puppy do just as well?

Transiting Saturn brings very similar patience and ease. The principal difference between Jupiter making the aspect and Saturn making the aspect is that transiting Saturn brings pre-existing Jupiter hopes to a reality, while Jupiter provides new expressions for Saturn responsibilities. The ease aspects are not indicators of events. They will give you the stamina and the humor to turn other stress/action aspects towards the most positive manifestation.

JUPITER-URANUS ASPECTS

You'll spend some time imitating the coyote in the road runner cartoons when you put these two symbols together. Coyote has deleted Saturn from his chart until after the fact. Try to keep sight of your natal Saturn during any connection between Jupiter and Uranus, because forethought is the only way to keep yourself intact during the crazy changes coming now.

Only transiting Jupiter moves fast enough to make this connection a complete surprise. If the aspect is from progressed Jupiter or transiting Uranus, it will last a year or more. You'll have time to get used to checking out the twigs before you climb out on them. If you simply plunge into this time you may find it exhilarating. It certainly won't do much good to worry about it, for Uranus contacts have a way of bringing the unexpected. Uranus is like the Heisenberg Uncertainty Principle of astrology. If you knew what it was going to do before it hit, it wasn't Uranus.

Now add that to the risk-taking, expansive, buoyant qualities of Jupiter and you could have an incredible time. Of course, depending on your point of view, it could be incredibly awful. It is up to you to develop enough flexibility to grab the opportunities and discard the trash during aspects between Jupiter and Uranus.

Variable: Conjunction (0°)

Don't try to make things stay the same during this conjunction. You've got a potentially wonderful time coming up, so let yourself enjoy it! You won't be able to control the direction of your life completely when Jupiter conjuncts Uranus, but unless you obsess about pre-planning every detail, you should be pleased with the results.

If the conjunction comes from transiting Jupiter, you'll find that new ideas are sprouting up all around you. Some of these schemes may work. You will have to exercise a little judgment, for there will be some pie-in-the-sky mixed in with the more feasible ideas. The creative little kid inside can provide some new beginnings. If your creative kid is a spoiled brat, you may throw some monumental temper tantrums during the conjunction. Screaming and yelling aren't likely to lead to positive results. Go off by yourself and figure out what you want. You can get it now if you rein in your temper.

If transiting Uranus is conjunct your Jupiter, you may find sudden opportunities to move into new areas, to develop new goals. You can use this conjunction to get supremely hidebound and righteous, but that's rather a waste of a combination that could be a lot of fun. Some of the unexamined articles of faith which you've let rumble around in the back of your head for quite a few years will probably change. Unless you have completely stifled your ability to question a belief system, you can make these changes without creating major inner trauma. Take a chance on change.

Tension: Semisextile (30°) and Inconjunct (150°)

During the semisextile or inconjunct between Jupiter and Uranus you may feel as if your only choices are the frying pan or the fire. Change involves risk, and you can't tell what you are risking. Refusing to change brings another set of problems, for then you are slowly smothering your ability to grow and your creative side. The underlying issue here is fear of the unknown. There won't be any answers to "What if" questions.

When the connection is the inconjunct you aren't talking about whether to change the color of the drapes. This combination indicates pretty big shifts in your concepts of personal freedom and personal growth. If you only knew what you wanted to change to, the period would be a lot easier. If you knew that, however, this wouldn't be a semisextile or inconjunct, it would be a stress/action aspect.

You're like a little kid standing on a diving board. You think you remember all that stuff about how to float and how to swim, but the water is pretty deep. You've got to grab your nose and just jump in. There probably aren't any piranhas in the pool. Don't drive yourself crazy standing there hesitating (while the big kids make fun of you). Jump!

Stress/Action: Semisquare (45°), Square (90°), Sesquiquadrate (135°) and Opposition (180°)

With this combination you can make some big changes in whatever area of your life you happen to focus on. It helps to think about what happens next, because the stress/action aspects between Jupiter and Uranus can get you into some pretty unbelievable situations. Assuming that you have a Saturn somewhere in your chart, remember to use it now. Otherwise you could pop off and tell the boss exactly where to go and have all these changes be no fun at all. It doesn't matter how right you are in your description of your boss's problems, engage your brain before you put your temper in gear.

During the stress/action aspects between Jupiter and Uranus a restless wanderlust can take up residence in your head. If you are right where you want to be, and your life is moving along pretty much according to plan, this little aspect can gnaw away at you, whispering about something more, something bigger, and what's it like over the next mountain range, anyway? If you aren't really close to where you would like to be, this aspect doesn't whisper, it shrieks discontent. It is usually better for you to take action now rather than wait for the universe to dump some action on you. There is a difference between choosing to go white-water canoeing and finding unexpected rapids during an afternoon paddle.

Ease: Sextile (60°) and Trine (120°)

The unique characteristic of the sextile or trine between Jupiter and Uranus is humor. You can slide through the events indicated by stress/action aspects occurring simultaneously, primarily because you can laugh about what is going on. This combination seems to provide a marvelous overview of nearly any situation. Sometimes that means you can find the gem in the muck, sometimes it means that you can chuckle over grubbing around in the muck whether or not there is a gem to be found. You get a charge out of the games you all play with friends, relatives and co-workers instead of getting cross about them. You won't excuse what is going down, but you won't get hooked into someone else's aggravation.

Instead of trying to figure out how to use this combination to grab some kind of gold ring, relax and let it happen. If you get a prize now it will come because you didn't pursue it, not because you broke your back over it. Unless you practice rudeness (calling it "frankness" or "honesty") you won't have any difficulties due to this particular aspect. Some people do use this to aim a few poison darts ("Just kidding. No harm meant."). The rest of you endure it and hope that the better side of the ease aspect will take over soon. Lots of sarcastic wit now indicates an underlying problem with some other part of your chart, namely Mars and anger.

JUPITER-NEPTUNE ASPECTS

This combination is like one of those giant cocktails they serve at Polynesian restaurants. You have to watch out for the ones with names like "Maiden's Prayer" or "Zombie." They taste sweet and mild, but then you can't stand up when it's time to leave. Almost any connection between Jupiter and Neptune feels nice until you want to go do something.

The Neptune transits are a little more subtle, because they stay close for so long. You can spend a year with transiting Neptune no more than two degrees from an aspect. Even if transiting Jupiter retrogrades over the aspect, it gets far enough away from the aspect to give you a breather. Your head clears for at least a little while, and you get to look at what this wonderful new (pick one) person, teacher, religion, philosophy or spiritual quest has behind it. When it comes from transiting Neptune you may have to go the whole nine yards before you find out what's really happening.

If your friends are telling you to be careful or to slow down, LISTEN to them. Regardless of how unspiritual they are, keep Saturn and Mars and Pluto in your chart—you may want them later.

Variable: Conjunction (0°)

Romance often blooms in this garden, particularly if you have Venus aspected by an outer planet transit or progression at the same time. If you don't have anything going on with natal or progressed Venus, you may have a dream lover now. Most people feel optimistic about nearly everything during this conjunction. Buoyed by the conjunction, you may develop your artistic or musical ability. If you choose to begin something like this during a conjunction of Jupiter and Neptune, you will learn more and produce better projects than at any other time. Your ability won't evaporate after the conjunction goes away.

If you have a tin ear, are color-blind and can't draw straight or wiggly lines, try sailing or swimming. Write poetry. Explore philosophical belief systems. Take sensitivity training. Don't sell your house and join a religious (so very spiritual) center. Get engaged, but delay the marriage until either the aspect passes or Saturn gets in some hard aspects, if not to your Jupiter, then to your Moon or Sun. If you are very, very lucky, you'll have this conjunction while transiting Saturn is in a stress/action aspect to your natal Venus. That's the recipe for a romance that can lead to a happily-ever-after. If nothing else is going on in your chart, enjoy the daydreams. Sooner or later you'll get a Saturn chance to make some of them real.

Tension: Semisextile (30°) and Inconjunct (150°)

The worry here is real enough, but the reasons for the worry are not easy to pin down. The focus usually comes from some other symbolism in your chart. This kind of free-floating anxiety can amplify any other hard aspects. The underlying problem involves some kind of incompatibility within your personal belief system. If, for example, you believe that all illness is the manifestation of a spiritual problem, you may have a very hard time admitting that you've got an ulcer. You may not go to get a physical exam, citing your belief system, while you are eating yourself up with worry that the thing you found is cancer or a sign of coronary artery disease or whatever scares you the most. If you can't make some adjustments between your spiritual beliefs and your faith or religion, you can drive yourself straight to the funny farm.

Medical problems due to an addiction make it difficult to keep denying a problem with alchohol or drugs. The period of the semisextile or inconjunct can make it harder to keep rationalizing. The combination of Jupiter and Neptune can be extremely inventive, coming up with all kinds of reasons why it isn't your fault. If you are fortunate, someone in the hospital will force Saturn upon you, so that you can face reality and let go of the addiction.

Stress/Action: Semisquare (45°), Square (90°), Sesquiquadrate (135°) and Opposition (180°)

The stress/action aspects beween Jupiter and Neptune indicate an unrealistic attitude towards what you can do. You may seriously over-extend as you promise everyone the world, without any possibility of delivering anything. Sometimes folks stall out as dreaming replaces doing and they sleep a lot. I'm not sure whether psychic ability increases or your imagination is stimulated, but the reasons that you didn't do something take on a fantastic hue. You bounce back and forth between optimism and escape.

If you get involved in a new relationship during the stress/action aspects between Jupiter and Neptune, you go from stars in your eyes to a glazed look all in the space of a day or two. You may go off on all sorts of tangents rather than finish needed work. If you want to use this, take a course in creative writing or painting or music. Provide yourself with some kind of area that lets you question and explore imagination, philosophy, alternate fields of reality. Form or join a group studying the more esoteric areas of life. You won't completely understand the stuff you're working with, but you will deflect the confusion so that the rest of your life doesn't get turned upside down.

Ease: Sextile (60°) and Trine (120°)

You tend to take these periods of time for granted. Sextiles and trines don't indicate events, so you are not likely to have anything you can attribute to this particular combination of Jupiter and Neptune. You'll find that your life is smoother, for you can combine spiritual belief and faith with optimism. Another benefit is a global view and a quiet humor about the state of affairs.

The ease aspect doesn't indicate that you'll have any problems, but can come in handy if transiting Saturn, Uranus or Pluto is making rotten aspects to absolutely everything else in your chart. Spiritual beliefs or religion form a basis from which you can cope with other difficulties. Sometimes the support is quite tangible, as your clergyman and members of the congregation come over to hold your hand through a period of crisis. This combination is non-denominational, in that it doesn't matter what you call the spiritual or religious group. It may surprise you that a bowling team that gets together after the games and talks about the meaning of life may function as a spiritual group. Take a look at who provides the help you need during this aspect. They are the bedrock of your belief system.

JUPITER-PLUTO ASPECTS

You can't beat this combination for sustained effort. The difficulties with Jupiter-Pluto connections usually come from biting off more than you can chew. You may surprise yourself by being able to finish the impossible number of things you've undertaken. When the aspect is from transiting or solar arc Pluto, you are changing something about your means of relating (in a philosophical sense) with others, or you are changing a basic religious/philosophical belief system.

If the aspect is from transiting, solar arc or progressed Jupiter to your natal and progressed Pluto, you are amplifying your concept of power. If you do this in an unconscious manner, without examining your behavior, you can stomp all over everyone else in your life. Since Pluto is a master of manipulation, you may whine and plead, or pretend you are sacrificing your time and energy, all to get your own way. You may become pretty self-righteous about using the power at your disposal. Not only can you make people do what you want them to do, you may insist that it is for their own good and they had better like it. Only the progressed position hangs around long enough to develop into a real pain for the folks who love you. If the progression starts to get obnoxious, you'll hear about it from anyone who can get up the courage to tell you. If you don't hear about it, it will be because you have driven away all of the people who could qualify as true friends.

Variable: Conjunction (0°)

Playing around with Jupiter and Pluto keywords can be quite illuminating when you're thinking about the conjunction. Power and expansion. Manipulation and faith. Force and optimism. Growth and permanent change. This conjunction has to be looked at within the context of the entire chart, because the possible manifestations depend on what you've done with your personal power sense and your optimistic, philosophical, expansive self.

Pluto isn't only the big stick kind of power. Folks who deny their own power often use the power of the weak with Pluto. This involves groveling and pleading until they get their own way. An alternate tactic mixes heavy sighs and martyred expressions as they go about not letting you have any peace until they get their way. If you add Jupiter to that, the grovelers and whiners may have you over a barrel, because they will be able to be very righteous about whatever you were supposed to do for them.

If transiting Jupiter conjuncts a negative natal Pluto, all the manipulation of the past twelve years comes to a head. The office drudge who stays late to do your work but won't let you pay off the debt (and you know there is something owed to this kind of person) often doesn't understand why you don't want the help. When transiting Jupiter hits this person's natal Pluto he or she tries even harder to do both jobs. You will have to do something to get away from what you probably see as interference with your position. The drudge will get even more frantic, and the putdown is inevitable. If you are the one who is unappreciated at work or at home during transiting Jupiter conjunct your natal and progressed Pluto, stop trying to do everyone else's job. Pull your own life and your own power into focus.

There is another set of possibilities that can occur with either transiting Pluto conjunct natal or progressed Jupiter or transiting Jupiter conjunct Pluto. If you can center yourself and decide what you want to do, you can get whatever you want. You don't have to sneak around or make other people do it for you. During the conjunction it is possible to simply go out there and get what you want. That may sound far too simple, but ask yourself why you can't do just that. If your answers all begin with "Yes, but," you really enjoy exactly what you are doing and don't want to do anything else. If you are playing the "worse" game, your problems are worse than anyone else's problems. You win this game when everyone throws up their hands and concedes that there is no solution to your problems. In other words, you win by being the biggest loser in the whole world. The conjunction provides an opportunity to quit either the "yes, but" game or the "worse" game. Are you ready to get off the merry-go-round?

Tension: Semisextile (30°) and Inconjunct (150°)

Power plays cause incredible tension now. You may be the heavy or the victim. Whichever end you're on, you've got to make some philosophical adjustments in your response to power. When do you stand up for yourself? How do you go about doing that? If you thought you had that part of yourself pretty well together, you may listen or watch in disbelief as your mother or father speaks through your mouth or body, pushing other people's buttons exactly the way those external parents pushed your buttons. It's like digging around in a box of clothes that has been stowed under the eaves for years. There isn't any elastic left in the underwear, and the moths have eaten all the sweaters. This stuff is so bad that when you stuck it in the attic even the poor, naked, starving people in third world countries couldn't use it. Here you are, trying those things on once more. The tension arises because it is so darned hard to throw out stuff like this.

If you become good and stubborn, refusing to relinquish old manipulation techniques, all the petty details of life can collect to overwhelm you. People may just leave, and you have to sort out the junk yourself. All of you have mental attics in which you collect old junk. The junk may be labeled "philosophy" or "religion" or "important prejudgments." You will have to sort it out now so that you can get on with your life.

Stress/Action: Semisquare (45°), Square (90°), Sesquiquadrate (135°) and Opposition (180°)

Big changes are in the wind whenever Jupiter and Pluto form stress/action aspects for any length of time. Of course, if transiting Jupiter is simply running by the aspect, and won't come back to aggravate you, the event probably will not be earth shattering. If Jupiter is going to come back and tromp around for a while, or the aspect is from solar arc or progressed Jupiter, the matters being enlarged all have to do with heavy-duty self-will and power. They may not look like this on the surface, but the events cause enormous inner angst precisely because they make you look at exactly what you want. Jupiter transits the zodiac once every twelve years, so there are seven times during the twelve years that it makes a stress/action aspect to your natal and progressed Pluto. When one of these times involves a station of Jupiter within a degree of the aspect, you won't be able to get away from looking at your own Pluto power.

When transiting Pluto gets into a stress/action aspect to your natal Jupiter, you find your whole method of relating on a philosophical level turned upside down. The good news is that you won't get very many of these aspects during your life. And you do have quite a while to get used to making the changes. Before the aspect is exact, start weeding your righteous garden of beliefs. If you can approach the aspect with a flexible attitude, you may find that you can make major changes without excessive anxiety.

Ease: Sextile (60°) and Trine (120°)

Do whatever you want to do; it will work when you have Jupiter and Pluto in a sextile or trine by transit, solar arc or zero-orb progression of

Jupiter. In a way this may be difficult, because if you don't think about what you are doing, you may not want what you thought you wanted after the aspect passes. Every folk heritage has tales of people getting what they thought they wanted, only to discover that they had missed the point when they made their wish lists.

One of my clients had a huge wish list, precisely detailed, about the ideal man. He was to be in his fifties, well-heeled, capable of taking over the details of her pretty chaotic life, tall, reasonably good-looking, a tennis player, interested in the symphony, ballet, opera, etc. She found him. He adored her. He sent forty roses to her office. He nagged her incessantly about her smoking, and slowly started to take over every part of her life. After about a year (after the trine from Pluto to her natal Jupiter had passed) she couldn't stand it anymore. She discovered that as screwy as her life was without a strong hand at the helm, she'd rather do the steering herself. As hard as it was to make ends meet on a secretary's salary with a couple of kids, she'd rather juggle her own budget than explain why she spent two hours on the phone talking to her girlfriend in another state.

CHAPTER 11

Who's in
Charge Here?
SATURN ASPECTS

Saturn progresses about 7 minutes per year when in fast, direct motion. It will only move about 8 degrees in sixty-five years. Saturn won't make new aspects by secondary progression. If your natal Saturn is approaching several aspects in your chart, the year that each of the aspects becomes exact by secondary progression will be the year that you focus on sorting out the meaning of your natal aspect. Transits to the natal and progressed positions tell you about the events occurring.

Transiting Saturn travels around the zodiac every twenty-nine years. The Saturn cycle is one of the most important cycles of life. It dovetails with the progressed Moon's cycle, which takes about the same number of years to complete. The progressed Moon cycle marks periods of emotional growth,[24] while transiting Saturn marks periods of ethical growth.

Saturn has a cyclical transit pattern to every planet in your chart. Every seven years or so it conjuncts, squares or opposes each planet. You didn't go to the dentist when you needed to? When Saturn comes along you'll get to see a lot of the dentist. Saturn isn't always awful, but it isn't known as the greater malefic for nothing. It is the toughest teacher in the chart. Saturn makes you look at the reality of your coping mechanisms.

------

[24]The progressed Moon cycle is described in *Secondary Progressions, Time to Remember*.

SATURN-SATURN ASPECTS

The only difference between solar arc Saturn and transiting Saturn aspects to your natal Saturn is that the solar arc aspects are not part of a cycle. You'll find that the situations manifesting during a solar arc connection are quite similar to the situations you've encountered when transiting Saturn was making the same aspect to your natal Saturn.

If your progressed Moon conjuncts, squares or opposes its natal position during the time that transiting Saturn is making the same aspect to its natal position, the stress is enormous. You have to deal with difficult experiences on an emotional level while you have to accept more responsibility for your behavior patterns. When the two cycles are more than six months apart, you have the opportunity to do the two growth symbols separately. If the progressed Moon aspect comes first, you hit the emotional needs and changes before you have to deal with the responsibility part. When transiting Saturn makes the aspect first, you have time to do what you need to do before you have to sort out how you feel about this new set of circumstances. I've never been able to sort out which is nicer, Saturn first or the progressed Moon first. It really doesn't matter, because you're going to get them whichever way your own chart works. If they are going to hit together, simplify your life before they get close. You'll have plenty of events to occupy your time without setting yourself up to go crazy.

Variable: Conjunction (0°)

Saturn conjuncts its natal position for the first time when you are about twenty-nine, then again when you are approximately fifty-six, and for the last time when you are about eighty-four. Each of these conjunctions signals a change in your responsibility status. The first conjunction signals the onset of maturity. Depending on the cultural bias, childhood may end at the first Saturn-Saturn opposition (about age fourteen) or the second square (about age twenty-one), but maturity doesn't arrive until you have completed one cycle. By the first conjunction, you can realistically evaluate what you can accomplish, based on what you have accomplished since the second square. This is the time that you realize whether or not you can set the world on fire, and whether or not you want to.

Career issues become paramount at each conjunction. At the first conjunction you consolidate your choices. At the second conjunction you prepare for the next change (to retire or not to retire). At the third conjunction you figure out what you want to do with the years left to you. Each conjunction also provides a time for you to evaluate what your responsibilities are and will be for partners, children, parents. It tells you to make your kids take responsibility for themselves. If you won't listen, your kids may become permanent burdens. You have to accept some duties, reject others. Saturn collects for the "shoulds and oughts" that you didn't do and rewards for the "shoulds and oughts" you did do.

Tension: Semisextile (30°) and Inconjunct (150°)

When Saturn is semisextile or inconjunct its natal and progressed position, you struggle with issues of control. The semisextile is a little more subtle, gnawing away at your control over the material world or over your unconscious, critical parent. The waning semisextiles occur two to three years before the conjunctions, the waxing semisextiles two to three years after the conjunctions. These aspects don't cause events, but set up an uneasy background against which other stress/action aspects play themselves out. The semisextile between transiting Saturn and natal Saturn is the Monday morning quarterback for all of your Sunday games. You pick at sins of commission and omission in areas of responsibility. You have to remind yourself that you are not responsible for the health, wealth, and happiness (or lack thereof) of the entire world, or even of the people right around you. You have to balance the two extremes of Saturn. You can neither accept responsibility for everything nor refuse responsibility for anything. That's the problem of both the semisextile and inconjunct.

The inconjunct is rarely as hidden as the semisextile. Most of us feel like a chicken whose clutch of ducks just went swimming. You get the very first one of these when you hit the beginning of puberty. Daddy and your teachers start to pick on you. You want to be in control of more areas of your life, but are not sure how to do it. The second inconjunct hits between ages fifteen and sixteen. How do you control sexuality? Can you control what others do? Can you control what you do?

The second set of inconjuncts brackets the period of life recently labeled "midlife crisis." Sometime between age forty-one and forty-two, you get the waxing inconjunct again, and then at about forty-five or forty-six, you get the waning inconjunct. You become more aware of your own mortality during the inconjunct aspect. Your kids are growing up and flying out of the nest, parents are approaching retirement. You are in the middle, facing down the spectre of middle age. The tension of releasing control peaks during the inconjuncts. Do you really want to tote that barge and lift that bale forever? If you simply refuse to release control, you may set yourself up to carry a load of responsibility for the rest of your life.

Stress/Action: Semisquare (45°), Square (90°), Sesquiquadrate (135°) and Opposition (180°)

The open stress/action aspects (square, opposition, conjunction) make up the seven-year cycle pattern of transiting Saturn. The hidden squares (semisquare and sesquiquadrate) form another seven-year cycle of stress which hits between each of the open aspects. Everyone sees the open aspects, including us. The semisquare and sesquiquadrate may not be very visible, but we feel their effects as keenly.

Each of the aspects carries its own set of characteristics. The waxing squares occur when you are approximately seven, thirty-five and sixty-three. The oppositions hit around age fourteen, forty-two and seventy. The second (waning) squares involve ages twenty-one, forty-nine and seventy-seven. The Saturn cycles resemble a tune you first learn on a tin whistle. As your life unfolds you play it out with a larger group of instruments. By the last cycle period, you have a full orchestra playing, but it is still the same underlying melody. That melody involves personal responsibility and personal control. To follow this analogy a little further, the semisquare and sesquiquadrate play the descant to the melody. During these aspects you find the variations on the theme which bring you back to the main melody.

At each of the squares, the problems and events manifesting involve responsibility appropriate for your age. The first square when you are about seven years old requires that you become responsible for yourself in school. When you are thirty-five, you have to be responsible for yourself at work, and at parenting. When you are sixty-three you have to be responsible for what you will do when you retire and no longer have an established routine. At each of these junctures the events manifesting will push you into that acceptance of personal responsibility.

In exactly the same fashion, the first opposition at age fourteen forces you to acknowledge authority. You have to push against the authority in order to grow. While doing this, you learn to accept the consequences of your personal choices. The second opposition at forty-two demands that you sort out your professional life. What is the authority, where does it come from, what kinds of control do you have in professional situations? Many of us also are dealing with the end of our childbearing time, and looking at this change. The physical changes for women don't usually start at the opposition, but the idea of bearing a child changes. I think the last opposition may have a lot to do with whether or not you're going to let someone else (no matter how well intentioned) take over running your life.

The waning squares hit you with things that really deal with separation connected to parenting issues. The first one, at twenty-one, brings with it separation from parents. If you have not moved away from home, you are itchy to establish separate control. It is time to get on with your own separate life, setting up a career, family of your own, a place of your own. At forty-nine, you deal with another set of separations. The second waning square gets you when your kids (human or psychological kids, your career) have to be released. You have to find another set of things to build your routine and your responsibility around.

Some of us don't accept the responsibility of Saturn. Each of the stress/action aspects brings difficulty. After a while it gets harder and harder to pass the buck. At some point it really is your own fault. That point crashes down on you when Saturn is in one of the stress/action aspects. Some of you latch on to Saturn responsibility with a death grip. This reaction is very common in people who grew up in dysfunctional families and who always assumed the responsiblity. These people have just as much trouble with the stress/action aspects as the buck-passers. It is as if the universe says "So you think you can fix everything? Try this one!" The lessons of Saturn for the over-achiever involve knowing when to quit.

Saturn is a tough task-master. Somewhere in the next plane of existence there is the perfect balance of control and release. Part of the process of growth on the human level is learning to balance between running everything and running nothing. Saturn lessons are the hardest for the stressed-out business executive and the beach bum, those at the extreme ends of the scale. Those of us who fall somewhere in the middle tend to muddle through, as Saturn catches us whenever we lean towards one or the other end of the scale.

Ease: Sextile (60°) and Trine (120°)

Astrologers tend to pay so much attention to the stress/action aspects from transiting Saturn to natal Saturn that they ignore the ease aspects. The sextile and trine don't signify events, so they aren't as spectacular as the stress/action aspects. However, during the ease connections you can accomplish the mission impossible. The period of the sextile or trine symbolizes an ability to pull together authority, duty, responsibility, and make these things work for you. If you have set up your life at one of the Saturn extremes, where you either feel responsible for running everything or accept responsibility for nothing, you'll move towards a more middle position during the ease aspects. If you are not living on an edge of Saturn, your life will simply hum along the way it is supposed to.

This combination provides the way through difficulties. Suppose you have transiting Pluto square your Sun while you have transiting Saturn sextile its own position. The Pluto-Sun square says that you are in the process of changing your outlook in a very fundamental and permanent fashion. However, the Saturn sextile says that you can take charge of the direction of the changes. You won't have the trauma with the change that someone else might have without the Saturn release valve.

SATURN-URANUS ASPECTS

Neither of these planets moves fast enough by secondary progression to make a new aspect to each other. If they are completing a natal aspect, the year in which the aspect is exact will be the year in which you focus on how to cope with this natal aspect. Solar arc aspects are a little easier to handle than transiting aspects from either planet, because the transits usually last a lot longer than the three months of the solar arc aspect.

Control, forethought and responsibility don't mix awfully well with sudden change, self-will and explosive behavior. Those are the two symbols you are combining when you have a connection between Saturn and Uranus. When the aspect comes from transiting Uranus to natal and progressed Saturn, your concept of control gets turned inside out. It feels like your life has gone into the twilight zone. Every time you try to flex your Saturn, life turns bizarre.

Whenever transiting Saturn connects to your natal and progressed Uranus, your two-year-old self inside gets to stand in the corner for a while. Whenever you try to do something original, odd or a little crazy, here comes Saturn to ask whether it will work, how it will work, and why you want to do it in the first place. Not an easy connection.

Variable: Conjunction (0°)

When transiting Uranus comes along to conjunct your natal and progressed Saturn, all the things you thought that God told you to run in this life fall apart. If you've been managing a department in a large business fairly competently, the business gets sold and you inherit a boss. Don't get smug about it unless you will never have this conjunction during your life. In that case, keep your smugness to yourself. Those of you who will have the conjunction don't need to listen to what you may or may not have done on a metaphysical level to have your lives disrupted. The reality is that you're left at loose ends, not because you didn't do things right, but because it is time to change horses. There doesn't have to be any cause and effect with this conjunction. If you see it coming up in your life, the best you can do is brace yourself. Don't brace yourself by pouring concrete around your feet, though. If you can accept the concept of change, you can get on with a whole new set of life circumstances. You won't be stuck in a rut anymore.

All of us have transiting Saturn conjunct our natal and progressed Uranus once every twenty-eight or twenty-nine years. Nobody gets to be righteous about this one forever. We've all got a rebellious kid inside, left over from when we physically were that kid. That inner kid wants to do things itself, and in its own way. When Saturn comes along, the kid runs headlong into structure. If this means that you have to take your creative ideas and make something out of them, the conjunction can be very helpful. If you are stuck in the rebellious side of creativity, the conjunction can be pretty difficult. You can respond to the conjunction by telling off your boss, the cop, the judge, and Saturn will clamp down on your Uranus. You can choose to respond differently, taking the Saturn input and rearranging the ideas from the kid. Then the Saturn conjunction signals a time of new beginnings.

Tension: Semisextile (30°) and Inconjunct (150°)

The kind of internal destruction that happens to your automatic transmission when you stand on the gas pedal and the power brake at the same time is similar to the difficulty you encounter when Saturn and Uranus are in a tension aspect to each other. Uranus wants to get going, Saturn wants to be in complete control.

When the tension is from a semisextile, you are likely to fret about lack of control over budget items, for you may be hit with a couple of unexpected bills. The more orderly you are, the more you live within your means at all times, the harder it is to accept or cope with these fiscal surprises. If your normal state of finance is fairly chaotic, you will be caught short. Go easy with the plastic before this aspect gets tight.

When the tension is from an inconjunct, you may wish it was only an unbalanced checkbook. Your kids, spouse, pets, boss and/or parents wander off and "do their own thing" while you fume on the sidelines. It's no use to try to make things conform to your idea of what is right, proper or expected. Nothing will work that way. You don't have to force an explosion or accident, but if you are determined to make everything run the way it "should" run, you can ruin your insides during this inconjunct. Let go. You'll be happier in the long run.

Stress/Action: Semisquare (45°), Square (90°), Sesquiquadrate (135°) and Opposition (180°)

The stress/action aspects between Saturn and Uranus are like the first time you drive a standard shift car. You lurch ahead, then stall. Most of us do manage to get where we want to go, but the ride is a bit bumpy. By the time the aspect separates, you may have mastered the clutch. If the aspect is from transiting Saturn, you'll find out whether you got the hang of it the next time Saturn hits a stress/action aspect to your Uranus, in about three-and-a-half years. Uranus takes about eleven years to go the 45 degrees to the next hit. That's a long time to remember how to run this aspect. Most of us don't remember, and find each Uranus hard aspect a new surprise lesson.

The stress/action aspects pry apart over-control situations, often in a sharp manner. Look at where the two are located in your chart and what they rule. This information tells you what part of your life is involved. Transiting Saturn in the third, opposing Uranus in the ninth (ruler of the fifth), resulted in my car being totalled by my son while I was lecturing in another country (Uranus in the ninth). So much for being the perfect parent. Can you prevent this sort of result? You can certainly try. Sometimes you'll succeed. Sometimes the hard aspects bring a dose of reality into your life, and you recognize a need to direct or focus your creative energy. If you think about the areas of life involved before the aspect is exact, you can develop a more flexible attitude towards change in those areas. This is the key to redirecting the stress into action.

Ease: Sextile (60°) and Trine (120°)

Now is the time to try out all those interesting projects you've had rumbling around the back of your brain. While you have an ease connection between Saturn and Uranus, you can use your creative inner kid to get some solid results. The ease aspects don't make things happen, but they help you take charge of any events occurring now.

The sextile or trine between these two planets relieves any tendency to become overly obsessive, because it gives you the option of combining flexibility and control harmoniously. If you hate to take responsibility for anything you do, the ease aspect won't seem to do much at all. You're not too likely to get into difficulty with authorities while the aspect is present. The ease aspects present the best opportunities for the folks who have already done Saturn and feel accountable for their own choices. Then the sextile or trine indicates that you automatically make choices that work well for you.

SATURN-NEPTUNE ASPECTS

Saturn crystallizes, creates form, brings things into reality. Neptune softens, dissolves, brings life to another concept of existence. The combination of these symbols works like heavy-duty paint stripper, taking away all the ugly, chipped layers that interfere with your ability to enjoy life. Of course, if you were not planning to strip the paint, you may be uncomfortable during the process.

There are times when the combination of Saturn and Neptune dissolves so much of the outer coating that you discover the underlying reality wasn't even close to what you thought you had. You may find that the pearl was paste, or, alternately, that the rhinestone was a diamond. The discovery of reality occurs slowly as the aspect separates. While the aspect is present, you're in the middle of the layers. No other combination can confuse you the way this one can. Whatever you're positive is real may disintegrate, while whatever you've scoffed about happens in front of your eyes. During the aspect you may suspect that someone has scrambled your brains. Try to avoid imposing your previous concept of reality on friends and relatives, because you'll have to change your mind after the aspect passes.

Variable: Conjunction (0°)

Transiting Saturn conjuncts your natal and progressed Neptune once every twenty-nine years or so. When this occurs, take a look at your Neptune dreams and ask "Why not?" Saturn can help you bring your Neptune into focus. If you've overdone Neptune, Saturn can appear as an authority figure. Then you may lose your driving license for drunk driving, or lose your job for incompetence. You may lose anything you have not cared enough to be responsible about. This conjunction tells you precisely where you have taken responsibility in your life. It also tells you where that assumption of responsibility is foolish.

Neptune will make one conjunction at most to your Saturn. More than half of us will never have transiting Neptune conjunct our natal or progressed Saturn. If Neptune does conjunct natal and progressed Saturn, you'll find yourself slowly changing your concept of reality as Neptune effectively strips away the layers between you and the universe. You may be quite tempted to take up drinking or try a few recreational drugs. These substances will dull the perception of change, but they won't prevent the action of Neptune. You have to deal with the "bare bones" reality of your own life. After the conjunction passes, you will see the results of your choices during the conjunction.

Tension: Semisextile (30°) and Inconjunct (150°)

These are frustrating connections, for just when you've figured out how to play the game (Saturn), Neptune changes the rules. When Neptune changes the rules, nobody tells you until you've blundered. At least that's how it feels.

Often there isn't much you can do about the events occurring during the tension aspects between Saturn and Neptune. Because you can't control the direction of events occurring now, the underlying stress may become enormous. You have to reassess your whole script concerning personal responsibility. The family fixer, driven to rescue everyone, won't be able to do it now. The family dilettante, for whom others pick up the slack, finds that the rest of the family quits. Both of these expressions of Saturn and Neptune have problems. The family fixer has to learn that he or she can't fix everything. The dilettante has to grope around to figure out how to do the things that have to be done.

Those of you in the middle of this road hit both ends in different contexts. Whatever you didn't take responsibility for has to be done, and whatever you completely controlled escapes into the ether. You can't make a sick family member well, but you don't have to get sick, too.

Stress/Action: Semisquare (45°), Square (90°), Sesquiquadrate (135°) and Opposition (180°)

These connections between Saturn and Neptune challenge all of your nice theories of reality. Each of us has some ideas about what constitutes reality. These beliefs are central to our existence. We expect that tables stay solid. We don't expect our kitchen tables to suddenly fly up to the ceiling and stick there, or to melt into puddles on the floor. If a table did one of these things, most of us would get ready to sign ourselves into the closest funny farm.

The stress/action aspects hardly ever make the kitchen table go nuts, but they do start you wondering about how tightly you are wrapped. Sometimes the manifestation comes from another person who is engulfed in a drug or alcohol problem. This other person presents an alternate reality view, about which you can do nothing. A variation of this manifestation occurs when you choose to ignore problems with loved ones. Denying that a problem exists hardly ever cures it. However, it is possible to do lots of other things during a stress/action aspect between Saturn and Neptune, by refusing to recognize the core issue. The avoidance route is more likely during a semisquare or sesquiquadrate than during a square or opposition. By the time that transiting Saturn or transiting Neptune gets to the open aspect (square or opposition), you won't be able to hide from reality anymore.

Ease: Sextile (60°) and Trine (120°)

The ease connections between Saturn and Neptune provide strong resiliency. Most of the other aspects occurring simultaneously are likely to manifest positively. When the background connection combines softness and duty in harmony, you respond easily to any events. Most of us won't even notice the sextile or trine because it works so well. We don't get too concerned about what we are "supposed" to do, because we did it. This is a wonderful antidote for guilt. We're pleased to have the old, chipped paint stripped away by Neptune.

Trust yourself during the ease connections. You can figure out the best way to get things done. You won't have to struggle over choices, for the path of least resistance is very likely to be the most productive path anyhow. If the aspect is from transiting Neptune to your natal and progressed Saturn, you may have transiting Pluto in a sextile or trine at the same time. Then you have a combination that's hard to beat, because you're adding power to the easy assumption of control. The only difficulty possible with this pattern comes from the fact that you may not notice the extent of your own power.

SATURN-PLUTO ASPECTS

When the symbol for power and permanent change connects to the symbol for control and responsibility, you have an unforgettable combination. Back up through the ephemeris and look at the times transiting Saturn aspected your natal Pluto. The events surrounding these aspects tell you how you have reacted to this combination in the past. If you are about to have transiting Pluto aspect your natal and progressed Saturn, it's doubly important to look at what happened during the cycle of Saturn to Pluto. Pluto will bring similar events, but about forty times stronger.

When Saturn aspects Pluto or Pluto aspects Saturn, you have an opportunity to flex your power muscles. You can decide to manipulate instead of using overt power, or you can decide to be forced or manipulated rather than use your Pluto. Many of us have been taught that power is a nasty thing which only nasty people have. So we have to sneak around the edges, manipulating everyone in order to get what we want. If you can't use Pluto directly, and you can't use it covertly through whining and manipulating, you have to be the doormat for the world. When Saturn comes along to aspect your Pluto, or Pluto touches off your Saturn, the world will wipe its feet on you. It's time to change that script and get up off the floor.

Variable: Conjunction (0°)

This combination can indicate a major power/control struggle in just about every area of your life. Fortunately, for the next few years transiting Neptune will trail in after the conjunction of transiting Pluto, connecting to Saturn by sextile. The sextile will let you soften your rigid stance, allowing the Pluto change to occur with less trauma. You have to let go of some control issues when Pluto conjuncts your natal and progressed Saturn. When Saturn conjuncts your natal and progressed Pluto, the situation is only slightly different. This conjunction brings up the use of power, and how to control your desires. If someone proceeds to hammer you into the dust (literally or figuratively) during the conjunction, you are not letting yourself use your Pluto. Even if you can't bring yourself to take out the big stick, at least examine the possibilities. Transiting Saturn will be in a semisquare in three-and-a-half years, and you'll need to be able to use your power then.

When Pluto conjuncts your natal and progressed Saturn, it's like the universe wants you to stop running things. The more you resist letting go, the more areas this conjunction affects. If you never ran anything in your life, having come as close as possible to deleting Saturn from your chart, you'll find that Saturn is alive and well, and manifesting in a great big authority figure.

Tension: Semisextile (30°) and Inconjunct (150°)

Although the semisextile isn't as difficult as the inconjunct, neither of these connections is very easy. When you try to strong-arm a person or a situation, you find yourself up against iron man. Nothing budges. If you try to maneuver around the obstacles, you find your path blocked. Given the persistence of both of these symbols, most of us spend a lot of time pounding on walls during the tension connections between Saturn and Pluto.

The constant frustration of losing control leads to intense inner pressure. Find a hot tub or masseuse—you need some way to release this tension. Back up to take a better look at the situation. You can make yourself quite ill if you won't let go of the power/control issues culminating now.

An even more insidious possibility arises during these connections. You may be so intent on whatever your current problem involves that you ignore where you are and what you are doing. You may be a victim looking for a mugger. Don't wander down dark alleys while you have an inconjunct between these two planets. Pay attention to where you are and what is going on. With a minimum amount of awareness, you won't experience the worst manifestation of these two.

Stress/Action: Semisquare (45°), Square (90°), Sesquiquadrate (135°) and Opposition (180°)

The immovable object has just met the irresistible force, particularly if the transiting planet is Pluto. When transiting Saturn makes a stress/action aspect to your natal and progressed Pluto, it is one of a cycle series. You'll get quite a few chances to try this one on for size. Check back through a few of these aspects in your past to see whether you usually manifest through a difficult authority figure or through taking on more responsibility. If your boss got nasty during the last few stress/action hits from transiting Saturn, it may be time to do your work ahead. Then you can use the coming aspect for something else.

Transiting Pluto may bring you a complete change in your reality structure. That translates to "hold on to your hat," the roller coaster is about to start down the first hill. You may have time to wonder what possessed you to get on the roller coaster, but mostly you'll be too busy hanging on to think about whether or not you wanted to be there. Never mind trying to control where the roller coaster goes. Let go of whatever isn't needed; don't worry about the rest. It will be quite a bit easier if you don't dwell on the things you can't do anything about.

Ease: Sextile (60°) and Trine (120°)

One way or another you'll get anything you really want when you have a sextile or a trine between Saturn and Pluto. You won't necessarily find automatic fulfillment (no genie in a bottle, sorry to say), but you will have the drive and persistence to find a way to get what you want. Make sure you really want what you think you want, because it can be awfully disappointing to get it and then find out you don't like it.

One of the possible drawbacks to this combination comes from the nearly unconscious way we usually use sextiles and trines. These aspects flow so easily that it's harder to see them acting. You may not recognize your ability to control or persuade the people around you. If you really are putting the screws to everyone around you during the ease aspects, you may be in big trouble when that sextile turns into a square or that trine turns into an inconjunct. If you want long-term positive results from either of these transiting connections, observe the golden rule. Don't do to someone else something you would hate to have done to you.

CHAPTER 12

The Slip 'Twixt Cup and Lip: URANUS ASPECTS

Uranus progresses too slowly to make any new aspects by progression, averaging only about 4 degrees per year. The impact of transiting Uranus is usually stronger than the impact of solar arc Uranus, simply because the transit is there longer.

Uranus takes eighty-four years to go around the zodiac. It will hit all of your natal planets sooner or later. Uranus is the planet that shakes up the bottle of soda pop just before you open it. Natal Uranus symbolizes your own inner child as well as your areas of creativity; transiting or solar arc Uranus indicates the child in the universe. This is the mischievous kid who introduces random chance into events that might otherwise move smoothly.

Sudden, abrupt change is a hallmark of Uranus. Most of us don't like it much when the universe turns over the chessboard, particularly if we were up a couple of pieces. It is extremely difficult to be accurate with predictions when Uranus is making the major aspect. Thus, it is simultaneously the ruler of and the downfall of astrologers. Uranus manifests through anything wild, weird, strange or unusual. The newer a technology, the more likely it is to be connected to Uranus.

URANUS-URANUS ASPECTS

The eighty-four year cycle of Uranus sets some clear time frames for delineating stages of life.[25] When transiting Uranus aspects your natal Uranus, your inner child comes under scrutiny. This is the kid who throws temper tantrums, but it is also the kid who finds wonder in a grasshopper, joy in a discarded box. You create with this freedom-loving kid. Every so often that kid really needs a big hug. We are socialized into repressing this crazy, uncooperative part of ourselves. We do have to get along with the other people in our environment, so some sort of control has to be exercised with natal Uranus. But if that part of yourself is locked in a closet and never let out, the result is rage. It doesn't matter who shut that kid in the closet. You can only blame Mom and Dad up to a point. After you get to be a grownup, you can unlock that kid.

When you are afraid of what that part of you might do, it is difficult to let it out. If you are ever going to be able to experience the exhilarating sense of accomplishment which accompanies a leap into the unknown, you have to embrace your inner child. You have to own your natal Uranus.

Variable: Conjunction (0°)

It's like a book, I think, this bloomin' world,
Which you can read and care for just so long,
But presently you feel that you will die
Unless you get the page you're readin' done,
An' turn another—likely not so good;
But what you're after is to turn 'em all.

—Rudyard Kipling
Sestina of the Tramp-Royal

You'll be in the neighborhood of eighty-four by the time transiting Uranus gets around to the conjunction to its natal position. Maybe you'll

---

[25]See Betty Lundsted, *Planetary Cycles* (York Beach, Maine: Samuel Weiser, Inc., 1984), for a discussion of the planetary cycles. Lundsted's book has a more complete description of the aspects between the outer planets and their own natal positions than there is room to include in this book.

finally stop worrying about whether something is silly, and simply go out and do it. By the time the conjunction comes around, you've been here in this reality long enough to do just about anything you want to do with the conjunction. The kinds of things you'll attempt probably have lots more to do with your actual physical ability than with what you would like to try.

We all hope that when we come around to the conjunction we'll find it fun. If we've taken care of our perpetual child inside, maybe we will!

Tension: Semisextile (30°) and Inconjunct (150°)

The first semisextile between transiting Uranus and natal Uranus, the only tension connection which you don't impose upon yourself, happens when you are four-and-a-half to five years old. That's when grownups start to teach you about controlling the tantrum-throwing Uranus kid. Watch the hard aspects from transiting Mars to your natal Uranus during tension aspects from transiting Uranus to natal Uranus. Uranus moves so slowly that you always have Mars triggers during this aspect. The tension aspect sets the stage for an accident, because we usually repress our inner children whenever we are uncomfortable or worried about how we will respond in an unknown situation. We are really pretty angry about something when we encounter either the semisextile or inconjunct. It may be easier to let Mars trigger a major accident than to look at why we are so angry right now.

Temper tantrums are a much easier way to handle a combination of transiting Uranus and transiting Mars. Some of us simply won't allow ourselves to do a full-bore temper tantrum. You don't have to do it in public, you know. You can take a pile of old jars down to the cellar and throw them against the wall. You can beat up an old pillow or take karate lessons. You don't have to let the universe (or anyone inhabiting this universe) do a tantrum on you.

Stress/Action: Semisquare (45°), Square (90°), Sesquiquadrate (135°) and Opposition (180°)

The challenges of the stress/action aspects from transiting Uranus to natal and progressed Uranus all involve how you choose to use your own uniqueness. Stress/action aspects usually manifest as events, and the Uranus connections are certainly no exception. The problem for the practicing astrologer arises because Uranus events regularly defy prediction.

While accidents are more probable during a stress/action connection, they are not always the way we choose to work out these periods.[26] The highest probability for an accident occurs when transiting Mars joins the mixture, triggering the stress/action aspect from transiting Uranus. A high probability isn't a guarantee, or even a prediction, because you could have many mitigating aspects occurring simultaneously.

Look at the other aspects before you get too wound up about stress/action connections with Uranus. If you have ease aspects to your Sun, Moon, Midheaven or Ascendant, the stress/action aspect from Uranus is more likely to indicate a sudden, very positive event in your life. In this case, Mars will simply get the ball rolling.

Ease: Sextile (60°) and Trine (120°)

During the sextile or trine from transiting Uranus to natal Uranus, you tend to make peace with your inner child. You can enjoy playing, you can try new things. This connection provides an ability to come up with creative solutions, which smooths out any hard aspects occurring simultaneously. Sometimes the ease connection simply indicates a flexibility that lets you ride the waves, turning potentially aggravating situations into opportunities.

Change the way you analyze other aspects if there is a sextile or trine present from transiting to natal Uranus. The ease aspect won't make anything happen by itself, but it will introduce an element of surprise to other aspects. In this case, the unexpected is not unpleasant. Suppose you have transiting Saturn opposing your natal Sun and you're feeling about as low as the vest pocket of a snail. If you also have a trine from transiting Uranus to your natal Uranus, you could take that Saturn and turn it into the beginning of a company, book or relationship which, while tough at the beginning, could grow spectacularly as soon as Saturn gets out of the way.

---

[26]See Chapter 3, chart 5, Kay's second concussion.

URANUS-NEPTUNE ASPECTS

Uranus wants to go a hundred miles per hour through Neptune's dense fog. Uranus really can't make the fog evaporate. Neptune tends to gloss over the realities of change. Sometimes the combination can result in important spiritual change, but usually this is mixed with a generous dose of sheer weirdness.

When transiting Neptune makes the aspect, rearranging your creative child very subtly, the combination can send you into a spin at any moment. If you have developed your creative child, and use this part of yourself productively, the addition of Neptune energy confuses and scatters, but eventually adds a new dimension to your creative efforts. If you have not done much to encourage your inner child, Neptune brings a vague awareness of lack.

When Uranus transits touch your natal and progressed Neptune, it's time to go out and play with Neptune toys. Music, art, poetry, sailing, swimming are nice Neptune areas. Drugs, alchohol, deceit are the back alleys of nasty Neptune. You can avoid the negative side of Neptune if you consciously develop some positive outlets for yourself. You don't have to be Milton, Mozart or Modigliani to use Neptune in poetry, music or art. Grandma Moses did alright, and so does Dolly Parton. We aren't talking about great art, we're talking about staying sane.

Variable: Conjunction (0°)

When transiting Uranus conjuncts your natal and progressed Neptune, your fundamental concept of spirituality is changing. This doesn't usually happen with a flash of insight and a word from on high. Rather, it occurs while you are busy doing something else and feeling a little uncomfortable with your old way of thinking about things. If you have no interest in the spiritual side of life, you may find this conjunction considerably different. Be careful with drugs—you can become addicted easily or you may react adversely to simple over-the-counter compounds (even aspirin can cause physical reactions). You will be more susceptible to infections now.

The conjunction from transiting Neptune to natal and progressed Uranus generally works a bit differently. Neptune obscures the action of your Uranus, so you may be unaware of the demands you place on both yourself and others. Uranus symbolizes self-will as well as creativity. This part of you can be very stubborn about independence. When transiting Neptune comes along, you may not notice that you are regularly dragging out your soapbox. If your desire for freedom interferes with everyone else's lives, your creative kid may be in for hard times after Neptune goes away.

Tension: Semisextile (30°) and Inconjunct (150°)

Tension aspects between Uranus and Neptune don't need much in the way of a triggering aspect to get into deep water. If you have any problem with drugs (including alcohol) you may hit a crisis when transiting Mars or any other planet touches off a semisextile or inconjunct between Uranus and Neptune. The semisextile is not as difficult as the inconjunct, but either aspect sets up a background of discontent between what you want (Uranus) and how you escape reality (Neptune). Folks who have never indulged in mind-altering substances are tempted to during the semisextile or inconjunct.

Neptune symbolizes any kind of drug or chemical, while Uranus symbolizes sudden events. Drug or chemical sensitivity is a little more likely when the aspect is from transiting Uranus to natal and progressed Neptune, but can happen either way. If you break out in a wretched rash, suspect your laundry detergent before you run off to a shrink. If you have to take a broad-spectrum antibiotic and you are female, you'll probably need something else to get rid of the yeast infection which is likely to follow the antibiotic. Read all of those little pieces of paper that come with over-the-counter drugs. Ask your druggist if you are at all unsure of any combination. If it can react, it is more likely to do so now.

Stress/Action: Semisquare (45°), Square (90°), Sesquiquadrate (135°) and Opposition (180°)

Anyone who is involved in a Neptune-related career or hobby loves the stress/action aspects from transiting Uranus to natal and progressed Neptune, for they usually bring an explosion of creativity. The stress part of the combination pops up if you are doing Neptune when you are supposed to be doing Saturn (that is, at work). If you are not a self-employed musician, your boss may not like it one little bit if he or she discovers you writing music instead of filing bills. Somehow you have to fit in the activity around the rest of your life.

When the aspect comes from transiting Neptune to natal and progressed Uranus, you need a new outlet for your creativity. If you are working on personal growth, you may find this a marvelous time to take psychic development courses, for you are open to bringing your spontaneous side out of the closet.

The down side of the stress/action connections between Uranus and Neptune involve drugs or escape. It is easy to rationalize irresponsible behavior during hard aspects from transiting Uranus to natal and progressed Neptune, or from transiting Neptune to natal and progressed Uranus. If you don't do it yourself, you may have to deal with someone (friend, relative, co-worker) who does.

Ease: Sextile (60°) and Trine (120°)

Ease aspects don't signify events, but rather provide a soft background against which the other transits and progressions play. If you are using the sextile or trine between Uranus and Neptune positively, you find creative musical or artistic pursuits which allow you to escape whatever daily pressures are present from other sources. If you are not using these symbols in a particularly responsible manner, you fog out on grass or alchohol and blame it on the stress of the other aspects. While the ease aspect is present, you won't hit any crisis from the drugs you're ingesting. You think everything is just fine, and are likely to laugh at anyone who disagrees.

If you have this aspect present, ask yourself a couple of questions. Are you having cocktails with dinner every night? How would you feel if there wasn't any booze or grass in the house? Would you go get some, or would you really wait until next Saturday when Uncle Harry comes to dinner?

In the phraseology of the sixties, there are lots of "natural highs" available to you now. You won't find them if you've deadened your senses with chemicals.

URANUS-PLUTO ASPECTS

Whenever these two symbols combine, you have to make some decisions about what you want and how you're going to get it. Your creative kid can become a real brat when transiting Pluto aspects your natal and progressed Uranus, or you can decide to do something you've always wanted to do. You have to decide how to use power whenever transiting Uranus connects to your natal and progressed Pluto. The decisions you make during Uranus-Pluto aspects usually end up affecting the rest of your life, although they may not appear Earth shattering when you make them. Robert Frost could have been talking about the combination of Uranus and Pluto in his poem *The Road Not Taken*. The last verse reads "I shall be telling this with a sigh/Somewhere ages and ages hence:/ Two roads diverged in a wood, and I/ I took the one less traveled by,/ And that has made all the difference."

Often the choices you make are influenced by things which turn out to be trivial. The combination of mathematical ability, a crush on a ninth-grade science teacher, and an indifferent high school English department can get you into a career in hard sciences. If your real inner bent is writing, you'll get nudged in that direction with every connection between Uranus and Pluto. Whether you'll ever be able to abandon the science area for the humanities depends on all the intermediate choices you make during your life.

Variable: Conjunction (0°)

Uranus conjuncted Pluto September 10, 1965, April 5, 1966, and July 1, 1966. Everyone born between 1901 and 1965 will have transiting Uranus conjunct natal Pluto, and won't have transiting Pluto conjunct natal Uranus. Those born after 1966 will have transiting Pluto conjunct natal Uranus long before transiting Uranus makes the conjunction. Thus, once in our lives we get this combination of power, pressure and change. Whatever happens during the conjunction will affect the rest of our lives.

I don't have much information from clients who have had transiting Pluto conjunct natal Uranus, because most of the people born between 1965 and 1969 had the conjunction occur before they were eight years old. For some, it accompanied the start of school, for others a family move. Those born in 1974 and 1975, with natal Uranus at the end of Libra, had the transiting Saturn-Pluto conjunctions of 1982 and 1983 hit their Uranus positions. Their experiences can't be used to delineate Pluto by itself. Pluto is just starting to transit the natal Uranus position of the kids born after 1975.

The conjunction symbolizes a time in your life during which you have to assert your own individuality in spite of extreme pressure to abandon your inner child. If the conjunction occurs in childhood, the pressure can come from parents, teachers or siblings. If the conjunction occurs after you have become an adult, the pressure comes from the society around you. Whatever the source of pressure, you will have to rebel to avoid being crushed. Rebellion is not necessarily negative. The older you are when the conjunction occurs, the more experience you have with this particular version of reality called life. You have more options for directing the changes.

You won't be able to slide around or duck this aspect. If you prepare yourself in advance, you can make changes that you want to make. If you don't do anything at all, the universe will decide what to change in your life. You may not like the changes that occur by themselves.

Tension: Semisextile (30°) and Inconjunct (150°)

When you have an semisextile or inconjunct between Uranus and Pluto the tension centers on two things. First, you have to figure out exactly what you want. This may not be easy, for the wants of Pluto or Uranus don't involve material goods, but inner needs for power and personal expression. Second, you have to find out which approaches work when you are after something. The approaches you have used up to now (persuasion, pleading, power pushes) probably won't work anymore. The people who used to respond to guilt or pressure move out or grow up or quit allowing you to manipulate them. It might be you who moves out or grows up or quits allowing someone else to push your buttons.

Although there is a sinister possibility of mugging or rape with the inconjunct between these two, most people don't experience this manifestation unless there are simultaneous hard aspects to their Suns. Even when there are tough aspects to your Sun, you should be able to avoid the worst manifestation by being more careful. It will help a lot if you explore the whole power issue instead of waiting to see if anything happens with the inconjunct. There may be people out there who really don't have any concerns about power. I have not met any. Most of us do the best we can to walk somewhere between doormat and tyrant.

Stress/Action: Semisquare (45°), Square (90°), Sesquiquadrate (135°) and Opposition (180°)

When Uranus and Pluto are hooked together in a stress/action aspect, every other transit can become a test of power or a contest of wills. It's amazing to watch a perfectly nice transit of Jupiter to natal Venus turn into a test of one-upmanship while Pluto and Uranus are square each other. I have had a few cases of accidents or other physical mayhem during a stress/action aspect between these two outers. However, the far more common effect places stress on even the best aspects occurring during the year.

It is as if the action required is a complete overhaul of one of two parts of yourself, neither of which you nor I nor anyone else likes to think about. You may have to pull out your inner rebellious child and pay attention to the needs, expression and any unresolved rage this kid has. It is hard enough to acknowledge this kid, let alone take care of it. Alternately, this combination may force you to deal with your own petty power plays. None of us likes to pay attention to that pushy, greedy, stubborn part which won't give in at all. So we let the stress/action aspect sour all the rest of the combinations in our lives. Sooner or later we may figure out that we are causing all of our misery. Then we can do the action part and get rid of our hidden agendas. Some of us hate the process of looking at ourselves so much that we don't let go. Then we can spend years and years (up to the end of our lives) being bitter about all the miserable things that are our lot in life.

By the way, nobody can make anyone else look at him- or herself. If this aspect is going on with someone you love, and you think he or she isn't doing it very well, your tactful suggestions may cause an enormous fight. Further, your loved one may transfer the whole mess to your shoulders. Unless you are ready to carry the other person's bitterness and rage around for the rest of your life, keep your nose out of it.

Ease: Sextile (60°) and Trine (120°)

Your ability to persuade and to change things will never be greater than it is during the sextile or trine between Uranus and Pluto. This isn't an action aspect. However, with this aspect in the background, you can use any other stress/action aspect to your advantage and growth.

The only possible exception to the above occurs if you have transiting Pluto trine Uranus while transiting Neptune opposes Uranus. If you have this combination, you are likely to be quite confused about exactly what you want, yet you have a strong ability to get it. If you decide to find the lost gold of the Wicky-wacky tribe in central Borneo, your best hope of finding backing comes during the Uranus-Pluto sextile or trine. The sextile or trine won't find the gold, however.

Promotions, pay raises, new businesses, anything you start close to the time when this ease aspect is exact will flow fairly easily. The connection between Uranus and Pluto doesn't say anything about the eventual outcome. Even if you don't want to begin a new venture, you can keep things humming merrily during these aspects. Use your power and creativity joyfully. This is the best possible use of an ease connection between Uranus and Pluto.

CHAPTER 13

Spiritual Snakehandling:
NEPTUNE ASPECTS

Neptune is the fickle muse who prompts us to write poetry and music, and seduces us into escape and drugs. Neptune brings us the highest and the lowest of human behavior possibilities. Although Neptune does not have an exclusive on lying (Jupiter does a pretty good job at prevarication), Neptune is notorious for sliding past the truth. Neptune may provide the penchant for denial common with drug/alcohol abuse, but frequently our friend Venus is more prominent when we are indulging our pleasure centers.

Neptune is allegedly involved in spiritual awareness and spiritual opening. As an observer of the "new age cultures" of twenty years ago, I wonder how much of the "awakening" of the sixties and early seventies was spiritual and how much was LSD and other assorted mind-altering substances. Neptune makes you let go of preconceived notions, not by ripping them away or by exploding your world, but by dissolving your defenses. When you discover that your mighty shield is paper, you have to trust the universe. When you trust the universe, Neptune shows you the kaleidoscope of other realities, other places. Then Neptune lets you see the wonder of yourself. Neptune slips in and takes apart the ego. When you have found that you can live without that ego, Neptune gives it back to you.

NEPTUNE-NEPTUNE ASPECTS

Neptune takes about 146 years to go completely around the zodiac. Thus, its cycle can't complete (come to a conjunction) during a lifetime.[27] The only conjunction from transiting or progressed Neptune to natal Neptune possible occurs if your natal Neptune is at a station or about to make a station. Then transiting Neptune will conjunct natal Neptune during the first year of your life. If you will have a conjunction by progression, your Neptune is unlikely to move more than two degrees during your life. You may have a 0° 0′ orb conjunction for two years. Since the intensification of Neptune is a little like an intensification of fog, most of you simply don't notice it very much. When you can't see anything anyway, you can't see less, no matter how thick the fog gets.

The periods of semisextile, semisquare, sextile, square and trine from transiting Neptune to natal Neptune provide times to evaluate, fuss over, smooth out, disrupt, and finally, come to ease with your spiritual inclinations in this life. Even if you don't think you have any spiritual inclinations, you have a reality structure. The more you want life to be predictable, real, grounded, the harder it is to cope with Neptune whispering in the back roads of your mind. Do you chain yourself to the mast in order to ignore the call of the siren, or do you follow the muse?

Variable: Conjunction (0°)

This will not occur during adult life.

Tension: Semisextile (30°)

Sometime between the ages of fourteen and sixteen, the only semisextile from transiting Neptune to natal Neptune occurs. I think this is planned so that you won't get through adolescence without some sort of difficulty. If you cope with your progressed Moon opposition wonderfully, handle

---

[27]See Betty Lundsted, *Planetary Cycles* (York Beach, Maine: Samuel Weiser, Inc., 1984), for a discussion of the planetary cycles. Lundsted's book has a more complete description of the aspects between the outer planets and their own natal positions than there is room to include in this book.

the Saturn opposition with aplomb, launch yourself into the second Jupiter cycle effortlessly, you still have to do something with the semi-sextile from transiting Neptune to natal Neptune.

If you are growing up in some sort of vacuum (drugs are not available in your school), you'll probably get the Neptune that looks at your parents' religious or spiritual beliefs and makes rude noises. This is the great kid who doesn't do any awful stuff, but needles parents about their lack of spiritual basis. Many kids turn to mystical religions, or the mystical side of whatever religion they have been exposed to, during the semisextile. So you are reformed Jewish and your kid becomes orthodox and makes you get separate dishes for him or her. Or, you are a Unitarian and your kid starts going to the "Jesus Saves" church on the other side of town and quotes Bible verses to you. Of course, if you are a member of the "Jesus Saves" church, your kid becomes interested in Hinduism and refuses to eat turkey at Thanksgiving.

As irritating as these manifestations may be to parents, the other way to do the semisextile is infinitely more destructive to mind and body. You can start experimenting regularly with alcohol and/or drugs. This manifestation is much harder to grow out of if you happen to be the one in three persons for whom addiction is a strong possibility.

Most of us do try a couple of drinks, maybe a joint or two during the semisextile. If you are also in a very difficult progressed Moon cycle, you can slide into an emotional mess that provides an excuse for alcohol or drug abuse. If the stress comes from the Saturn cycle, you may get into control issues, again having an excuse to escape through Neptune.

There is no solution to the semisextile, only the ability to live through it and learn from it. If your parents let you explore different spiritual belief systems, you can provide yourself with some interesting insights. If you can establish control in other areas of your life, you can question from a basis of acceptance.

Stress/Action: Semisquare (45°) and Square (90°)

The semisquare hits sometime in your early twenties, the square in your early forties. During the stress/action aspects it's very difficult to decide who you are or what you want. Thus, the action part is almost funny—

except while it is there. If you have a very strong responsibility index, you won't be able to sit still. So you row anyway, even though you haven't the vaguest notion of what you are rowing into or out of.

The best solution to the stress/action combinations is to wait them out, observe the challenges to your spiritual beliefs and reserve judgment until the year of the semisquare or square has passed. Most of us are not blessed with that amount of patience. We struggle with the hard aspects, trying our darnedest to make sense out of life while Neptune is undermining the whole concept.

We certainly don't have to give up and drown our troubles in a bottle or beat them to death with chemicals. If you are doing one of these things with Neptune, don't blame the stars. Look at your own attitudes. You may not be able to control much of life during the hard aspects from transiting Neptune to natal Neptune, but you certainly can control your response. No one will hold you down and pour stuff down your throat. Run to your phone book and look up Alcoholics Anonymous. Then go to the meetings.

Ease: Sextile (60°) and Trine (120°)

During the ease aspects from transiting Neptune to natal Neptune you actually feel comfortable with whatever reality structure you believe in. Most of us don't worry about our spirituality during ease aspects, because everything flows comfortably. What this usually means is that you have found a group of friends who agree with you. So if your reality includes nature spirits and wood nymphs, you find a whole group of people who talk to nature spirits and live near you. If your reality is computers and machines, you live in a whole community of high-tech people. It isn't that you seek out the compatibility; during the sextile or trine you discover that it is there all around you.

Most of us reinforce our own levels of artistic ability or appreciation during ease aspects. If beauty resides in brass elephants, you find them. You simply don't expect, nor do you usually experience, resistance to the unfolding of your personal spiritual self during these aspects.

Because this isn't an action connection, most of us don't notice a sextile or trine from transiting Neptune to natal Neptune until it is long gone. It is just easy to live with.

NEPTUNE-PLUTO ASPECTS

Most of you have a natal aspect between Neptune and Pluto. During the 1920s and 1930s the aspect was a semisquare; since the 1940s the aspect has been a sextile. For those with a natal aspect, power is inextricably entwined with your concept of spirituality. The closer the natal aspect is, the harder it is for you to consider personal power without considering spiritual issues. The aspects stay in orb for so long that each pattern marks a generation, rather than an individual. Yet as the wheel turns and the two outer planets aspect your natal positions by transit, you respond as an individual.

Transits of Neptune or Pluto last at least a year, sometimes longer. In contrast, solar arc directions are usually done within a three-month period maximum. If you are reading the aspect delineation with a solar arc direction in mind, remember that the effect will be shorter and probably sharper than the transiting aspect. Hard aspects from transiting Neptune to natal Pluto or from transiting Pluto to natal Neptune set a background for change. This background is usually triggered by a faster transit or by the progressed Moon. As long as the transit is within a 1 degree orb, other transits or the progressed Moon, when exact, can set events in motion.

Variable: Conjunction (0°)

Everyone who was born the same year as you were born will have transiting Pluto conjunct their natal Neptune during the same year you have the conjunction.[28] If your natal Neptune does not aspect any of your inner planets or angles, you may not find that the conjunction affects you in a personal fashion. Nonetheless, you will be more aware of changes in the goals of the people around you during the conjunction.

The spiritual goals of society are constantly shifting, albeit slowly. In the 1960s we went through a period of social awareness and an upswing in drug use, in the 1970s we "found ourselves," and in the 1980s we were concerned with making money. When transiting Pluto

---

[28]The last Neptune-Pluto conjunction took place in 1891 to 1892. Since Neptune passed Pluto in the sky at that time, those of us alive now will only have transiting Pluto conjunct natal and progressed Neptune, as Pluto catches up to the natal Neptune position.

conjuncts your natal Neptune, you notice the shifts that have already occurred. You now feel pressured to accept or reject whatever social mores are fashionable at the time of the conjunction. Neptune does not symbolize religion, but the spiritual values underlying the desire for religion in people. When transiting Pluto conjuncts Neptune, you choose which of these underlying values to embrace, and which to discard.

Tension: Semisextile (30°) and Inconjunct (150°)

Like the conjunction, the tension aspects between Neptune and Pluto occur at approximately the same time for everyone born during the same year. Unless these aspects are tied to inner planets through very tight aspects (such that the transiting planet will aspect the inner planet within a few months of the aspect to the outer) you notice a discontent mirrored in the lives of all the people you know who were born during the same year. Although this provides grist for mutual gripe sessions, individual responses are not symbolized by the connections between transiting Neptune or transiting Pluto and natal Neptune or natal Pluto.

As Neptune transited Sagittarius, it inconjuncted natal Pluto in Cancer (people born between 1913 and 1939). Now that Neptune is in Capricorn, it is inconjunct natal Pluto in Leo, the generation born between 1939 and 1957. Perhaps this aspect marks a time in our lives when we romanticize the "good old days." The adjustments we make are connected to personal power and current spirituality.

Stress/Action: Semisquare (45°), Square (90°), Sesquiquadrate (135°) and Opposition (180°)

These aspects provide a generational background (they happen at approximately the same time to everyone born during the same year). Unless the aspect is closely connected to personal planets, you will notice a change in the perception of personal power or the direction of spiritual interest during this time. You are more likely to notice who is in charge during the aspect. If your natal Pluto or Neptune is not connected to inner planets, the aspect brings up only observational input, not events that are connected to you in a personal manner.

Watch other transits and progressions during the year that transiting Neptune is in a stress/action aspect to natal Pluto, or transiting Pluto is in a stress/action aspect to natal Neptune. These other aspects will play against a background of change in perception for you. During the stress/action aspect between the two outermost planets, you are more likely to make sweeping changes in your personal perception of spirituality than you would if the same aspects occurred when you had no hard aspect between Neptune and Pluto by transit.

Ease: Sextile (60°) and Trine (120°)

During the ease aspects we tend to trust the underlying power/spirituality concepts we've been taught. We can use your inner belief systems as a steady background, for we are less likely to find major discontinuities between what we believe and what is occurring out there in the world. Since these connections happen at the same time to everyone born during the same year, it is very interesting to observe the differences in perception between people who are more than five years apart in age. While not as striking as the differences between people who have the outer planets 30 degrees apart (and who thus have completely different patterns occurring) the five-year jumps move the outers just enough to observe a wave pattern between periods of content and periods of discontent with belief systems.

CHAPTER 14

The Carrot and the Stick:
PLUTO ASPECTS

Pluto moves so slowly that it won't make any new aspects by secondary progression. The position of Pluto in most ephemerides is accurate to a few minutes of arc (usually within 10 minutes). Although this is certainly precise enough for predictions involving transits, it can throw a solar arc aspect off by a month or more, and can practically invalidate any progressed aspect, for you may not be able to figure out the year in which the progressed aspect is exact to the minute, let alone the month during the year. A computer program will give you a month and day because it was programmed to do just that. The difficulty with this wonderful feat of science is simply that as of this writing (1989) the date given is irrelevant. The date on your printout is irrelevant simply because at this time your program cannot calculate the position of Pluto to an accuracy that can be measured in seconds of arc. Don't pay any attention to dates given by your computer, your ephemeris, or your favorite astrology teacher for progressed Pluto aspects. They are all probably wrong. Dates for solar arc Pluto will be within a month of accurate. Use secondary progressed or solar arc Pluto aspects as a background. Unless you want egg all over your face, don't predict based on a date for a progressed or solar arc Pluto.

PLUTO-PLUTO ASPECTS

Pluto's eccentric orbit means that Pluto does not spend equal amounts of time in each sign. Pluto spent roughly twenty-six years in Cancer, eighteen years in Leo, fourteen years in Virgo, twelve years in Libra, and will stay about thirteen years in Scorpio.[29] The age at which the aspects from transiting Pluto to natal Pluto occur is dropping rapidly. Most folks with natal Pluto in Cancer had transiting Pluto square its natal position when they were in their mid- to late-fifties. Folks with natal Pluto in Leo are getting the same square while they are in their early forties. In 1983, transiting Pluto trined the natal Pluto for those born in 1913 (who were seventy years old), but by 1988 Pluto was trining natal Pluto for those born between 1923 and 1925 (people between the ages of sixty-three and sixty-five). In 1996, when Pluto enters Sagittarius, it will be trining natal Pluto for people only fifty-seven years old.

At the same time that transiting Pluto has speeded up in orbit, life expectancy has increased globally. The older perception of Pluto as a devastating aspect (particularly when in square aspect to its natal position) probably has to be revised. While transiting Pluto square natal Pluto still indicates major internal change, for most people it does not accompany physical difficulties.

Tension: Semisextile (30°) and Inconjunct (150°)

People who are currently in their mid-nineties may have transiting Pluto inconjunct their natal positions of Pluto in early Gemini. Any conditions connected to that inconjunct could be more accurately connected with being over ninety years old. You won't be able to draw any conclusions on a personal level until after the year 2000, because until Pluto enters Capricorn, the inconjunct aspect will be complicated by factors of age.

The semisextile from transiting Pluto to natal Pluto hit the Pluto-in-Cancer generation while they were in their twenties (perhaps the Second World War?). The Pluto-in-Leo generation got the semisextile while they were in high school. Those with natal Pluto in Virgo, Libra or Scorpio have their first opposition from the progressed Moon and/or their first opposition from transiting Saturn complicated by the semisextile from transiting Pluto to natal Pluto. This semisextile symbolizes an

---

[29]See *Planetary Cycles* for a discussion of the planetary cycles. Lundsted's book has a more complete description of the aspects between the outer planets and their own natal positions than there is room to include in this book.

internalization of power scripts, particularly for those with a close sextile between natal Pluto and natal Neptune. Many of the Pluto-in-Leo generation sorted this out during the drug-filled sixties. There may be a correlation between the age at which children are exposed to drugs (which has steadily dropped since the mid 1960s) and the semisextile aspect between transiting Pluto and natal Pluto.

Stress/Action: Semisquare (45°) and Square (90°)

Most astrological knowledge comes from taking the experiences of a block of people who have had a certain aspect, and inferring from this information what will happen to others. You cannot directly transfer a set of experiences from a group that has a semisquare to a group that has a sextile, for the combination of aspects is quite different. Those of us who have natal Pluto semisquare natal Neptune got the stress/action aspect from transiting Pluto doubled, as transiting Pluto formed another stress/action aspect to natal Neptune at approximately the same time. All of us born after 1940, when Pluto and Neptune moved into the sextile relationship with each other, will not have transiting Pluto make stress aspects to both natal Neptune and Pluto within the same year. Instead, we have transiting Pluto semisextile natal Neptune around the time that transiting Pluto squares its natal position.

The stress/action connection from transiting Pluto to natal Pluto forces us to change the way we acknowledge our power and our deepest self-will. Examining how we get what we want is not usually easy. Furthermore, the stress/action aspects seem to require that we choose what we want to be when we grow up. It seems fairly normal to ask that kind of question with the semisquare, but we are asking again when we are in our forties! During this square we may need to completely re-evaluate our positions relative to everyone else in our lives.

Ease: Sextile (60°) and Trine (120°)

The sextile and trine from transiting Pluto to natal Pluto are not as likely to indicate similar events as the two aspects do with other planets, because those people with Pluto in Cancer natally have transiting Neptune opposed natal Pluto, while the people with natal Pluto in Virgo have transiting Neptune trine their natal Pluto positions, as well as having transiting Pluto conjunct their natal Neptunes. In spite of these problems, a few patterns seem to be emerging.

The group with the sextile wants to utilize personal power. Some of these, of course, are the young "yuppies," making their mark through conspicuous consumption. A few are delving into various areas of occult study, while others are reassessing their personal ways of avoiding real issues. The folks with the sextile all seem to be trying to *do* something to make changes in their lives or awareness, while the folks with the trine seem much more content to wait and see what this phase of their lives brings them.

PART THREE:

The Case
of Too
Many Aspects

CHAPTER 15

A *Predictor's*
Nightmare:
TONI'S CHART

As I worked on this book, I realized that few people could tolerate having me shine a spotlight on their lives. It's easy to get permission to use specific events as examples in a book, but I wanted more. I needed a year full of dated events and a birth time from some sort of record (not rectified), but more importantly, I needed a person who would let me honestly analyze her natal chart and background. She had to be grown up enough to have stopped parent-bashing, no matter how wonderful or awful her parents had been. She had to be mature enough to acknowledge mistakes, confusion or just plain bad judgment without falling apart. At the same time, she had to be assertive enough to tell me when my analysis was wrong or did not fit the facts. This kind of analysis strips the example person of pretense, is often unflattering, yet is the best possible teaching tool. It is far simpler to use data from someone who has died. That person can't come back and complain about the analysis after the book is published. At the same time, unless the individual involved has read and understood the analysis, the student is left with the possibility that my interpretation may be completely flawed in the eyes of the person being analyzed.

While I searched my mental list of clients, friends and relatives, trying to come up with this super someone, two of my students dropped in for a visit. Since both of them are in their early thirties, we started to talk about the kinds of things that happen when the progressed Sun is semisextile the natal Sun (which sometimes overlaps either the progressed Moon cycle or the transiting Saturn cycle). Toni spoke about the wretched year she had experienced just before her Saturn return. She could provide dates for all the major events. She had worked most of it through in therapy. Her birth time came from hospital records.

This chapter exists because of the generosity of the person called Toni.

I've called this chapter "A Predictor's Nightmare" because it would have been just that. As I put together Toni's transits, progressions and solar arc positions for the year, I found myself mumbling "thank you" to whatever gods there be that I didn't have to forecast something based on these aspects. There were too many aspects. Whenever a client has this number of things going on, I know I'm in for a long session. I'm glad it isn't me. I pray that the client isn't one of those skeptical people who won't tell you anything because you might find out what's going on.

When every possible area of the chart is being activated, just about anything can and will happen. When I see this kind of activity in a client's chart, I take out my list of therapists, what they charge and where they live before the client walks in the door. If the chart belongs to a cardinal person I drink forty-seven cups of coffee so that I can keep up with her intensity. If the chart belongs to a mutable person I prepare myself by doing a centering exercise five or six times because he will run off in a hundred different directions as soon as I open my mouth. If the chart belongs to a fixed person I try to fortify myself with soothing herb tea and a lot of Bach's Rescue Remedy because we're in for a real blow.

When there is this much activity in a chart, compressed into so short a period of time, the universe teaches humility to the astrologer. We can tell when and for how long, but may not be able to tell which of the probable manifestations really will occur. As you read this chapter, keep in mind that at each junction, at each hard aspect, Toni could have made different choices. I don't say this to judge the choices Toni made, but to tell you that the "what happens next" isn't determined solely by the aspects, but also by the choices made at each aspect. It is precisely this reality that makes a year-long prediction so difficult when there are too many major aspects occurring. After you have gone past the first and second major aspects trying to predict events, you are lost, simply because you don't know what the client will decide to do. So you might get a month or two into the year ahead and be very accurate, but then the client changes his or her course of action and the rest of what you said doesn't make sense anymore. Yet your dates still will be right.

At this point you need to be able to stress that the number of events, the number of choices, is bewildering. The client needs to know that he or she can make it through the problems, and that there is a specific duration of time for difficulty. Bracket the times of relative sanity so that your client knows when he or she can put together some of the pieces. Anyone going through this many changes has to have someone to talk to. Unless you are trained in therapy, the person your client needs is probably not you.

If the chart with all the aspects is your own, and you are a student of astrology (or a practicing astrologer), watch out for the astrologer's particular brand of avoidance behavior. We can spend hours daily pouring over our own charts, particularly when our lives are chaotic. We can spend so much time progressing and transiting and directing and midpointing and adding asteroids that we avoid any responsibility (or even thought) about what we ourselves are doing at particular times or in specific situations. Your chart doesn't act; you do. Your chart can't make choices; you can. Your chart will never relate to other people; you do.

A YEAR IN THE LIFE OF TONI

Any analysis of a living person must be understood within the context of the time period under discussion. Toni is very much alive and growing. She will not be the same person in 1997; in fact, she is not now the person described here, who lived between 1983 and 1984. This chapter is like a videotape of parts of that year in her life. It is also a record of events which occurred in childhood, events which correlate to the choices Toni made in 1983.

Toni has taken the time to analyze and learn from the events of this year. By allowing us the privilege of sharing these events and their ramifications, Toni's year can influence more than her own life and her own circle of friends, relatives and associates. You have the opportunity to follow an astrologer through an analysis of both a personality and an event-filled year. You will be able to see where traditional analysis shines and where it is incomplete. And you will learn when an astrologer should ask questions instead of making assumptions, and when an astrologer should follow through on a symbol until the manifestation becomes clear to both the astrologer and the client.

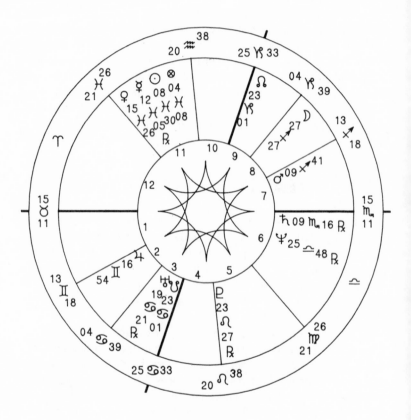

Chart 18. Toni's natal chart drawn for February 27, 1954, 9:10 AM CST, 86W54, 41N43. Birth data from hospital records; Placidus Houses.

Toni did not have her first astrological reading until 1986. Her first chart was based on an incorrect birth time (given to her from memory). After she had written to the hospital to get the hospital records, her chart made quite a bit more sense. As you read the analysis, you will see why I believe the time recorded in the hospital records may be about five minutes later than when Toni was actually born. This type of error is unfortunately the norm rather than the exception. I've included the earlier cusps in the text, but did not do a formal rectification of this chart for this chapter.[30]

Before we start to analyze the progressed chart and transits for 1983 and 1984, we need to understand the natal chart (Chart 18 on page 270) and Toni's background.[31] Toni's mother is a social worker; her father teaches. Toni is a white Anglo-Saxon Protestant, who grew up in the American midwest. Toni has two brothers, one a year older and the other three years younger than herself.

Analysis of Toni's Natal Chart and her Childhood

Before a client arrives, I spend time working on the natal chart, the progressed chart and the transits for the upcoming year. I want to have a basic grasp of the chart and of the major issues before I sit down with the client.

Toni has her natal Sun in Pisces, Moon in Sagittarius and Taurus rising. She has a yin majority, indicating that she prefers to collect information before responding to situations. The conflict between the yin Sun and yang Moon indicates an emotional inner response nature, or a high po-

☉ ♓, ☽ ♐, ASC ♉
Yin majority

☉ ♓ □ ☽ ♐
(57' arc, separating)
Mundane square indicates conflict

---

[30]This book doesn't deal with rectification, and more importantly, when the birth time is close but not exact, you can still work with progressions, directions and transits. It takes several hours to do a good job rectifying a natal chart. Yet you can do quite respectable astrological work without rectifying a close birth time. If any readers are interested in testing methods of rectifying this chart, the dates included in the text provide plenty of information.

[31]In *Secondary Progressions: Time to Remember*, I described the method of chart analysis I'm using here. Other source books for natal chart analysis include Hone, Sakoian and Acker, Lundsted, etc.

tential for internalizing emotion. She may brood over situations. The Sagittarian Moon may mean that she doesn't allow the validation of her own feelings, for she may assume that it could be worse, regardless of how difficult the emotional stress gets.

Toni's Sun-Mercury-Venus conjunction in Pisces combines with the Sagittarian Moon and the Taurean Ascendant to put up a good defense whenever analysis of emotion is involved. This means that Toni learns both psychological and astrological buzz words very quickly, using them as protection against experiencing the feeling part of emotion until she understands or can deal with whatever is being analyzed.

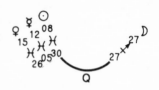

The primary father symbolism in a natal chart involves the Midheaven, Saturn and the Sun. Toni's natal Saturn is angular (conjunct the seventh house cusp), but it is not otherwise severely afflicted. The semisextile from Saturn to Mars suggests some underlying tension about control of energy or anger, but Saturn trines Toni's Sun-Mercury-Venus conjunction, indicating that Daddy provided quite a bit of background support. The North Node conjunction to the Midheaven could indicate growth through the father as well as growth through the development of life direction and career choices.

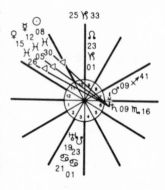

Natal Moon, IC and Sun combinations give a picture of the relationship with Mom. Toni's Moon trines Pluto, sextiles Neptune and quintiles the Sun, indicating a friendly relationship with her mother. There is a possible sesquiquadrate between the Moon and the Ascendant (it is 2° 44' apart, Moon approaching). If the sesquiquadrate is actually present (if the birth time is off by a few moments), Toni could find that somehow her relationship

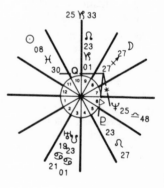

with her mother is never completely comfortable, for the Ascendant symbolizes how you interact with the environment immediately around you.

⛢ ♂ IC could mean Mom is unstable or abusive; ☋ ♂ IC gives up something at mothering point.

If her birth time is close to accurate, the major difficulty within the parental symbolism centers on Toni's Uranus-South Node-IC conjunction. I have seen Uranus angular in many cases of child abuse, but the other indicators (afflicted Sun, Moon or Saturn) that usually accompany charts of people who were abused as children are not present. Nonetheless, Uranus conjunct the IC could mean that Mom is unstable or abusive, while the South Node conjunct the IC can indicate a need to give up something at the mothering point in order to grow. I made a mental note to ask Toni about her childhood situation to find out how that Uranus manifested.

I knew that Toni had studied astrology for a while before she had her first reading. This is not unusual for someone with Saturn angular, for that Saturn position wants to establish some sort of control in advance. However, this kind of client sometimes comes just to hear validation of her own conclusions, not to discuss what kinds of things really are happening in her life. Such individuals don't want to talk about their fathers, they talk about Saturn. Mom is obliterated by words about the Moon. The more garbage you throw into the chart (asteroids, floating gravel, hypothetical planets, midpoints, solstice points, direct and converse solar arcs, dials, wheels, invisible people) the better they like it. I didn't know whether Toni, with her Mars in the seventh house, and the conflict between the Sagittarius Moon and the Pisces Sun-Mercury-Venus, would hit me with running arguments at every turn.

Fortunately for me, Toni didn't do any of the above. We started by discussing the Sun-Moon sign conflict. Toni recognized her defense mechanisms. When someone else (therapist, astrologer) gets painfully close to something Toni hasn't seen or can't quite cope with, she starts to distance herself, becoming extremely analytical. Later on, when she has time to think about what was said, she'll decide whether it has any truth to it or is merely a silly opinion.

Toni's natal Sun is square both Mars and Jupiter and semisquare the North Node. The square to Jupiter, although wide, is drawn in by the closer squares to Jupiter from both Mercury and Venus. This T-square indicates activity, curiosity and a certain volatility (otherwise known as temper, Mars square Mercury). The trine from natal Saturn steadies the Mars squares. Toni said that whenever she became angry or upset as a child, her father would put her to work to channel the energy. Even now, when she becomes upset, she starts cleaning the house.

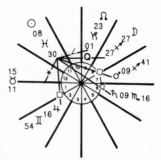

Toni sees her father as a traditionalist when it comes to the issue of women's roles. Although Toni's Mom was a feminist, her father tried to make Toni adhere to a more conservative interpretation of the female role. Toni contradicts herself repeatedly when she talks about either of her parents. First, Toni asserted that her relationship with her father was difficult because he wouldn't allow closeness, and she was afraid of him. Later, as we probed the relationship more deeply, she told me that her father had been a drinker until Toni was five years old, when he stopped drinking. Dad rescued people constantly, and brought them home to stay awhile. One of the men that her father rescued raped her older brother.[32] Dad was not a very good judge of character. Yet her father displayed more emotion than Toni's mother had. Dad was the one who played with Toni and listened to her while she was growing up.

Toni idealizes her mother. She feels close to her Mom, although she sees mother as very detached. Mother involved Toni in a boys-against-girls manipulation game with her father and brothers. In Toni's eyes, her Mom never let Toni's Dad get under her skin. Toni's Mom has both Sun and Moon in Aquarius. Toni's Mom has only one or two close friends, whom she never really lets in emotionally. With her Pisces Sun, Toni allows more closeness in her life, yet seeks emotional detachment. (Here the conflict between the Sagittarius Moon and Pisces Sun is quite clear.)

Toni's husband, Dwight, has an Aquarian Sun and Moon. Toni has married someone who symbolically recreates her mother in her life. Unlike her mother, however, Dwight won't leave, no matter what Toni does or doesn't do.

---

[32]Toni did not know until 1985 that her brother had been raped, when he underwent hypnosis as part of therapy, and remembered it.

At this point I asked Toni whether or not there had been violence against her during childhood. Her brother's rape could be the manifestation of Toni's Uranus-IC conjunction, but there might be more to it than that. In June 1959, when she was five years old, Toni came down with a bad flu virus. The family doctor was out of town, so Toni was taken to a very young MD who gave her an extremely strong antibiotic. Toni came down with Guillian-Barrs disease. Her nerves started to degenerate, causing extreme pain. No one knew what was wrong with her. The doctor treated her for polio, doing exactly the opposite of what needed to be done. Toni could not walk for six months. When she started to walk again, her muscles were extremely weak, so the doctor put her in a cast in order that she not create bone problems by walking without full muscular support. The cast was too tight. Toni cried and protested, but the medical community convinced her parents that she was only trying to get attention, or was manipulating her parents. Toni remembers one particular night when she was in the cast. She got up and tried to go to her mother, crying because the cast hurt so much. Her father would not let her go into her mother's bedroom, and made her stand in the hall. Finally he became exasperated and started to spank her. She covered her bottom with her hands and got the paddling on her hands, after which Dad sent her back to bed. At the end of the six weeks, when the doctor took off the cast, Toni had a blood blister which ran the entire length of her foot. It had started to infect, but the infection had not yet begun to move up her leg.

Shortly after the cast was removed, Toni started to have anxiety nightmares, which continued until she was thirteen years old. She would get up at night and run to her mother screaming "Mommy Mommy Mommy." As soon as she reached her mother she would pull back and cry, "No No No No." Then she would run to her father shouting "Daddy Daddy Daddy." Again, upon reaching him, she would pull back and scream, "No No No No." Her father would carry her to the bathroom and bring her out of the nightmare by washing down her arms and hands with warm water and soap. Toni remembers crying about her bad hands and remembers having a sensation of swollen hands during these nightmares. She isn't sure if the reference to her hands comes from that spanking or from the soap and water washing which brought her out of her anxiety attacks. Toni describes coming out of the nightmares as feeling as if she had received an electrical shock. The nightmares stopped when Toni's parents split up and Toni's mother moved out.

Toni was thirteen when her parents divorced. At that time, Toni's mother was politically active in causes that were not acceptable in a medium-sized midwestern city. Toni made ten or fifteen minutes' worth of rationalizations, excuses and evasions about her mother's participation in the custody battle. I didn't say anything. Sometimes waiting is the best thing you can do when somebody is trying to spit out something she can't bear. Finally, Toni admitted that it was possible that her mother really didn't want custody and had not used all the means at her disposal

Table 2. Events in Toni's Life

Major Events Preceding 1983
Spring 1977–January 1980: Acting school. August 26, 1979: Conceived Joseph (first child). December 31, 1979: Married, 11:30 A.M., Miami, Fla. May 15, 1980: Joseph's birth, 4:17 P.M., Boston, Mass. August 1, 1981: Bought house. September 20, 1982: Entered Radcliffe to study landscape architecture.
Events in 1983 and 1984
April 13, 1983: Abortion. April 17, 1983: Severe anxiety attack. May 10, 1983: Started therapy. July 1, 1983: Therapist went on two-month vacation; Toni stayed stoned for two months. July 23, 1983: Went to New York for three weeks with the baby, stayed with mother, visited father and stepmother. September 1, 1983: Started therapy again, stopped smoking pot. October 1, 1983: Dwight (husband) went into therapy with Toni. November 15, 1983: Toni threw Dwight out of the house. December 1, 1983: Toni saw a lawyer who convinced her that she had no means of support without Dwight. December 7, 1983: Dwight moved back in. December 20, 1983: Massive anxiety attack. February 14, 1984: Conceived second child.

to take the children with her. Toni's mother moved to New York City, where she got a job. Toni saw her on school vacations.

Toni doesn't fully acknowledge her sense of rejection from her mother. Even as a child, she knew that her mother could have used her father's bisexuality in court against him had she wanted custody. Mom could have chosen to get a job closer to home, allowing more contact with her children, if not full custody. Toni doesn't express or recognize anger towards her mother. Intellectually, Toni accepts that her Mom may not have wanted custody of the children, but emotionally she rejects this possibility. A year after the divorce, when Toni was with her mother during summer vacation, she confronted her mother, screaming "You are not my mother. My stepmother is my mother. She lives with us and cares about me." Her mother did not respond at all, but left the room.

Whenever Toni starts to see the anger or rage, she gets confused and loses direction. She acknowledges her anger with her parents and towards the medical profession for not protecting her when she was five years old.

By this point in the reading, I felt that Toni's true birth time was probably about five minutes earlier than the time given. A 9:05 A.M. birth time would place solar arc Uranus conjunct her IC when she was five years old, symbolizing the complete mishandling of her medical problems. Her MC would fall back to 24° Capricorn 21′; her Ascendant would be 13° Taurus 23′. This Ascendant would be exactly sesquiquadrate her natal Moon, symbolizing the situation with her mother. I could still use the dates I had already calculated for the secondary progression, *with the exception of the progressed angles*. Any aspects from the progressed angles would be a little over a year off for a five-minute change in birth time. That made my life a little easier, for the major aspects that didn't fit the chronology given above were from progressed angles. Of course, there were a couple of hits from the progressed angles for the later birth time, but removing them did not damage my argument nearly so much as keeping all of the aspects (like progressed Ascendant conjunct progressed Jupiter!) poked holes in the analysis.

The temptation to force shaky symbolism into matching known events is nearly irresistible. But the birth of Toni's second child or her completion of the college work both fit an Ascendant-Jupiter conjunction better than an abortion, a close call with a nervous breakdown or a near divorce—all of which were the real events of her life in 1983 and 1984. (See Table 2.)

Analysis of Toni's Progressed Charts, 1983 and 1984

The most straightforward way to determine whether a year is going to be a major-event year in a person's life is to count the number of aspects made by secondary progression, other than the aspects made by the progressed Moon. The progressed Moon makes aspects every year, but most years of our lives have relatively few aspects made from the other progressed planets to each other or to natal positions. See Table 3 on page 284. Toni has forty-one total aspects, twenty-two from progressed Moon, ten involving Ascendant or Midheaven. Eleven aspects do not involve Ascendant, Midheaven, or progressed Moon.

Between April 1, 1983, and April 1, 1984, Toni had twenty-two aspects between progressed planets or from progressed to natal positions. Nine of those aspects were from the progressed Moon; four involved the Ascendant or Midheaven. Even if we discount the Ascendant and Midheaven aspects, we have nine aspects other than those made by the progressed Moon. The progressed chart clearly outlines a stressful year. The five aspects from the progressed Sun show that Toni had to deal with the current manifestation of her life energy, with her current view of herself during this year.

On April 13, 1983, Toni had an abortion. She only told one or two close friends about it. Toni didn't want to have to justify her decision, particularly while she tried to deny her guilt feelings. She also didn't recognize her rage/anger about the situation. Instead, she focused on a fear of being judged. The Sagittarian Moon kicked in, discounting her own pain. Toni did not allow herself any space to mourn or to recover. She attempted to keep up her social life as if nothing had happened.

On the way to a dinner party four days later, Toni had her first massive anxiety attack. "I felt as if I were going to faint and my legs started this involuntary shaking. We ended up going to the hospital and found out I was reacting to hormonal changes. I was, of course, reacting to a lot more than that and didn't know it."

Outer planet transit
April 11-22

T ♄ ⊡ R ♃ April 11
T ♌ ☍ R ☽ April 12
T ♅ ☐ R ☉ April 22

R = radix or natal

In the aftermath of the abortion Toni's conflicting needs became much more apparent. She was too vulnerable to tolerate her husband leaving (another abandonment by Mom), even though he didn't want to leave. During this time, Toni recreated her parent's script, with the roles reversed. Her attitude and behavior towards Dwight duplicated her father's behavior towards her mother. Toni vacillated between making her husband want her and attempting to make her husband leave. Although Toni wanted her husband to change and display some of his feelings, she also wanted unconditional love, a love that would not change regardless of what she did.

Toni started therapy on May 10, 1983. Between May 10 and July 1, Toni started to understand some of her anger towards Dwight. Then her therapist went on a two-month vacation. Toni was pretty scared at this point. She felt she was on the verge of flying apart. She couldn't cope with her anger, and wasn't at all clear about its causes or possible resolution. Toni decided to say stoned for the two months that the therapist was gone.

This decision is probably no worse or better than gobbling up valium or librium during a therapist's absence. Toni was still having anxiety attacks, and experienced a feeling of terrible doom and depression. She was fighting these emotions with exercise and vitamins, but needed the escape that marijuana or tranquilizers provided. She found it impossible to meditate. All that Toni could do

T ⛢ □ R ☉ April 22
T ♃ ☌ R ♂ April 25
(anger increases)

T ♃ □ R ☉ May 7
(magnifies internal conflict)

T ♄ ⊡ R ♀ April 30
(estrangement in love situations)

T ♇ ⊡ R ☿ May 31
(digging out mental causes)

P ☽ ⅂ P ♇ June 21; ⅂ R ♇ July 7
(fear of doom; also fear of consequences of emotional expression — this effect is increased because P ☽ is in ♑)

SA ♄ □ R ☉
(restricts expression of self, fear of death)

T ♆ ☌ R ☽ July 5
(use of drugs to escape emotional responses; here ♆ ☌ ☽ cannot overcome P ☽ in ♑, P ☽ ⅂ ♇)

P ☉ ⊡ P ♇ August 3, 1983
P ☉ ⊡ R ♇ March 12, 1984
P ☉ ⊡ point between R and P ♇ November 23

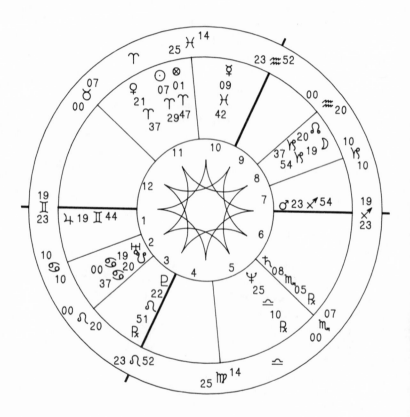

Chart 19. This is the progression of Toni's natal chart to April 1, 1983. The angles are progressed by the traditional (Naibod Arc) method. The latitude and longitude used are for place of birth.

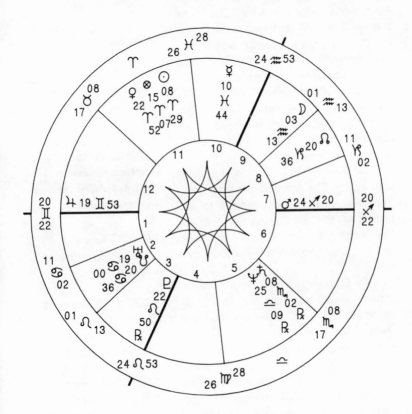

Chart 20. This is the progression of Toni's natal chart to April 1, 1984. The angles are progressed by the traditional (Naibod Arc) method. The latitude and longitude used are for the place of birth.

was to keep moving in an automatic, anesthetized manner.

On July 27, Toni went to New York with Joseph, her son, who was three years old. Toni and Joseph stayed with Toni's mother in the city. Toni's father and stepmother rented a beach house on Long Island for a month. Seeing both her parents helped a little, but Toni continued to suffer from anxiety and insomnia. Joseph's presence was a constant reminder of what it would be like to be a single mother, but at the same time, his needs connected Toni to reality. She couldn't let go and go crazy while he needed her. During this time, Toni centered her rage on Dwight. She didn't want to see him again.

On September 1, Toni started therapy again. She stopped smoking pot. Toni was serious about getting to the bottom of the depression. She felt she had nothing to lose at this point. She had to know who she was and own that self.

On October 1, 1983, Dwight entered therapy with Toni. Toni was livid with anger by this point. Dwight denied that there was a problem, except in Toni's head. Dwight insisted that everything was all right in the marriage, that all of the problems could be worked out if Toni simply got her head straightened out. During the therapy sessions, Dwight sat passively and said very little. He was trying to play a role of supportive helper, but refused to react to anything Toni said. After four weeks in joint therapy, Dwight stormed out, claiming that if

T ♇ ⊡ R ☿ May 31, 1983
T ♇ ⊡ R ☿ August 12, 1983
Station of ♇ 13' arc
from ⊡ ☿
(complete change in
self-perception/power
perception/thought patterns)

T ♄ SD July 3
16' arc from *R ☽

P ☽ ∠ R ♂ August 10, 1983
(centers anger on husband —
natal ♂ in 7th house)

P ☽ ∠ P ☿ August 22; P ☽
☐ P ♆ August 23
(emotional upheaval
combined with lack of clarity
and desire to escape)

T ♇ ⚹ R ☽ August 27
(starts gaining emotional
stability)

P ☿ ⊡ P ♆ September 5
(confused thinking)
P ☽ ☐ R ♆ September 10
(confused emotions)

T ♃ ☐ ☉ October 11
P ☽ ∠ ☿ October 15
P ☽ ⚻ P ♄ October 21
T ♃ ⊡ R ♆ October 23
P ☽ ⚼ R ☽ October 25

T ♃ ☐ R ☿ October 30
T ♆ ☌ R ☽ November 8

Toni really loved him she wouldn't say these things to him. Toni had been telling Dwight for two weeks that she didn't love him.

On November 15, Toni threw Dwight out of the house. Dwight returned home every day to be with his son Joseph, and followed Toni around the house crying and pleading for a reconciliation.

About the first of December, Toni saw a lawyer who convinced Toni that she had no means of supporting herself. With her self-confidence severely undermined (Saturn aspects) Toni allowed Dwight to move back in about December 7.

On December 20, Toni had another massive anxiety attack while Christmas shopping. "The other shoppers seemed alien, like bees in a beehive compulsively consuming the merchandise." Toni's legs started to shake and she almost fainted. At this time Toni began to realize how much money meant to her. Dwight was the source of money and security.

Between April 1, 1983, and April 1, 1984, Toni had thirteen quintiles or biquintiles from outer planet transits or progressions. These thread through all the difficulties outlined by the other aspects. During all the conflict occurring in her personal life, Toni was attending Radcliffe and attaining straight As in landscape architecture. Toni took three intensive seminars with students who had far more background in the field than she had. Nonetheless, she achieved the highest mark in each seminar. She felt "driven to do all that work." The courses

T ⚸ ∠ R ♌ November 9

T ♄ △ R ☉ November 10

T ♃ ☐ R ♀ November 15

T ♄ ☌ R ♄ November 16

T ♇ ⊡ R ♀ November 17

T ⚸ ☐ R ☉ November 17
(power/love conflict)
(change in self)

T ♄ ⊻ R ♂ November 20
(fear of anger)

T ♃ ☍ R ♃ November 21
(exaggerates everything)

T ⚸ ⊻ R ♄ November 30
(upheaval/tension concerning duty or control issues)

T ♃ ⊼ R ⚸ December 2
(fear of risk or change)

T ⚸ ☌ R ♂ December 7
(Dwight moves back in)

T ♄ ∠ R ☽ December 15
(emotional control becomes central issue)

T ♃ △ R ♇ December 20
(♃ enlarges the power issues underlying the conflicts concerning both emotional control and a desire to escape control)

T ⚸ ⊻ R ♄
(the ease line provides the escape route – back into the marriage)

Table 3. Toni's Progressed Aspects, 4/1/1983–4/1/1984

	Mo...	(Pr)	QNT	Sa...	(Pr)	Apr. 6, 1983	Mo...	20Cp05	Sa...	8Sc05
*	Ma...	(Pr)	SXT	MC...	(Pr)	Apr. 16, 1983	Ma...	23Sg54	MC...	23Aq54
*	Su...	(Pr)	QNT	MC...	(Na)	Apr. 16, 1983	Su...	7Ar32	MC...	25Cp32
	Sa...	(SA)	SQU	Su...	(Na)	Apr. 16, 1983	Su...	7Ar32	MC...	25Cp32
	Mo...	(Pr)	CONJ	No...	(Pr)	Apr. 20, 1983	Mo...	20Cp37	No...	20Cp37
	Mo...	(Pr)	QNT	Sa...	(Na)	May 8, 1983	Mo...	21Cp15	Sa...	9Sc15
	Mo...	(Pr)	SQU	Ve...	(Pr)	May 23, 1983	Mo...	21Cp49	Ve...	21Ar49
*	As...	(Pr)	BQT	MC...	(Na)	June 1, 1983	As...	19Ge32	MC...	25Cp32
	Mo...	(Pr)	QNX	Pl...	(Pr)	June 21, 1983	Mo...	22Cp50	Pl...	22Le50
	Mo...	(Pr)	CONJ	No...	(Na)	June 25, 1983	Mo...	23Cp01	No...	23Cp01
*	Sa...	(SA)	SQU	Su...	(Na)	June 29, 1983	Sa...	8Sg30	Su...	8Pi30
	Mo...	(Pr)	QNX	Pl...	(Na)	July 7, 1983	Mo...	23Cp26	Pl...	23Le26
	Mo...	(Pr)	SSQ	Su...	(Na)	July 9, 1983	Mo...	23Cp30	Su...	8Pi30
*	Su...	(Pr)	QNT	Ju...	(Pr)	July 12, 1983	Su...	7Ar47	Ju...	19Ge47
	Mo...	(Pr)	SSX	Ma...	(Pr)	July 23, 1983	Mo...	24Cp02	Ma...	24Sg02
	Mo...	(Pr)	SSX	MC...	(Pr)	July 28, 1983	Mo...	24Cp12	MC...	24Aq12
*	Su...	(Pr)	SQQ	Pl...	(Pr)	Aug. 3, 1983	Su...	7Ar50	Pl...	22Le50
	Mo...	(Pr)	SSQ	Ma...	(Na)	Aug. 10, 1983	Mo...	24Cp41	Ma...	9Sg41
	Mo...	(Pr)	SSQ	Me...	(Pr)	Aug. 22, 1983	Mo...	25Cp07	Me...	10Pi07
	Mo...	(Pr)	SQU	Ne...	(Pr)	Aug. 23, 1983	Mo...	25Cp09	Ne...	25Li09
	Mo...	(Pr)	CN	MC...	(Na)	Sep. 3, 1983	Mo...	25Cp32	MC...	25Cp32

Table 3. Continued.

*	Ju...	(Pr)	CN	As...	(Pr)	Ju...	Sep. 3, 1983	19Ge48	As...	19Ge48
*	Me...	(Pr)	SQQ	Ne...	(Pr)	Me...	Sep. 5, 1983	10Pi09	Ne...	25Li09
	Mo...	(Pr)	SQU	Ne...	(Na)	Mo...	Sep. 10, 1983	25Cp47	Ne...	25Li47
	Mo...	(Pr)	BQT	Ju...	(Pr)	Mo...	Sep. 10, 1983	25Cp48	Ju...	19Ge48
	Mo...	(Pr)	BQT	As...	(Pr)	Mo...	Sep. 10, 1983	25Cp49	As...	19Ge49
*	Su...	(Pr)	QNT	Mo...	(Pr)	Su...	Sep. 14, 1983	7Ar57	Mo...	25Cp57
	Mo...	(Pr)	SSQ	Me...	(Na)	Mo...	Oct. 15, 1983	27Cp05	Me...	12Pi05
*	Su...	(Pr)	QNX	Sa...	(Pr)	Su...	Oct. 21, 1983	8Ar03	Sa...	8Sc03
	Mo...	(Pr)	SSX	Mo...	(Na)	Mo...	Oct. 25, 1983	27Cp27	Mo...	27Sg27
*	Ma...	(SA)	SXT	Sa...	(Na)	Ma...	Oct. 27, 1983	9Cp15	Sa...	9Sc15
*	Pl...	(SA)	TRI	No...	(Na)	Pl...	Nov. 1, 1983	23Vi01	No...	23Cp01
*	Mo...	(SA)	SSQ	Me...	(Na)	Mo...	Nov. 20, 1983	27Cp05	Me...	12Pi05
*	Ve...	(SA)	SSX	As...	(Na)	Ve...	Dec. 28, 1983	15Ar11	As...	15Ta11
*	Ne...	(SA)	SXT	MC...	(Na)	Ne...	Jan. 1, 1984	25Sc32	MC...	25Cp32
	Mo...	(Pr)	SSQ	Ve...	(Na)	Mo...	Jan. 16, 1984	0Aq27	Ve...	15P127
*	MC...	(SA)	BQT	Ur...	(Na)	MC...	Jan. 20, 1984	25Aq20	Ur...	19Cn20
*	Me...	(Pr)	SSQ	MC...	(Na)	Me...	Jan. 22, 1984	10Pi32	MC...	25Cp32
*	Ma...	(Pr)	SSQ	Sa...	(Na)	Ma...	Jan. 25, 1984	24Sg15	Sa...	9Sc15
	Mo...	(Pr)	SQQ	Ju...	(Na)	Mo...	Feb. 24, 1984	1Aq54	Ju...	16Ge54
*	Su...	(SA)	SQQ	Pl...	(Na)	SU...	Mar. 12, 1984	8Ar26	Pl...	23Le26
	Su...	(SA)	SQU	As...	(Na)	Su...	Mar. 12, 1984	8Ar26	Pl...	23Le26
*	Ve...	(Pr)	TRI	Pl...	(Pr)	Ve...	Mar. 16, 1984	22Ar49	Pl...	22Le49

These are key aspects made by planets other than the progressed moon.

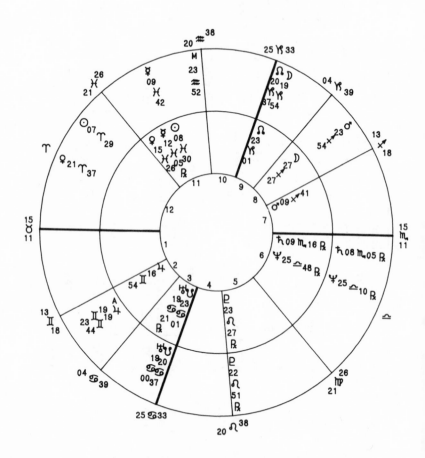

Chart 21. Toni's double wheel. Her natal chart is on the inside; her progressed chart for April 1, 1983, is on the outside. The transits for April 1, 1983 (from Mars out), are drawn in on the outside of the chart.

provided an escape from an intolerable home situation. "I worried about doing the work so well that the other people in the seminars wouldn't like me. I was opening up my mind to creating visuals, to creating an environment, creating a setting. I was waking up to something that I didn't know I had."

On February 14, 1984, Toni conceived her second child, Robert. Toni, in her own words, "ran home and slammed the door." Bobby became the symbol of capitulation to mothering, stability and living with her symbolic replacement for her own mother: her husband Dwight. At this point, Toni was determined to make the marriage and mothering work. She was still torn between her desire for children and her fear of staying in a bad marriage. Yet her fear of being a "welfare mother" overrode her other fears. She stayed with Dwight until 1987.

A FEW FINAL NOTES

The example of part of Toni's life brings us full round in the circle of what a predictive astrologer can and cannot do in the practice of astrology. From the examples used in the earlier sections of this book, you have seen events that could be forecast with accuracy. Yet the the last chapter demonstrates the limits of what astrological work can do.

In spite of the difficulty in attempting to predict accurately the events of a year such as Toni had, an astrologer can provide a client with a means of breaking down the series of events into smaller, more manageable chunks, by delineating the times when the difficulty eases. During those times, a client can assess the situation. The old cliché "nothing lasts forever" has a little more weight if you can tell a client when there will be periods of relative calm.

Often, when you see a client, there is one issue that seems paramount in the person's life. Then you are tempted to try to fit all of the aspects into explaining or analyzing that one situation. All of us live on many levels. Thus, the aspects at any one time in your life may symbolize different, but simultaneous situations. For example, you may have a series of extremely difficult aspects to your Midheaven and to the ruler of your Midheaven, while you have ease aspects to your Sun, Mercury and Venus. Your natural inclination will be to look for beneficial changes at work. However, I've found that this combination often symbolizes ease in a love relationship during a period when your work situation is rather stressful.

Astrologers can get locked into personal ideas or projections concerning a specific pattern. It's very important to remember that each individual responds differently to similar astrological events. I prefer to ask you questions about past cycles to find out exactly how you respond.

This brings us to what I need to know from you in order to predict with accuracy for you. Before you come to my office, I would rather know only your birth data. That way, I cannot prejudge your situation. I will devote the first hour of the reading to your natal chart. During this time, I will ask you questions about your marital status, work situation, siblings, children and your parents. If your father died fifteen years ago, those Saturn-Midheaven-Sun aspects probably indicate a situation at work. If you have no children, your oldest child won't drive you batty while Mars transits your fifth house.

Finally, I try to maintain some contact with everyday life while I am analyzing a chart. Pluto brings plumbing problems as often as it brings transformation. You may be quite a bit more useful as an astrologer if you mention this possibility before the ground freezes and your poor client is stuck with a jackhammer trying to get at a balky septic tank.

How to Do the Math

PROGRESSIONS MADE EASY

If there were a standard method of erecting a natal chart, the instructions for erecting a secondary chart would be extremely simple. Unfortunately, in our Uranian independence, we astrologers do astrological math with logs, with calculators, with plain old arithmetic, and all too often by using a formula we neither understand nor follow accurately. Many of us have abandoned math completely, relying on a computer (either through a computer service or our very own micro, programmed by someone else).

As if by diabolical intent, to further complicate what should be simple, there are five different Midheavens which can be calculated for the secondary progressed chart. Four of the five Midheaven calculations will arrive at a Midheaven within a degree or two of each other.

QUOTIDIAN PROGRESSION OF MIDHEAVEN

The fifth method, the Quotidian, moves the MC approximately 361° per year, reasoning that if a day equals a year, then the MC should move as it does in a day or about 361°. This last method is complicated to use unless you have a computer and not terribly useful for prediction because of it's very cumbersome nature. It is, however, a fascinating tool for "hindsight" astrology. When you know the date of an event, you can put up the Quotidian angles and see wonderful correlations for whatever the event was. Mohan Koparkar in his book *Precise Progressed Charts,* uses a method similar to Quotidian angles. Carl Stahl in *Introduction to Sidereal Astrology* and Fagin and Firebrace in *Primer of Sidereal Astrology* both give the math behind this method.[34] If you want to play with these angles, try these books.

---

[34]See Koparker, Mohan, *Precise Progressed Charts* (Mohan Enterprises, Rochester, New York, 1976); Stahl, Carl, *Introduction to Sidereal Astrology,* Stahl, Bay City, Michigan, 1969; Fagin, Cyril, and Firebrace, R. C., *Primer of Sidereal Astrology* (Littlejohn Publications, Isabella, Missouri, 1973).

A DEGREE FOR A YEAR

The four other methods of reaching a MC follow. The easiest of the four (and one which only puts you in the ballpark, hardly ever aspected exactly at the time of events) is to add one degree to the natal MC for every year of life elapsed. If you only know the birth time to an approximate hour ("Oh, he was born between three and four A.M.") and you haven't rectified the chart, it's silly to do much more than this. This method is extremely useful for verifying a birth time, because you can add a degree to the MC for each year of life in your head. You can look at the year of a major event, figure out how old the person was, add degrees equal to the age to the natal MC, then see if the progressed MC is within a degree of a major aspect. If it is, you know you've got a pretty accurate birth time.

SOLAR ARC MIDHEAVEN

The next easiest method of determining the progressed MC, and the method usually used by the major computer services unless you specify otherwise, is the solar arc Midheaven. To calculate the solar arc MC, count one day per year from birth in the ephemeris, then subtract the midnight position of the Sun on the progressed day. The resulting angle is the solar arc. Add this angle (degrees and minutes) to the natal Midheaven. The result is the solar arc Midheaven. (If you're still using a noon ephemeris, use the noon positions on the Sun.)

NAIBOD ARC
(SUN'S MEAN MOTION
IN RIGHT ASCENSION)

The next method of getting the MC is called the Naibod arc, or the Sun's mean motion in right ascension. This method averages the Sun's motion along the equator, adding about 3'57" per day. This is the same as the change in sidereal time on successive midnights (or noons). This is a method available from most major astrological computing outfits. For two reasons, all of the charts in this book use the Sun's mean motion in right ascension to progress the MC. Not only can all of you get this method of progression from most astrological computing services, it arrives at the same MC as the next method.

TRADITIONAL METHOD
(MEAN SIDEREAL TIME)

This method gives the Midheaven for the person's birthday every year. Simply put up a natal chart for the time and place of birth on the progressed day. Do the houses exactly as you would for a natal chart, changing only the sidereal time from that of the birthday to that of the day as many days after birth as years old the person is at the time of the progression. For someone who is fifteen, count fifteen days after birth. For someone who is thirty, count thirty days, and so on. The only reason this method is more difficult is that you have to erect another chart. If you have a computer, you just tell the computer to put up a new natal chart for the progressed date. The computer will never know you just fooled it into doing a progression. The chart it gives you will be the progressed chart for the birthday. I've engaged in many a friendly argument (and a few not so friendly fights) with adherents of the solar arc method of progressing the MC. I've used both this MC and the mean sidereal time MC in ninety degree work since 1974. I found that the mean sidereal time MC was more likely to be directly aspected (within 5' of arc) when events occurred, although the solar arc MC was usually within a degree. Unless you're using the ninety degree dial with your secondaries, you probably won't care about the small discrepancy. Again, unless you're pretty sure of the accuracy of the birth time, there is not much reason to do the extra work to get the mean sidereal time MC.

There you have all of the ways that I know to cast the houses for the progressed chart. The next step involves figuring out where the planets are at any time during the progressed year.

THE ADJUSTED CALCULATION DATE

It's often useful to know on which day the emhemeris positions will be exact for any person. If each day equals a year, then at some point during the year the ephemeris positions will be right. So rather than do a lot of arithmetic to figure out where the planets are, say on the birthday, why not figure out what day equals the ephemeris positions? Then you won't have to do any arithmetic for that day. It's nice to know this even if you have a computer, because sometimes you just want to look up what's going on without the bother of going through a lot of charts. If you know what day during the progressed year equals the ephemeris positions, you can get a quick fix on timing the events of the year.

Just as in the MC calculations, there are several methods of arriving at the right day, which is usually called the adjusted calculation date or ACD. Some people call it the limiting date. I don't think there's anything special or magic about the day itself; it's just an astrological convenience.

The easiest method of finding the ACD is not, of course, the method I use. That has nothing to do with accuracy, but with the way I was taught. Since I used the method I was taught for about eight years before I learned the easier way, I can never remember the easier way. I hope you learn the easier method first and always forget the method I use. This method is given in Marcia Moore's book *Astrology, the Divine Science*[35], although Robert Hand first taught it to me.

CAUTION: Step one, the same in both methods, is the critical step. Over 90 percent of the calculating errors which occur in finding the ACD are due to either skipping this step or doing in incorrectly.

1. Change the birth time to GMT. First, change your birth time to 24 hour notation. This just means that if you have a P.M. birth, you add 12 hours. Sometimes this is called U.T., or universal time. If the birth was *west* of Greenwich, add the hours (equal to the time zone) to the birth time. If the birth was *east* of Greenwich, subtract the hours (equal to the time zone) to get GMT (Greenwich mean time).

---

[35]See Moore, Marcia, *Astrology, the Divine Science* (Arcane Publications, York Harbor, Maine, 1978).

2. Subtract the GMT of birth from the following midnight (or noon).

3. To this answer add the sidereal time for Greenwich (the time given in the ephemeris) on the birthday to get the sidereal time of the ACD.

4. For a midnight ephemeris look backwards to the day which has this sidereal time in it. That is the ACD. For a noon ephemeris, look forward in the ephemeris to the day which has this sidereal time in it. (The days should be six months apart for noon and midnight.)

That's all there is to it. Simple, isn't it? If you never learned a way to do the ACD before you read this, *stop here. Go straight to the example*. I'm only including the method I use so that those of you who learned it but forgot exactly how to do it can be refreshed and reassured that it, too, gets the right answer (or very close).

1. CHANGE THE BIRTH TIME TO GMT. First, change your birth time to 24 hour notation. This just means that if you have a P.M. birth, you add twelve hours. Sometimes this is called U.T., or universal time. If the birth was *west* of Greenwich, add the hours (equal to the time zone) to the birth time. If the birth was *east* of Greenwich, subtract the hours (equal to the time zone) to get GMT (Greenwich mean time).

2. Divide the hours by 2, the minutes by 4.

3. For a midnight ephemeris or a noon ephemeris and a birth *after* noon, subtract the hours ÷ 2 from the month of birth, and the minutes ÷ 4 from the day of birth. The resulting day is the ACD. For a noon ephemeris and a birth *before* noon, add the hours ÷ 2 to the month of birth and the minutes ÷ 4 to the day of birth. The resulting day is the ACD.

The only reason that this gets complicated is that it sometimes runs into the previous year. That's really obvious with the first method, but not always obvious with the second. Now I'll run through an example, using both methods, so that you can see how they work.

EXAMPLE
John Doe, May 5, 1955, 14:30 GMT

```
  24 hrs  00 min
− 14 hrs  30 min
─────────────────
   9 hrs  30 min (is your answer)
```

```
  14 hrs 48 min 22 sec (= the sidereal time for midnight, 5/5/55.)
+  9 hrs 30 min 00 sec
────────────────────────
  23 hrs 78 min 22 sec (is your answer)
```

However, 23 hrs 78 min 22 sec needs to be further converted.

60 min = 1 hr, so
78 min = 1 hr 18 min =
24 hrs 18 min 22 sec =
00 hrs 18 min 22 secs (final answer)

Whenever you go over 24, you start again at 0 because the days form a circle. When you back up in the ephemeris to the day that has this sidereal time in it, you have to go all the way back to September 26, 1954 before you find it. So John Doe's ACD is September 26, the *year before*. Suppose you wanted to progress John Doe's chart to 1985. You would add 30 days (equal to thirty years) to the birthday. May 5 + 30 days = June 4. (May has 31 days.) The midnight ephemeris positions of the planets on June 4 equal the progressed positions for September 26, 1984. The midnight positions for June 5, 1955 equal the progressed positions on September 26, 1985.

If you were to use the other method, you would follow these steps:

1. 14:30 GMT of birth; 14 ÷ 2 = 7 and 30 ÷ 4 = 7

2. 1955 year   5 month 5 day
                   − 7 month 7 day

Since you can't directly subtract 7 days from 5 days or 7 months from 5 months, you have to borrow. 1955 year, 5 month, 5 day = 1954 year, 17 month, 5 day = 1954 year, 16 month, 35 day.

1954 year 16 month 35 day
—7 month   7 day
—————————————————————
1954 year 9 month 28 day

The ACD is September 28, the year before.

The reason the two answers are not precise (two days off) is that in the second method, months are rounded to thirty days each. Not only is the second method more cumbersome, it's not as accurate. So unless you are bound by habit, use the first method.

Now that you've found the ACD, you can *interpolate* to find where the planets are on specific days during the year. You'll want to do this primarily for the progressed Moon, which moves 12 to 15 degrees a year, depending on how close to the earth it is.

Make a list like this on your paper. I'm still using John Doe, so it starts September 26. Of course, your list will start on your ACD.

MOON: SEPT. 26, 1984 _____

OCT. 26, 1984 _____

NOV. 26, 1984 _____

DEC. 26, 1985 _____

JAN. 26, 1985 _____

FEB. 26, 1985 _____

MAR. 26, 1985 _____

APR 26, 1985 _____

MAY 26, 1985 _____

JUN. 26, 1985 _____

JUL. 26, 1985 _____

AUG. 26, 1985 _____

SEPT. 26, 1985 _____

Write in the Moon's position on June 4, 1955 from the ephemeris next to September 26, 1984. (The position is 25°♏22'8"). Write in the Moon's position on June 5, 1955 next to September 26, 1985. (The Moon's position is 7° ♐ 10'59".) Now subtract the June 4 position from the June 5 position:

$$7° ♐ 10'59" = 37°♏10'59"$$
$$- 25°♏22'08"$$
$$\overline{11°\quad 48'51"}$$

Divide this answer by 12 to get the monthly motion. To divide degrees, minutes and seconds, you need to change them to decimal parts of a degree. To do that, take your hand calculator and divide 51" by 60 to get decimal parts of a minute. (51 ÷ 60 = .85) Now you have 11°48.85'. Next you divide 48.85 by 60 to get the decimal parts of a degree (48.85 ÷ 60 = .8142) Now you know that the decimal motion of the Moon in the year is 11.8142°. Divide this by 12 months to get the monthly motion (11.8142 ÷ 12 = .9845°) We'd really be able to use this better if it was in minutes instead of decimal parts of a degree, so multiply this number by 60 to find out the minutes. (0.9845 × 60 = 59.071") You could quit here, but let's be precise, just for this example. To find the seconds, multiply .071 by 60. (.071 × 60 = 4.25") So now you know that you have to add 59'4" per month to get the monthly motion of the moon. Now you can fill in that chart you made earlier.

Moon:		
SEPT. 26, 1984	25° ♏ 22' 07"	
OCT. 26, 1984	26° ♏ 21' 12"	
NOV. 26, 1984	27° ♏ 20' 16"	
DEC. 26, 1985	28° ♏ 19' 20"	
JAN. 26, 1985	29° ♏ 18' 24"	
FEB. 26, 1985	00° ♐ 17' 28"	
MAR. 26, 1985	01° ♐ 16' 32"	
APR. 26, 1985	02° ♐ 15' 36"	

MAY 26, 1985	03° ♐ 14' 40"
JUNE 26, 1985	04° ♐ 13' 44"
JULY 26, 1985	05° ♐ 12' 48"
AUG. 26, 1985	06° ♐ 11' 52"
SEPT. 26, 1985	07° ♐ 10' 58" (Ephemeris = 7° ♐ 10'59")

You can interpolate all of the rest of the planets just like this if you want to.

There is just one more thing which can help you utilize your tools with maximum effectiveness. Some ephemerides have an aspectarian at the bottom of each page. It's a shame not to use this aspectarian to get the day that progressed aspects are exact, since it isn't too hard.

If one year = 24 hours, then 12 months = 24 hours and 1 month = 2 hours, and 15 days = 1 hour = 60 minutes. 1 day = 4 minutes. Are you with me? According to the aspectarian for June 4, 1955, the Moon trined Jupiter at 6:02 A.M. Six hours equal three months. (1 month = 2 hours) Two minutes isn't even a day, so we forget it. Add three months to the ACD (Sept. 26, remember?) and you get Dec. 26, 1984. That's when John Doe's progressed Moon will trine his progressed Jupiter. Another major aspect that occurs on June 4 is Moon inconjunct Mars, which happens at 10:33 P.M. Change that to 24 hour notation by adding 12 hours, so you don't get all mixed up, that is, 22:33.

22 hours equals 11 months (22÷2)
33 minutes equals 8 days (33÷4)
Sept. 26, 1984 plus 11 months 8 days = Sept. 3, 1985.

That's when John Doe's progressed Moon was inconjunct his progressed Mars and he probably picked a fight with some woman in his life.

BIBLIOGRAPHY

George, Llewellyn. *A to Z Horoscope Maker and Delineator*. St. Paul, Minn: Llewellyn Publications, 1970.

Greene, Liz. *The Astrology of Fate*. York Beach, Maine: Samuel Weiser, Inc., 1984.

Hand, Robert. *Planets in Transit*. West Chester, Penn.: Whitford Press, 1976.

Hastings, Nancy Anne. *Secondary Progressions: Time to Remember*. York Beach, Maine: Samuel Weiser, Inc., 1984.

Lantero, Erminie. *The Continuing Discovery of Chiron*. York Beach, Maine: Samuel Weiser, Inc., 1984.

Lundsted, Betty. *Planetary Cycles: Astrological Indicators of Crisis and Change*. York Beach, Maine: Samuel Weiser, Inc., 1984.

Negus, Joan. *Astro-Alchemy: Making the Most of Your Transits*. San Diego, Calif.: ACS Publications, Inc., 1985.

Sakoian, Frances, and Acker, Louis. *Predictive Astrology*. New York: Harper and Row Publishers, 1977.

ABOUT THE AUTHOR

Nancy Anne Hastings was born January 18, 1945, at 11:20 PM, EWT, in Attleborough, Massachusetts, 71W17, 41N57. She has been past president of the New England Astrological Association, an executive committee member on the national board for the National Council for Geocosmic Research, and past president of the Mass Bay Chapter of the NCGR. She is an astrologer accredited with the Gold Card from the American Federation of Astrologers. She is the author of *Secondary Progressions: Time to Remember,* also published by Weiser, and has published numerous articles in *Astrology Now, Your Astrology* and *Astrology Today.* She has lectured internationally as well as for NCGR and AFA national conferences. She has a B.S. in biology from Tufts University but has chosen to be a full-time astrological counselor and teacher. She currently lives in Concord, Massachusetts.